LEISURE ARTS PRESENTS

CHRISTMAS
merry & bright

Why settle for humdrum, everybody-has-'em Christmas trims when it's so easy to craft your own? Whether you're starting a new holiday collection or adding to your treasure-trove of favorites, you'll love our festive decorating themes — from traditional elegance to country whimsy, and even fun stuff for kids to craft! And to make the holidays even better, we've included lots of great gifts to make and scrumptious recipes to try. Make your Christmas merry & bright!

LEISURE ARTS, INC.
Little Rock, Arkansas

CHRISTMAS
merry & bright

EDITORIAL TEAM
Editorial Director: Susan Frantz Wiles
Senior Editor: Linda L. Garner
Technical Editor: Kristine Anderson Mertes
Foods Editor: Celia Fahr Harkey, R.D.

ART TEAM
Art Publications Director: Rhonda Shelby
Art Imaging Director: Mark Hawkins
Art Category Manager: Lora Puls
Freelance Artist: Jessica L. Puls
Art Imaging Technicians: Stephanie Johnson and
 Mark Potter
Publishing Systems Administrator: Becky Riddle
Publishing Systems Assistants: Clint Hanson,
 John Rose, and Chris Wertenberger

BUSINESS STAFF
Publisher: Rick Barton
Vice President, Finance: Tom Siebenmorgen
Director of Corporate Planning and Development:
 Laticia Mull Dittrich
Vice President, Retail Marketing: Bob Humphrey
Vice President, Sales: Ray Shelgosh
Vice President, National Accounts: Pam Stebbins
Director of Sales and Services: Margaret Reinold
Vice President, Operations: Jim Dittrich
Comptroller, Operations: Rob Thieme
Retail Customer Service Managers: Sharon Hall and
 Stan Raynor
Print Production Manager: Fred F. Pruss

International Standard Book Number 1-57486-366-5

10 9 8 7 6 5 4 3 2 1

TABLE OF CONTENTS

HOLIDAY DÉCOR

TABLE OF CONTENTS
(Continued)

98

HEARTFELT GIFTS

Seasonal Sweatshirt Vest • Fleecy
Winter Wear • Appliquéd Knit Dress
Sweet Baby Set • Snowman Dress
Santa Patches • Crocheted Vest
Covered Album • Masculine Desk Set
Hand-Painted Holiday Tableware
Luxurious Bath Set • Fragrant Bath
Tea Bags • Crocheted Angel Afghan
Memory Plate • Ornament Place Mats
Poinsettia Pillow • Poinsettia Afghan
Heart Coasters • Warm Wishes
Card Holder • Skating Santa Sled
Snowman Pillow • Winter Warmer
Mugs • Winter Warmer Towels
Winter Warmer Wall Hanging

132

EASY ENTERTAINING

All Wrapped Up for Christmas, 134

Spicy Cheddar Cheesecake with Apricot
Chutney • Two-Tone Cucumber Sandwiches • Fresh
Salsa Verde • Cherry Salsa • Savory Mushroom Pillows
Falafel Appetizers with Yogurt Mustard Sauce
Sparkling Champagne Punch • Vietnamese Spring
Rolls with Garlic-Ginger Sauce • Blue Cheese and
Bacon-Stuffed Artichokes • Sun-Dried Tomato Dip
Seasoned Pita Wedges • Make-Ahead Saucy Ribs
Nutty Blue Cheese Spread • Green Olive and
Jalapeño Roll-Ups • Hot Spiced Fruit Tea
Herbed Pimiento Dip • Cheesy Crab Puffs

New England Holiday Brunch, 142

Paella • Savory Tomato and Olive Pastries
Cranberry Champagne Cocktail • Cheesy
Triangle Puffs • Rosemary-Sweet Potato Soup
• Turkey Quiche Lorraine • Lemon-Dill Biscuits
• Minted Cranberry-Pear Relish • Stuffed Baked
Apples • Zucchini Medley Hazelnut Coffee Cake
• Pinecone Cookies • Marlborough Pie

HOLIDAY DÉCOR

It's easy to deck the halls (and the rest of the house, too!) in festive, handcrafted finery. Whether you prefer traditional holly and poinsettias, glorious gilded naturals, or whimsical surprises, you'll find the perfect accents for your holiday décor. You can select a theme — such as lacy angels and snowflakes — or pick and choose a variety of trimmings to supplement your customary Christmas décor. Either way, you're sure to make the season merry!

Keep Christmas in your ♥

Home is where you hang your heart.

Home is where y

7

MAKE AN ENTRANCE

*G*ive new meaning to the phrase "make an entrance" with creative entryway decor that's wonderfully entrancing! Begin with items borrowed from nature, such as evergreens, garlands of greenery, frosty snowballs, or luscious fruits; then use your imagination to develop a one-of-a-kind look. To create a sense of symmetry, arrange inviting decorations on either side of the doorway, or accessorize with a coordinating wreath or evergreen sprays. Instructions for creating three distinctive themes, including the farm-fresh style shown here, begin on page 12.

Even if you live in the middle of town, you can create a **Cozy Country Entrance** *(page 12)*. The wreath and garland combine rosy apples, checked ribbon, and galvanized stars for a charming provincial look. Complete the scene with rustic wooden reindeer, a weathered wheelbarrow, and buckets filled with country treasures.

For a **Winter Wonderland Entry** *(page 12)*, post **Cheerful Snowmen** *(page 13)* at the gate. They're sure to give guests a jolly welcome! A pair of slender artificial trees are wired together to form an impressive arch that's quick to decorate with **Cheery Snowballs** *(page 13)* and store-bought "candy canes," snowflakes, and icicles.

Festooned with gleaming ribbons, faux fruit, and sprigs of greenery, elegant spiral trees stand sentry in this Renaissance-style **Della Robbia Entry Collection** *(page 12)*. The luxurious flourishes are repeated in the evergreen sprays that grace the double doors in a matched set. Draped atop the doorway, a fruited garland completes the ensemble.

11

COZY COUNTRY ENTRANCE

(Shown on pages 8 - 9)

Welcome family and friends to your home with this cozy country Christmas entryway.

The jaunty wreath is certain to catch the eye of those who come to call during this happy season. Artificial apples and greenery picks are wired to a 24" dia. silk evergreen wreath. A 6"w galvanized star ornament hangs at its center. The wreath is adorned with a pretty bow fashioned from 1 1/2"w red-and-white checked wired ribbon, and is hung from a length of the same ribbon.

An artificial miniature apple garland is wired along the boughs of a silk evergreen garland and draped across the doorway. Large imitation apples, 6"w and 14"w galvanized silver stars, and lengths of ribbon also decorate the swag. A cheery bow is nestled in its center.

Star-spangled woodland critters stand ready to welcome your guests. Ribbon "bow ties," greenery, and star ornaments adorn the necks of two rustic wooden "reindeer."

To complete the down-home setting, store-bought trees and artificial apples fill galvanized buckets, while an old-fashioned wheelbarrow totes a treasured quilt and lush poinsettias.

DELLA ROBBIA ENTRY COLLECTION

(Shown on page 11)

When guests come to your door during this glorious holiday season, greet them with an entryway inspired by Renaissance sculptors. The garland, door swags, and spiraled trees, heavy-laden with fruits and berries and draped in sparkling ribbons, create an aura of elegance.

To create each of our splendid tree sentries, we began by wiring faux fruit, including apples, pears, peaches, and grapes, along the boughs of a purchased eight-foot-tall spiral tree. For added color, sprigs of cedar, mistletoe, and berries, cut in 6" to 9" lengths, are interspersed throughout the limbs and secured with glue. Streamers are fashioned from 2 1/2"w gold and sheer plaid wired ribbons. For each streamer, we cut a 1 yard length of each ribbon and wired the ends to a floral pick. The streamers are then secured to the tree with the floral pick and arranged in splendid style. The tree is then topped with bows fashioned from both gold and plaid ribbons. As a symbol of hospitality, a large pineapple adds the crowning touch to our Della Robbia trees.

For each of our festive door sprays, we cut three 24" lengths from a silk evergreen garland. The cut lengths are wired together 9" from one end. Luscious artificial fruits, gilded mistletoe, and brilliant berries are wired along each branch. A cheerful bow adds the finishing touch.

Finally, to complete our grand ensemble, golden mistletoe is sprinkled throughout a second garland and accented with fanciful bows with delicate streamers. This handsome swag is gracefully draped over the exquisite doorway.

WINTER WONDERLAND ENTRY

(Shown on page 10)

Even if the snow isn't falling where you live, you can transform your front door into a winter wonderland with our playful snowmen and snowball-decorated arch. Covered with everything that makes Christmas merry, from sweet candy canes to crimson icicles and dazzling snowflakes, this darling arrangement, along with our frolicsome snowmen, is sure to delight young and old alike.

The tops of two nine-foot-tall artificial slim noble fir trees are wired together to form the inviting arch. Purchased glitter-covered snowflakes, red acrylic icicles, and artificial cherry picks are wired among the boughs. Red-and-white checked ribbon accents the wintry branches.

The Cheery Snowballs add a frosty accent to this playful arched gateway, and they won't melt even in the mildest of climes!

The doorway is flanked with a pair of ribbon-tied "candy canes." For each pair, two 25" artificial candy canes are crossed and wired together, then accented with a bright red bow.

The whimsical arch is positioned around the door and two 4' x 8' pieces of whitewashed fencing extend from each side. Two Cheerful Snowmen are standing by, ready to invite your loved ones across your threshold to enjoy your happy holiday hospitality.

CHEERFUL SNOWMEN (Shown on page 10)

For each snowman, you will need 6 yds. of ¹/₂" thick sheet foam, 15" x 42" piece of lightweight cardboard, 12"h flowerpot, stapler, fiberfill, mittens, low-temperature glue gun, hat, black craft foam, tracing paper, scarf, and one Cheery Snowball or 25" artificial candy cane.

1. Cut one 24" x 33" piece, two 16¹/₂" x 24" pieces, and three 24" x 50" pieces from sheet foam.

2. For body, overlapping short ends, wrap cardboard around flowerpot; staple to secure. With one long edge even with bottom of cardboard, wrap one 24" x 50" foam piece around flowerpot; staple at back to secure. Cut a wavy edge along one long edge of each remaining 24" x 50" foam piece. Layer and wrap around first foam piece; staple at back to secure. Staple front and back, then side edges of body together at top for neck.

3. For each arm, roll one 16¹/₂" x 24" piece of foam from long end to long end; staple to secure. Lightly stuff each mitten with fiberfill. Pull a mitten over one end of each arm; glue to secure.

4. For head, matching long edges, fold remaining piece of foam in half. With fold at top, match short edges to form a tube; staple to secure. Place hat over folded edge of head.

5. Trace eye, nose, mouth, and button patterns onto tracing paper. Using patterns, cut shapes from craft foam. Glue shapes to snowman.

6. Staple arms to neck. Staple head to neck and arms. Knot scarf around neck. Glue snowball or candy cane to one mitten.

CHEERY SNOWBALLS
(Shown on page 10)

For each snowball, you will need a drawing compass, ¹/₂" thick sheet foam, 2" dia. or 3" dia. plastic foam ball, and a white chenille stem.

1. For small snowball, use compass to draw a 9" dia. circle on sheet foam; cut out. Gather sheet foam around 2" dia. foam ball. Use stem to secure gathers.

2. For large snowball, follow Step 1 using 3" dia. foam ball and cutting a 12" dia. circle from sheet foam.

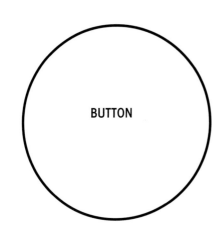

NOSE

BUTTON

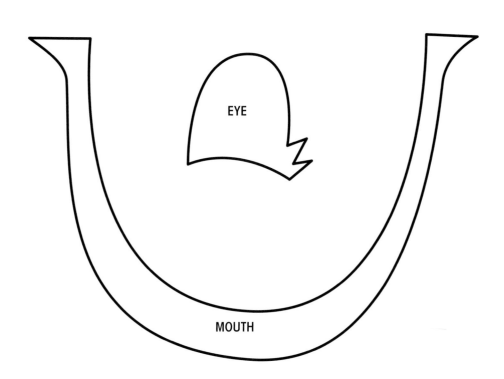

EYE

MOUTH

NATURE'S GLORY

Simple elements garnered from nature are enhanced by earth's precious metals to create this collection of opulent accents for the home. The dazzling display, which begins with a compelling centerpiece, abounds with nature's glory. A welcoming wreath blends grace and beauty, and a shimmering swag showcases a prized piece of artwork. A grouping of tailored topiaries creates a handsome vignette, and flickering candles dress the mantel in luxurious style. Creating natural beauty has never been this easy! Instructions begin on page 18.

An artful arrangement of painted dried fruit and leaves, our **Nature's Glory Centerpiece** *(page 18)* begins with a swath of luxurious fabric. Vintage unmatched silver candlesticks enhance the formal display, which is softened by the addition of a **Silvery Bird Nest** *(page 18)* and a plump, sleek quail. *(Opposite)* Equally elegant, the coordinating **Bountiful Wreath** *(page 18)* embraces an abundance of natural elements.

A contrast of color and texture, this **Picture Swag** *(page 16)* naturally accents a painting. Gleaming ribbons crown the piece with richness.

Moss, ferns, and pomegranates form the humble beginnings of these **Gilded Topiaries** *(page 19)*, which are displayed together to create a stately setting.

(Opposite) Elements from the collection are combined with gossamer fabric and glowing candlelight for **A Glorious Mantel** *(page 19)*. A hurricane globe filled with hazelnuts and trimmed with a silvery ribbon holds a sponge-painted pillar.

NATURE'S GLORY CENTERPIECE

(Shown on page 14)

A length of rich jacquard fabric provides the foundation for this bountiful centerpiece. The fabric flows softly across the table, drawing the viewer's eye to the treasures nestled in its folds.

To recreate this sumptuous centerpiece, fill your favorite silver bowl to the brim with nature's glory. Dried pomegranates, artichokes, and assorted leaves sprayed with Design Master® silver, gold, and copper spray paint provide a dramatic focal point for an exquisite table decoration. Accent these natural riches with pinecones, assorted nuts, and a plump 4" tall quail.

You'll set a peaceful mood for your holiday gatherings when you display our earthly wealth in all its splendor. Nearby, artificial eggs painted silver rest serenely in a purchased nest. An assortment of candlesticks offers a flicker of light to chase away the shadows.

BOUNTIFUL WREATH

(Shown on page 15)

You will need floral wire; wire cutters; 18" dia. sweet huck wreath; Design Master® silver, gold, and copper spray paint; items to decorate wreath (we used dried fern, hydrangea, salal leaves, pomegranates, mini artichokes, pinecones, assorted nuts, gold silk ivy garland, and a 4"h artificial quail); hot glue gun; one Silvery Bird Nest; and five 14" lengths each of 1"w silver mesh wired ribbon, 1 1/2"w gold mesh ribbon, and 1 3/4"w copper mesh wired ribbon.

Note: Allow paint and glue to dry after each application.

1. For hanger, bend an 18" length of wire in half. Twist wire together 2" from bend to form a loop. Keeping loop at back of wreath, wrap wire ends around wreath; twist ends together to secure.
2. Paint items to decorate wreath as desired. Glue eggs in nest.
3. Using floral wire and glue, attach items to wreath.
4. Tie one each of silver, gold, and copper ribbon lengths together into a bow. Repeat to make a total of five bows. Arrange bows evenly around wreath; glue to secure.

SILVERY BIRD NEST

(Shown on page 14)

For each nest, you will need Design Master® silver spray paint, two artificial eggs, hot glue gun, and an artificial nest.

1. Spray eggs silver; allow to dry.
2. Arrange and glue eggs in nest.

PICTURE SWAG

(Shown on page 16)

You will need Design Master® silver, gold, and copper spray paint; assorted items to decorate swag (we used dried fern, hydrangea, salal leaves, a pomegranate, mini artichokes, pinecones, brazil nuts, and gold silk ivy); floral wire; wire cutters; 32" twig swag; hot glue gun; and 42" each of 1"w silver mesh wired ribbon, 1 1/2"w gold mesh ribbon, and 1 3/4"w copper mesh wired ribbon.

Note: Allow paint and glue to dry after each application.

1. Paint items to decorate swag as desired.
2. Using floral wire and glue, attach items to swag.
3. Tie ribbon lengths together into a bow; glue to top of swag.

GILDED TOPIARIES (Shown on page 16)

POMEGRANATE TOPIARY

You will need an 18"h twig topiary form, 18" of 1/2" dia. dowel rod, floral foam, 4 yds. of gold cord, 52" of 1"w silver mesh wired ribbon, floral wire, wire cutters, Design Master® copper spray paint, dried pomegranates, 10" dia. lichen-covered wreath, sheet moss, 12" dia. urn, and a hot glue gun.

Note: Allow paint and glue to dry after each application.

1. Paint pomegranates.
2. Trimming to fit, fill urn with floral foam. Glue wreath to foam. Insert dowel into foam. Fill center of wreath with sheet moss. Glue pomegranates around wreath.
3. Place topiary form over dowel. Spot gluing to secure, wrap cord around topiary.
4. Follow **Making a Bow**, page 187, to make a bow with four 7" loops and two 12" streamers. Glue bow to topiary.

MOSS TOPIARY

You will need Design Master® silver spray paint, two dried salal leaves, 6" dia. pot, floral foam, hot glue gun, sheet moss, 22"h moss topiary form with trunk, 4 yds. of silver cord, and 1 yd. of gold cord.

Note: Allow paint and glue to dry after each application.

1. Paint leaves.
2. Trimming to fit, fill pot with floral foam. Glue moss over top of foam. Insert trunk of topiary into foam.
3. Spot gluing to secure, wind 3 yds. of silver cord around topiary from top to bottom, then bottom to top.
4. Tie gold and remaining silver cords together into a bow; knot cord ends. Glue bow and leaves to top of topiary.

FERN TOPIARY

You will need Design Master® silver spray paint, dried salal leaves, 12" dia. wire urn, sheet moss, floral foam, hot glue gun, two 26" lengths of 1/2" dia. dowel rod, 2 1/2 yds. of 1 3/4"w copper mesh wired ribbon, and a 26"h vine-wrapped fern topiary form.

Note: Allow paint and glue to dry after each application.

1. Paint leaves.
2. Line urn with sheet moss. Trimming to fit, fill urn with floral foam. Glue moss over top of foam. Insert dowel rods into foam.
3. Insert leaves under vine on topiary form; glue to secure. Gluing ends to secure, wrap ribbon around topiary. Place topiary over dowels.

A GLORIOUS MANTEL
(Shown on page 17)

Glimmering tulle spills over the edge of this mantelpiece and reflects the light from this shining collection. Stacks of leather-bound books complement the gilded fruit, glittering bead garland, and Silvery Bird Nest. A hurricane lamp plays host to dried naturals as it sports a glistening ribbon. An assortment of candlesticks spreads the radiance.

Keeping this little slice of heaven firmly on earth, twig balls and Gilded Topiaries remind us of the simple beauty of nature.

CRIMSON AND ICE

Enrich your home's interior with the warmth of deep crimson and the icy crispness of white in this collection. At the center of the radiant display is a poinsettia-covered tree sprinkled with snowflakes, icicles, and other winter treasures. Sharing the spotlight are exquisite topiaries and luxurious embossed velvet accessories. You'll also marvel at garlands of frosty flowers and branches and packages tied up with big shimmery bows. You can create this snowy Christmas wonderland using the project instructions beginning on page 24.

Slip something special into our **Embossed Velvet Stocking** *(page 27)*! It's elegantly embellished with a snow-white cuff and trimmed with a gold tassel.

An **Embossed Velvet Pillow** *(page 24)* featuring gold fringe and dimensional paint highlights will warm up any nook or cranny.

Our **Crimson and Ice Tree** *(page 24)* is dressed up in glittering **Frosted Glass Ornaments** *(page 24)*, elegant **Snow-Edged Poinsettias** *(page 25)*, and shiny **Red Berry Ornaments** *(page 24)*. Decorative **Bow-Tied Tassels** *(page 25)* and eye-catching **Shimmering Snowflakes** *(page 25)* are among the adornments. Purchased garlands of jewels and icicles, along with icicle ornaments and clear glass orbs filled with shredded white Mylar™, add frosty flair to this exquisite evergreen.

Make a bold holiday statement with a centerpiece created using a striking **Beaded Topiary** *(page 26)*, a round **Poinsettia Topiary** *(page 26)*, and a hand-painted **Hurricane Candle Holder** *(page 26)* that features a frosty snowflake design. Surround these unique accents with festive **Floral Arrangements** *(page 26)* and **Frosted Glass Ornaments** *(page 24)*, made using white paint and glitter. White globe candles and wintertime garlands complete this feast for the eyes.

CRIMSON AND ICE TREE
(Shown on page 27)

Crisp, powdery snowfalls and the warming glow of the hearth – these are the images brought to mind by this crimson-and-ice tree. Bead and icicle garlands wind around its 7 1/2-foot height. More icicles along with golden glass teardrops sparkle among the branches.

Bright Frosted Glass Ornaments gleam in three different designs and sizes. Shiny Red Berry Ornaments and glistening Snow-Edged Poinsettias nestle beside Shimmering Snowflakes and Bow-Tied Tassels. Clear glass ornaments filled with shredded white Mylar™ reflect the glow of a jacquard fabric "snowdrift" beneath the tree.

RED BERRY ORNAMENTS
(Shown on page 22)

For each ornament, you will need red spray paint, 2" dia. plastic foam ball, 10" of 5/8"w gold mesh wired ribbon, floral pin, artificial frosted juniper sprigs, wired artificial red berry picks, wire cutters, hot glue gun, and red and white bead garland.

1. Spray paint foam ball; allow to dry.
2. For hanger, fold ribbon in half to make a loop. Use floral pin to pin loop and three juniper sprigs to top of ball.
3. Leaving 1/2" stems, use wire cutters to cut berries from picks. Apply glue to each stem and insert in ball to cover ball.
4. Cut beads from garland. Glue beads and additional juniper sprigs to top of ornament.

EMBOSSING VELVET

Note: Velvet must be 100% rayon.

1. For each design, trace desired pattern onto tracing paper. Use carbon paper to transfer pattern to linoleum printing block.
2. Use a colored pencil to lightly color in all areas to be cut away.
3. Holding block steady, use a carving tool with a medium U-shaped blade and shallow strokes to make initial cuts and a carving tool with a large U-shaped blade and deep strokes to scoop out colored areas of block. Use a toothbrush to brush away cuttings.

FROSTED GLASS ORNAMENTS
(Shown on page 22)

SMALL ORNAMENT
You will need white dimensional paint, 2 1/4" dia. red glass ornament, and white crystal glitter.

Paint a "snowcap" over top of ornament. Generously sprinkle glitter over wet paint; allow to dry. Gently shake ornament to remove excess glitter.

MEDIUM ORNAMENT
You will need water-based crystal glaze, 2 1/2" dia. red glass ornament, fine iridescent glitter, artificial variegated holly pick, and a hot glue gun.

1. Drip glaze over top of ornament. Sprinkle glitter over wet glaze; allow to dry. Gently shake ornament to remove excess glitter.
2. Remove five leaves from pick. Glue leaves around ornament cap.

LARGE ORNAMENT
You will need a craft stick, white dimensional paint, 4" dia. red glass ornament, an artificial dusty miller stem, hot glue gun, and 14" of 2 1/2"w sheer white wired ribbon.

1. Use craft stick to apply paint to each leaf and top half of ornament; allow to dry.
2. Use paint to make dots on and below painted area of ornament.
3. Remove six leaves from stem. Glue leaves around ornament cap. Tie ribbon into a bow through hanger on ornament.

4. For pattern placement, use chalk to mark center of each design on wrong side of velvet.
5. Place block, design side up on flat surface. Place velvet over block, with mark on velvet over center of design. Lightly mist wrong side of velvet with water. Using a hot, dry iron, press velvet for 10 to 15 seconds until impression is made; do **not** slide iron.

EMBOSSED VELVET PILLOW
(Shown on page 22)

You will need tracing paper, carbon paper, linoleum printing block, colored pencil, carving tools with medium and large U-shaped cutting blades, old toothbrush, chalk, 20" x 25" piece and a scrap piece of red 100% rayon velvet, polyester fiberfill, 25" of 6"w gold bullion fringe, fabric glue, and gold glitter dimensional paint.

1. Follow **Embossing Velvet**, this page, to prepare velvet.
2. Matching right sides and short edges, fold velvet in half. Using a 1/2" seam allowance and leaving an opening for turning, sew raw edges together. Turn pillow right side out. Stuff pillow with fiberfill. Sew opening closed.
3. Cut fringe into two 12 1/2" lengths. Turning cut ends of fringe under 1/4" to wrong side, glue a length of fringe along each end of pillow; allow to dry.
4. Dot paint in center of each embossed design; allow to dry.

EMBOSSING PATTERN

SHIMMERING SNOWFLAKES

(Shown on page 22)

For each ornament, you will need tracing paper, tape, clear shrinking plastic, white dimensional paint, ultra-fine iridescent glitter, sharp needle, and 6" of clear nylon thread.

1. Trace desired snowflake pattern onto tracing paper. Tape pattern to work surface. Tape plastic over pattern. Paint over lines of pattern on plastic. Sprinkle wet paint with glitter; allow to dry. Gently shake plastic to remove excess glitter.
2. Cut snowflake from plastic. Use needle to pierce snowflake and pull thread through hole; knot ends together.

SNOW-EDGED POINSETTIAS

(Shown on page 22)

For each poinsettia, you will need wire cutters, 9" dia. red artificial poinsettia stem, floral tape, dimensional paint applicator, Aleene's™ True Snow, and coarsely cut iridescent glitter.

1. Use wire cutters to trim stem to 5" long. Wrap stem with floral tape.
2. Fill applicator with True Snow. Apply a line of "snow" along edges of red leaves and on tips of green leaves. Sprinkle glitter over wet snow; allow to dry. Gently shake poinsettia to remove excess glitter.

BOW-TIED TASSELS

(Shown on page 22)

For each tassel, you will need 24" of ¹/₈" dia. pre-strung clear iridescent beads, 6" white tassel, hot glue gun, 1"w red and gold braid, and 16" of 1 ¹/₄"w red wired ribbon with gold edges.

1. Cut bead strand into six 4" lengths. Working around tassel below knot, glue one end of each string to tassel. Covering ends of beads, glue braid around top of tassel.
2. Tie ribbon into a bow around hanger of tassel; notch ends.

SNOWFLAKES

BEADED TOPIARY
(Shown on page 23)

You will need red spray paint; 16"h plastic foam cone; 5" dia. terra-cotta flowerpot; wood-tone spray; floral foam; hot glue gun; utility knife; 18" of $1/2$" dia. dowel rod; 18" of $5/8$"w white satin ribbon; $2 3/4$ yds. each of white and red bead garland, $1/4$" dia. velvet cord with $1/2$" lip, and $1/8$" dia. satin twist cord; two plastic foam snowflake ornaments; two white foam berry picks; fiberfill; snow texture paint; paintbrush; artificial snow; artificial holly pick; $1 1/4$"w red velvet wired ribbon with gold edges; spray adhesive; and 25" of $3/8$"w red velveteen cord.

Note: Allow paint and wood-tone spray to dry after each application.

1. Spray paint cone and flowerpot red. Lightly spray flowerpot with wood-tone spray. Fill pot with floral foam; glue to secure. Use utility knife to carefully shape each end of dowel to a point. Apply glue to one end of dowel; insert in center of pot. Apply glue to opposite end of dowel. Leaving 4" of dowel exposed for trunk, insert dowel in bottom of cone. Gluing ends to secure, wrap trunk with satin ribbon.
2. Beginning at top of cone and gluing in place, wind velvet cord, satin cord, and bead garland around cone. Glue one snowflake and one berry pick to top of cone.
3. Glue fiberfill over foam in pot. Paint fiberfill with texture paint. Sprinkle artificial snow over wet paint. Insert holly and remaining berry pick in flowerpot. Tie wired ribbon into a bow. Glue bow and remaining snowflake to flowerpot.
4. Lightly apply spray adhesive to topiary; sprinkle with artificial snow.
5. Knot ends of velveteen cord. Form three loops at center of cord; knot one streamer around center of loops. Glue bow to top of cone.

POINSETTIA TOPIARY
(Shown on page 23)

You will need red spray paint, $3 1/2$" dia. x 5"h terra-cotta flowerpot, floral foam, hot glue gun, spray adhesive, 6" dia. plastic foam ball, sheet moss, several 15" lengths of frosted twigs, fiberfill, snow texture paint, paintbrush, white plastic foam berry picks, artificial snow, flocked artificial holly picks, seven 9" dia. red artificial poinsettias, and 25" of $3/8$"w red velveteen cord.

Note: Allow paint to dry after each application unless otherwise indicated.

1. Spray paint flowerpot red. Fill pot with floral foam; glue to secure. Apply spray adhesive to foam ball; cover with moss.
2. For trunk, apply glue to one end of each twig and insert in center of pot. Leaving 6" exposed, insert remaining ends into ball.
3. Glue fiberfill over foam in pot. Paint fiberfill with texture paint. Sprinkle artificial snow over wet paint. Insert holly and white berry picks in pot.
4. Remove leaves from poinsettias. Beginning near bottom, arranging leaves from largest to smallest and overlapping as necessary, glue leaves to ball. Insert holly picks in top and bottom of ball. Insert remaining berry picks in top of ball.
5. Lightly apply spray adhesive to topiary and sprinkle with artificial snow.
6. Knot ends of velveteen cord. Form three loops at center of cord; knot one streamer around center of loops. Glue bow to top of ball.

FLORAL ARRANGEMENTS
(Shown on page 23)

For each arrangement, you will need floral pins, a 6"w triangle of 1" thick white plastic foam, artificial juniper sprigs, one Snow-Edged Poinsettia without green leaves (page 25), and white twigs.

1. Using floral pins to secure, cover foam with juniper.
2. Insert poinsettia at center of foam.
3. Using floral pins, arrange and secure juniper sprigs and white twigs around edges of poinsettia.

HURRICANE CANDLE HOLDER
(Shown on page 23)

You will need tracing paper, tape, 6" dia. x 7"h hurricane globe with gold stand, white dimensional paint, ultra-fine iridescent glitter, and a red pillar candle.

1. Trace large snowflake pattern onto tracing paper. Tape pattern inside globe.
2. Paint over lines of pattern on outside of globe. Sprinkle wet paint with glitter; allow to dry. Gently shake globe to remove excess glitter. Remove pattern. Place candle in globe.

STOCKING CUFF

EMBOSSED VELVET STOCKING (Shown on page 20)

You will need tracing paper, carbon paper, linoleum printing block, colored pencil, carving tools with medium and large U-shaped cutting blades, old toothbrush, chalk, 18" x 24" piece and a scrap of red 100% rayon velvet, 18" x 24" piece of white satin for lining, 10" x 28" piece of white satin for cuffs, two 18" lengths of $1/8$" dia. gold cord with lip, 12" of $1/8$" dia. twisted gold cord, 5" gold bead tassel, and gold glitter dimensional paint.

Note: Use a $1/4$" seam allowance for all sewing, unless otherwise indicated.

1. Using embossing pattern, page 24, follow **Embossing Velvet**, page 24, to prepare velvet.

2. Aligning arrows and dotted lines, trace stocking top and stocking bottom patterns onto tracing paper. For seam allowance, draw a second line $1/4$" outside first line around sides and bottom of stocking. Cut out pattern along outer line.

3. Matching right sides and short edges, fold velvet in half. Using pattern, cut stocking pieces from velvet. Repeat using satin for lining.

4. Leaving top edges open, sew stocking pieces together. Clip curves and turn stocking right side out. Repeat to sew lining pieces together; do not turn.

5. Follow **Making Patterns**, page 186, to trace cuff pattern onto tracing paper; cut out. Matching short edges, fold satin for cuffs in half. Matching long edges, fold in half again. Using pattern, cut four cuffs from satin. Matching lip with raw edge,

baste one 18" length of cord along curved edge on right side of one cuff piece. Repeat using remaining cord length and a second cuff piece.

6. Matching right sides and using a zipper foot, sew one cuff with cord to one plain cuff along curved edge; turn right side out. Repeat using remaining cuff pieces.

7. Place lining inside stocking. Place one cuff inside lining with center of cuff at toe seam; pin in place. Place second cuff inside lining with center at heel seam; pin in place. With raw edges even, sew stocking and cuffs together. Pull cuff out from stocking. Topstitch seam in place. Fold cuff down over stocking.

8. For hanger, knot ends of twisted cord together. Sew knot of hanger inside stocking at heel seam. Tack tassel to cuff on front of stocking.

9. Dot paint in centers of each embossed design; allow to dry.

STOCKING BOTTOM

STOCKING TOP

RADIANT WHITE CHRISTMAS

Wrap your home in the rare and radiant wonder of a sparkling snowy landscape with inspiration from this frosty collection. The star of our glistening fairyland is a striking evergreen filled with the elegant innocence of icicles and angels. The dreamy scene is accented with pristine packages topped with shimmering bows, a silvery stocking cuffed in white satin, and unforgettable greeting cards dusted with snowflakes. Instructions for the projects shown here and on the following pages begin on page 32.

For unbeatable holiday greetings, acknowledgments, and gift enclosures, send your wishes on **Radiant White Christmas Cards** *(page 32)*, topped with crocheted snowflakes and edged with silvery rickrack.

Our **Radiant White Christmas Tree** *(page 32)* is frosted with one-of-a-kind **Crocheted Snowflake Ornaments** *(page 33)*, captivating **Crocheted Angel Ornaments** *(page 35)*, picture-perfect **Silvery Rose Clusters** *(page 32)*, and crafty **Hand-Painted Jingle Bells** *(page 32)*. The lustrous image is enhanced with silver rope and iridescent bead garlands, snowflake and star ornaments, acrylic icicles, and star burst mini-lights.

A white satin cuff edged with lacy crochet trims our **Silver Jacquard Stocking** *(page 34)*, which is sure to catch Santa's eye.

Puffy bows in organza and brocade crown **Shimmering Packages** *(page 32)*. For an elegant accent, add handmade paper roses or a crocheted angel.

RADIANT WHITE CHRISTMAS TREE

(Shown on page 29)

Start dreaming of your own White Christmas with an eight-foot-tall flocked spruce tree. We entwined strands of white mini-lights and white mini star burst lights on tree branches. Then we draped silver rope and white iridescent bead garlands around the tree.

We added Silvery Rose Clusters to charm even the crustiest old scrooge and painted glittering holly berries on Hand-Painted Jingle Bells to ring in the holidays.

Lacy Crocheted Snowflake Ornaments and Crocheted Angel Ornaments (page 35) grace the branches with the essence of timeless perfection.

Five yards of frothy white fabric became soft snowdrifts when we strategically placed crinkled tissue paper beneath this downy wrap-around Christmas tree skirt.

We tied simple bows from 28" lengths of 2 1/2"w white and silver plaid wired ribbon and nestled them in the foliage. We then topped the tree with an ornate bow. To make the bow, we used four yards of ribbon and followed **Making a Bow** instructions (page 187), making a 4" center loop, twelve 9" loops, and two 15" streamers.

To complete the tree, we tucked purchased flocked twig branches, white pearl acorn picks, and crystal stems among tree branches for fullness. Glass snowflakes, porcelain star ornaments, and acrylic icicles lend a frosty elegance to this Radiant White Christmas.

SHIMMERING PACKAGES

(Shown on page 31)

You will need wrapped gifts, desired silver and white ribbons (we used checked, brocade, mesh, and organza wired ribbons), **Paper Twist Roses** (page 187) or a Crocheted Angel Ornament (page 35), white crochet thread (optional), and a hot glue gun.

1. Follow **Making a Bow**, page 187, to make a bow for package.
2. If desired, glue roses to bow or use crochet thread to tie angel to bow.

RADIANT WHITE CHRISTMAS CARDS

(Shown on page 28)

For each card and envelope, you will need bristol board, one 7" square each of background fabric and paper-backed fusible web, silver baby rickrack, hot glue gun, and a small Crocheted Snowflake Ornament.

Note: If mailing card, envelope should be marked "HAND CANCEL."

CARD

1. Cut a 6 1/4" x 12 1/2" piece from bristol board. Matching short edges, fold card in half.
2. Fuse web to wrong side of fabric. Cut a 5 1/2" square from fabric. Fuse fabric square to front of card. Glue rickrack along edges of fabric square. Use a needle and thread to tack snowflake to front of card.

ENVELOPE

1. Cut a 7 1/2" x 14" piece from bristol board.
2. For flap, fold one short edge of board 1" to one side. Clip each corner of flap diagonally.
3. For pocket, fold opposite short edge 6 1/2" toward flap. Glue side edges to secure.
4. Place card in envelope. Glue flap to pocket to secure.

SILVERY ROSE CLUSTERS

(Shown on page 30)

For each decoration, you will need a sprig of white holly with berries, silver spray paint, silver glitter paint, paintbrush, two or three white **Paper Twist Roses** (page 187), silver paint pen, and a hot glue gun.

1. Spray paint holly sprig silver; allow to dry. Lightly paint leaves with glitter paint; allow to dry.
2. Use paint pen to add accents to rose petals; allow to dry. Glue roses to holly stem.

HAND-PAINTED JINGLE BELLS

(Shown on page 30)

For each ornament, you will need a 3 1/2" dia. jingle bell with center rim, white spray paint, tracing paper, transfer paper, green paint pen, black permanent medium-point marker, silver glitter dimensional paint, silver glitter, 12" length of 1"w silver ribbon, foam brush, and craft glue.

Note: Allow paint to dry after each application.

1. Spray paint bell white.
2. Trace holly pattern onto tracing paper. Use pattern and transfer paper to transfer pattern to bell.
3. Use paint pen to paint leaves green. Use marker to outline leaves and berries and to draw detail lines on leaves. Use glitter paint to paint berries and a thin line around rim of bell. Brush a thin layer of glue over top of bell; sprinkle glitter over glue. Shake off excess glitter and allow to dry.
4. Thread ribbon through ring at top of bell. Tie ribbon into a bow.

CROCHETED SNOWFLAKE ORNAMENTS (Shown on pages 28 and 30)

For each ornament, you will need bedspread weight (#10) white cotton thread, steel crochet hook size 7 (1.65), tracing paper, corrugated cardboard or plastic foam sheet, plastic wrap, fabric stiffener, one-pint plastic bag with zipper closure, rustproof straight pins, and tape.

Note: Refer to **Crochet**, page 188, for abbreviations and general instructions.

SIX-POINT SMALL SNOWFLAKE

Ch 6, join with sl st to beginning ch to form a ring.
Rnd 1 (Right side): Ch 3 (**counts as first dc, now and throughout**), dc in ring, ch 1, (2 dc in ring, ch 1) 5 times; join with sl st to beginning dc: 6 ch-1 sps.
Rnd 2: Sl st in next dc, sl st in next ch-1 sp, ch 3, (dc, ch 2, 2 dc) in same sp, ch 1, ★ (2 dc, ch 2, 2 dc) in next ch-1 sp, ch 1; repeat from ★ 4 times **more**; join with sl st to beginning dc: 12 sps.
Rnd 3: Sl st in next dc, sl st in next ch-2 sp, ch 3, (dc, ch 2, 2 dc) in same sp, ch 3, skip next ch-1 sp, ★ (2 dc, ch 2, 2 dc) in next ch-2 sp, ch 3, skip next ch-1 sp; repeat from ★ 4 times **more**; join with sl st to beginning dc: 12 sps.
Rnd 4: Sl st in next dc, sl st in next ch-2 sp, ch 3, (dc, ch 2, 2 dc) in same sp, ch 7, skip next ch-3 sp, ★ (2 dc, ch 2, 2 dc) in next ch-2 sp, ch 7, skip next ch-3 sp; repeat from ★ 4 times **more**; join with sl st to beginning dc: 12 sps.
Rnd 5: Sl st in next dc, sl st in next ch-2 sp, ch 1, in same sp work [sc, ch 3, tr, (ch 6, sl st in third ch from hook) 5 times, ch 3, tr, ch 3, sc], ch 3, in next ch-7 sp work [2 sc, (ch 3, sl st in third ch from hook, 2 sc) 3 times], ch 3, ★ in next ch-2 sp work [sc, ch 3, tr, (ch 6, sl st in third ch from hook) 5 times, ch 3, tr, ch 3, sc], ch 3, in next ch-7 sp work [2 sc, (ch 3, sl st in third ch from hook, 2 sc) 3 times], ch 3; repeat from ★ 4 times **more**; join with sl st to beginning sc; finish off.
Using Blocking Pattern A, follow **Finishing Snowflakes** to stiffen snowflake.

EIGHT-POINT SMALL SNOWFLAKE

Ch 8, join with sl st to beginning ch to form a ring.
Rnd 1 (Right side): Ch 1, (sc in ring, ch 8) 8 times; join with sl st to beginning sc: 8 ch-8 sps.
Rnd 2: Sl st in next 4 chs, ch 1, sc in same sp, ch 12, ★ sc in next ch-8 sp, ch 12; repeat from ★ 6 times **more**; join with sl st to beginning sc: 8 ch-12 sps.
Rnd 3: Sl st in next ch-12 sp, ch 1, in same sp and in each ch-12 sp around work [3 sc, (ch 3, sl st in third ch from hook, sc) 3 times, (ch 5, sl st in third ch from hook) 3 times, ch 8, sl st in eighth ch from hook, ch 3, sl st in third ch from hook (ch 5, sl st in third ch from hook) twice, ch 2, sc, (ch 3, sl st in third ch from hook, sc) twice, ch 3, sl st in third ch from hook, 3 sc]; join with sl st to beginning sc; finish off.
Using Blocking Pattern B, follow **Finishing Snowflakes** to stiffen snowflake.

EIGHT-POINT LARGE SNOWFLAKE

Ch 6, join with sl st to beginning ch to form a ring.
Rnd 1 (Right side): Ch 4 (counts as first dc plus ch-1), (dc in ring, ch 1) 7 times; join with sl st to third ch of beginning ch-4: 8 ch-1 sps.
Rnd 2: Sl st in next ch-1 sp, ch 1, sc in same sp, ch 8, ★ sc in next ch-1 sp, ch 8; repeat from ★ 6 times **more**; join with sl st to beginning sc: 8 ch-8 sps.
Rnd 3: Sl st in next 4 chs, ch 1, sc in same sp, ch 12, ★ sc in next ch-8 sp, ch 12; repeat from ★ 6 times **more**; join with sl st to beginning sc: 8 ch-12 sps.

BLOCKING PATTERN A

BLOCKING PATTERN B

Rnd 4: Sl st in next ch-12 sp, ch 1, in same sp work [sc, 7 hdc, ch 6, sl st in sixth ch from hook, (ch 10, sl st in sixth ch from hook) 3 times, ch 10, sl st in tenth ch from hook, ch 6, sl st in sixth ch from hook (ch 10, sl st in sixth ch from hook) 3 times, 7 hdc, sc], ch 6, sl st in sixth ch from hook, ★ in next ch-12 sp work [sc, 7 hdc, ch 6, sl st in sixth ch from hook, (ch 10, sl st in sixth ch from hook) 3 times, ch 10, sl st in tenth ch from hook, ch 6, sl st in sixth ch from hook, (ch 10, sl st in sixth ch from hook) 3 times, 7 hdc, sc], ch 6, sl st in sixth ch from hook; repeat from ★ 6 times **more**; join with sl st to beginning sc; finish off.
Using Blocking Pattern B, follow **Finishing Snowflakes** to stiffen snowflake.

FINISHING SNOWFLAKES

1. Make one blocking pattern for each snowflake by tracing indicated Blocking Pattern onto tracing paper. Tape traced patterns on cardboard or foam sheet. Cover patterns with plastic wrap.
2. Place one snowflake and a small amount of stiffener in a plastic bag. Squeeze plastic bag and snowflake until snowflake is completely soaked with stiffener. Squeeze excess stiffener from snowflake. Pin snowflake over blocking pattern with right side up, making sure spokes of snowflake are centered over pattern lines and interior sections of snowflake are even and smooth. Repeat for remaining snowflakes. Allow snowflakes to dry completely. Remove pins.

SILVER JACQUARD STOCKING (Shown on page 31)

CROCHETED EDGING

You will need bedspread weight silver/white cotton thread and steel crochet hook size 6 (1.80) **or** size needed for gauge.

Note: Refer to **Crochet**, page 188, for abbreviations and general instructions.

Gauge Swatch: 1 5/8"w x 2 1/2"h
Work same as edging for five rows.

Ch 11, place marker in last ch made for st placement, ch 4: 15 chs.
Row 1 (Right side): Working in back ridges of beginning ch (**Fig. 1**), dc in sixth ch from hook, ch 2, skip next 2 chs, sc in next ch, ch 2, skip next 2 chs, (dc, ch 2, dc) in next ch, skip next 2 chs, dc in last ch: 5 sts and 4 sps.

Fig. 1

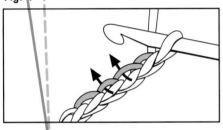

Row 2: Ch 3 **(counts as first dc, now and throughout)**, turn; (dc, ch 2, dc) in next ch-2 sp, ch 5, skip next 2 ch-2 sps, (dc, ch 2, dc) in next sp: 5 dc and 3 sps.
Row 3: Ch 5, turn; (dc, ch 2, dc) in next ch-2 sp, ch 2, sc in next ch-5 sp, ch 2, (dc, ch 2, dc) in next ch-2 sp, skip next dc, dc in last dc: 6 sts and 5 sps.

Row 4: Ch 3, turn; (dc, ch 2, dc) in next ch-2 sp, ch 5, skip next 2 ch-2 sps, (dc, ch 2, dc) in next ch-2 sp, place marker around last dc made for st placement, ch 1; working in end of rows, dc in next ch-5 sp, (ch 2, dc in same sp) 4 times, ch 1, sl st in marked st, remove marker: 10 dc and 9 sps.
Row 5: Turn; sc in first ch-1 sp (sc in next dc, 2 sc in next ch-2 sp) 3 times, ch 7, **turn**; skip first 5 sc, sl st in next sc, **turn**, 8 sc in next ch-7 sp, ch 5, **turn**; skip first 3 sc, sl st in next sc, **turn**; (4 sc, ch 3, 4 sc) in next ch-5 sp, 5 sc in remaining sp of ch-7 sp, sc in next dc, 2 sc in next ch-2 sp, sc in next dc and in next ch-1 sp, sl st in next dc and in next ch-2 sp, place marker in last sl st made for st placement, ch 5, dc in same sp, ch 2, sc in next ch-5 sp, ch 2, (dc, ch 2, dc) in next ch-2 sp, skip next dc, dc in last dc.
Row 6: Ch 3, turn; (dc, ch 2, dc) in next ch-2 sp, ch 5, skip next 2 ch-2 sps, (dc, ch 2, dc) in next sp, leave remaining sts unworked: 5 dc and 3 sps.
Repeat Rows 3-6 for 16", ending by working Row 4.
Last Row: Turn; sc in first ch-1 sp, (sc in next dc, 2 sc in next ch-2 sp) 3 times, ch 7, **turn**; skip first 5 sc, sl st in next sc, **turn**; 8 sc in next ch-7 sp, ch 5, **turn**; skip first 3 sc, sl st in next sc, **turn**; (4 sc, ch 3, 4 sc) in next ch-5 sp, 5 sc in remaining sp of ch-7 sp, sc in next dc, 2 sc in next ch-2 sp, sc in next dc and in next ch-1 sp, sl st in next dc; finish off.

STOCKING

You will need 2/3 yd. of white satin for cuff and lining, tracing paper, 1/2 yd. of 45"w silver jacquard fabric for stocking, 20" of 3/16" dia. cord, and 7 1/2" of 1"w white satin ribbon.

1. From satin, cut a 2" x 22" strip for welting and a 7 1/2" x 15" piece for cuff.
2. Aligning arrows and dotted lines, trace stocking top and stocking bottom patterns onto tracing paper. For seam allowance, draw a second line 1/4" outside first line around sides and bottom of stocking. Cut out pattern along outer line. Fold stocking fabric piece in half with right sides together. Use pattern to cut stocking from fabric. Repeat using satin fabric for stocking lining.
3. (**Note:** Use a 1/4" seam allowance for all sewing.) Leaving top edge open, sew stocking pieces together. Clip curves and turn stocking right side out. Repeat to sew lining pieces together; do not turn.
4. For welting, press one end of satin strip 1/2" to wrong side. Beginning 1/2" from folded end, center cord on wrong side of strip. Fold strip over cord. Beginning 1/2" from folded end, use a zipper foot to baste close to cord along length of strip. Trim seam allowance to 1/4".
5. For cuff, match right sides and stitch short edges of cuff fabric piece together; press seam open. Matching wrong sides and raw edges, fold cuff in half.
6. Matching raw edges and cuff seam to heel seam, place cuff over stocking. Beginning with pressed end of welting at cuff seam, pin welting along top of stocking. Trimming to fit, insert unfinished end of welting into folded end. Use zipper foot to sew around top of stocking as close to welting as possible. Press seam allowances to inside of stocking.
7. For hanging loop, fold ribbon in half. Tack loop inside stocking at heel seam. Fold top edge of lining 1/4" to wrong side; press. Place lining in stocking. Hand sew pressed edge of lining to seam allowance of welting. With ends of edging on back of stocking, tack top of crocheted edging to cuff just below welting.

STOCKING TOP

STOCKING BOTTOM

CROCHETED ANGEL ORNAMENTS (Shown on page 30)

For each ornament, you will need bedspread weight (#10) white cotton thread, steel crochet hook size 6 (1.80), 1" plastic ring, nine 4mm silver beads, ³/₈"w silver ribbon, hand sewing needle, and white thread.

Note: Refer to **Crochet**, page 188, for abbreviations and general instructions.

JOINING WITH SC
When instructed to join with sc, begin with a slip knot on hook. Insert hook in a stitch or space as indicated, YO and pull up a loop, YO and draw through both loops on hook.

HEAD
Rnd 1 (Right side): Join thread to plastic ring with sc; work 40 **more** sc in ring; join with sl st to first sc: 41 sc.
Note: Mark last round as right side.
Neck: Ch 1, turn; sc in same st and in next 8 sc, leave remaining 32 sc unworked; do **not** finish off: 9 sc.

RIGHT WING
Row 1: Ch 14, dc in sixth ch from hook, ch 1, skip next ch, ★ dc in next ch, ch 1, skip next ch; repeat from ★ 2 times **more**, sc in last ch; with **right** side facing, sl st in first sc on Neck.
Row 2: Ch 1, turn; sc in first sc, ch 1, (dc in next dc, ch 1) 4 times, skip next ch, dc in next ch: 5 ch-1 sps.
Row 3: Ch 4 (counts as first dc plus ch-1, now and throughout), turn; (dc in next dc, ch 1) 4 times, sc in last sc, sl st in **same** sc on Neck.
Row 4: Ch 1, turn; sc in first sc, (ch 1, dc in next dc) across.
Row 5: Ch 4, turn; (dc in next dc, ch 1) 4 times, sc in last sc, sl st in **next** sc on Neck.
Row 6: Repeat Row 4.
Row 7: Repeat Row 3.
Row 8: Repeat Row 4.
Row 9: Repeat Row 5; finish off.

DRESS
Row 1: With **right** side facing, join thread with sl st in first dc on Row 9 of Right Wing; ch 23, dc in sixth ch from hook, ch 1, skip next ch, (dc in next ch, ch 1, skip next ch) 8 times; working in sts across Row 9, (dc in next dc, ch 1) 5 times, sc in last sc, sl st in same sc on Neck: 15 sps.
Row 2: Ch 1, turn; sc in first sc, ch 1, (dc in next dc, ch 1) 14 times, skip next ch, dc in next ch: 15 dc and 15 ch-1 sps.
Row 3: Ch 4, turn; (dc in next dc, ch 1) 14 times, sc in last sc, sl st in **next** sc on Neck.
Row 4: Ch 1, turn; sc in first sc, (ch 1, dc in next dc) across.
Row 5: Ch 4, turn; (dc in next dc, ch 1) 14 times, sc in last sc, sl st in **same** sc on Neck.
Row 6: Ch 1, turn; sc in first sc, (ch 1, dc in next dc) across.
Rows 7 - 17: Repeat Rows 3 - 6 twice, then repeat Rows 3 - 5 once **more**. Finish off.

LEFT WING
Row 1: With **right** side facing, skip first 10 dc on Row 17 of Dress and join with sl st in next dc; place marker around dc just worked into for Edging placement, ch 4, (dc in next dc, ch 1) 4 times, sc in last sc, sl st in **next** sc on Neck: 5 ch-1 sps.
Row 2: Ch 1, turn; sc in first sc, (ch 1, dc in next dc) across.
Row 3: Ch 4, turn; (dc in next dc, ch 1) 4 times, sc in last sc, sl st in **same** sc on Neck.
Row 4: Ch 1, turn; sc in first sc, (ch 1, dc in next dc) across.
Row 5: Ch 4, turn; (dc in next dc, ch 1) 4 times, sc in last sc, sl st in **next** sc on Neck.
Rows 6 - 9: Repeat Rows 2 and 3 twice. Finish off.

EDGING
To work Cluster: Ch 3, YO, insert hook in third ch from hook, YO and pull up a loop, YO and draw through 2 loops on hook, YO, insert hook in same ch, YO and pull up a loop, YO and draw through 2 loops on hook, YO and draw through all 3 loops on hook.

With **right** side facing, join with sl st in marked dc on Dress; ch 2, dc in same st, (sl st, ch 2, dc) in top of dc at end of first 8 rows on Left Wing; working in sts across Row 9, (sl st, ch 2, hdc) in first 5 dc, sl st in last sc; working in unworked scs on Head, sl st in first 3 scs, work Cluster, (skip next 2 sc, dc in next sc, work Cluster) 8 times, skip next 2 sc, sl st in last 3 sc; working in free loops of beginning ch on Right Wing, (sl st, ch 2, hdc) in first ch (opposite sc), skip next ch, ★ (sl st, ch 2, hdc) in next ch, skip next ch; repeat from ★ 3 times more, (sl st, ch 2, dc) in next ch; (sl st, ch 2, dc) in top of dc at end of first 8 rows on Right Wing, sl st in top of dc at end of last row, ch 2; working in free loops of beginning ch on Row 1 of Dress, skip first ch, (sl st in next ch, ch 2, skip next ch) 9 times, (sl st, ch 2, dc) in next ch; (sl st, ch 2, dc) in top of dc at end of first 16 rows on Dress, sl st in top of dc at end of last row, ch 2; working in sts across Row 17, (sl st in next dc, ch 2) 9 times; join with sl st to joining sl st, finish off.

ANGEL FINISHING
1. Weave ribbon through spaces on Row 1 of Dress and every other row. Weave ribbon through spaces next to Edging on Wings; use needle and thread to secure all ribbon ends.
2. Tie an 8" length of ribbon into a bow. Sew bow and beads to Angel.

REDWORK REVIVAL

*T*his charming collection of old-fashioned redwork embroidery reflects the revival
of a crisp, clean Scandinavian style of outlining simple designs in red. It's a wonderful
way to spread seasonal cheer to the bedroom! If your room is too small for a full-size tree, don't
worry — just stitch fewer ornaments and decorate a tabletop tree. You'll find everything you
need to make your Yuletide merry, from personalized stockings, tree ornaments, and pillowcases
to a table topper that wishes a Merry Christmas to all. We've even captured the charm of
redwork in a lace-trimmed alphabet sampler. Instructions begin on page 40.

Sewn from red and white cotton ticking, our **Personalized Stockings** *(page 40)* feature embroidered cuffs fashioned from
a linen tablecloth. *(Opposite)* Four festive designs are embroidered on muslin to create the stuffed **Pillow Ornaments**
(page 40) that decorate the **Redwork Christmas Tree** *(page 40)*. Torn fabric bows, bouquets of baby's breath, holly sprigs,
and a lacy garland add a sense of sweetness. A chenille bedspread wraps the tree in snowy softness.

(Opposite) Designs from the pillow ornaments and lines from a classic holiday verse adorn our **Redwork Pillowcases** *(page 43)* and **"Merry Christmas" Table Topper** *(page 40).* The projects are holiday time-savers because they're made using purchased linens. *(Above)* Stitched on muslin, the motifs also border a simple alphabet in our **Redwork Sampler** *(page 42),* which is finished with Battenberg lace doilies.

REDWORK CHRISTMAS TREE

(Shown on page 37)

Our Redwork Christmas Tree will bring back memories of a time when your Mother or Grandmother patiently guided you in your first embroidery stitches. The pretty button-trimmed Pillow Ornaments and simple lace garland help recapture those sweet moments.

White lights twinkle cheerily through the boughs, and holly berry sprigs and bouquets of baby's breath add timeless beauty. Tied from torn fabric strips, red ticking bows make this tree a "candy cane" classic.

The tree skirt couldn't be more simple! It's a soft chenille bedspread draped around the base of the tree.

"MERRY CHRISTMAS" TABLE TOPPER

(Shown on page 38)

You will need vinegar, a red iron-on transfer pencil, tracing paper, 32" square linen table topper, embroidery hoop, red embroidery floss, sharp needle, $1/2$" dia. red buttons, and 45" of $1/4$"w red grosgrain ribbon.

Note: Refer to **Embroidery Stitches**, page 188, and **Stitch Key** and use two strands of floss for all embroidery stitches.

1. Mix 1 tablespoon vinegar in 8 ounces of clear water. Soak floss in mixture to release excess dye. Allow to air dry.
2. Use transfer pencil to trace the following patterns onto tracing paper: bell, page 41; bow, page 42; long border, page 43; and "Merry Christmas to all. . . ," page 44. Arrange patterns on table topper. Follow pencil manufacturer's instructions to transfer three bells, two bows, and "Merry Christmas to all. . ." patterns to right side of table topper. Repeating transfer as necessary, transfer long border around table topper.
3. Place table topper in hoop. Embroider design; remove from hoop.
4. Use floss to sew one button to each corner of border. Spacing evenly along length of ribbon, tie three bows in ribbon. Tack ribbon to table topper.

PERSONALIZED STOCKINGS

(Shown on page 36)

For each stocking, you will need vinegar, tracing paper; $1/2$ yd. each of red-and-white striped ticking for stocking and bleached muslin for lining; one 5" x 15" piece each of bleached muslin for cuff lining, paper-backed fusible web, and white linen for cuff (we used a piece from the border of a linen tablecloth); red iron-on transfer pencil; embroidery hoop; red embroidery floss; sharp needle; three $1/2$" dia. red buttons; 15" of $3/4$"w lace; and 8" of $1/4$"w red grosgrain ribbon.

Note: Use a $1/4$" seam allowance for all sewing. Refer to **Embroidery Stitches**, page 188, and **Stitch Key** and use two strands of floss for all embroidery stitches.

1. Mix 1 tablespoon vinegar in 8 ounces of clear water. Soak floss in mixture to release excess dye. Allow to air dry.
2. Aligning arrows and dotted lines, trace stocking top and stocking bottom patterns, page 27, onto tracing paper; cut out.
3. Matching right sides and short edges, fold fabric piece for stocking in half. Using pattern, cut stocking from fabric. Repeat using muslin for stocking lining.
4. Leaving top edge open, sew stocking pieces together. Clip curves; turn right side out. Repeat to sew lining pieces together; do not turn.
5. Fuse cuff lining to wrong side of linen. Matching short edges, fold cuff in half. Use straight pins to mark center and seam allowance. Use transfer pencil to trace letters for name from alphabet, page 45, onto tracing paper. Repeating design to extend border to 8", trace long border, page 43, onto tracing paper. Centering design between pins, arrange patterns on cuff with end of border at one short edge. Follow pencil manufacturer's instructions to transfer name and border to cuff.
6. Place cuff in hoop. Embroider design; remove from hoop. Use floss to sew buttons to cuff.
7. Topstitch lace along bottom edge of cuff. Matching right sides, sew short edges of cuff together. Matching raw edges and wrong side of cuff to right side of stocking, place cuff over stocking. Sew cuff to stocking. Press seam allowance to wrong side of stocking.
8. For hanging loop, fold ribbon in half. Tack ribbon ends to top of stocking at heel seam.

9. Press top edge of lining $1/4$" to wrong side. Place lining in stocking. Hand sew pressed edge of lining to seam allowance of stocking.

PILLOW ORNAMENTS

(Shown on page 37)

For each ornament, you will need vinegar, red iron-on transfer pencil, tracing paper, two 10" squares of bleached muslin, embroidery hoop, red embroidery floss, sharp needle, four $1/2$" dia. red buttons, polyester fiberfill, and two 10" lengths of $1/4$"w red grosgrain ribbon.

Note: Refer to **Embroidery Stitches**, page 188, and **Stitch Key** and use two strands of floss for all embroidery stitches.

1. Mix 1 tablespoon vinegar in 8 ounces of clear water. Soak floss in mixture to release excess dye. Allow to air dry.
2. Use transfer pencil to trace desired pattern onto tracing paper. Follow pencil manufacturer's instructions to transfer pattern to center of one fabric square.
3. Place square in hoop. Embroider design; remove from hoop.
4. Sew one button to each corner of design. Matching right sides and leaving an opening for turning, sew squares together $1/2$" from design. Clip corners; turn right side out.
5. Lightly stuff ornament with fiberfill. Hand sew opening closed.
6. For hanger, fold one ribbon length in half. Sew ribbon ends to back of ornament. Tie remaining ribbon length into a bow. Sew bow to front of ornament.

STITCH KEY	
Stitch Name	**Symbol**
French Knot	⊙
Lazy Daisy	⬯
Running Stitch	- - - -
Back Stitch	———

BELL ORNAMENT

BALL ORNAMENT

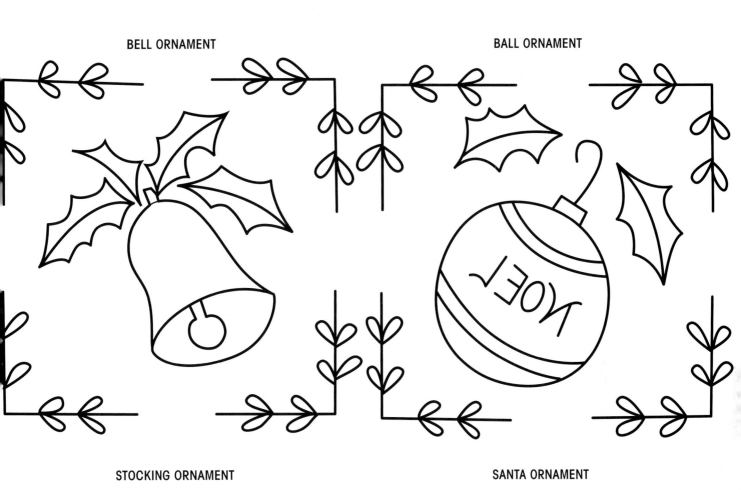

STOCKING ORNAMENT

SANTA ORNAMENT

41

REDWORK SAMPLER

(Shown on page 39)

You will need vinegar, 18" x 20" piece of paper-backed fusible web, two 18" x 20" pieces of bleached muslin, red iron-on transfer pencil, tracing paper, embroidery hoop, red embroidery floss, sharp needle, two $9\frac{1}{2}$" dia. linen doilies with Battenberg lace trim, $\frac{1}{4}$"w and $\frac{1}{2}$"w paper-backed fusible web tape, $19\frac{1}{2}$" x 21" piece of red-and-white striped ticking for backing, straight pins, two yds. of $\frac{3}{4}$"w flat lace, four $\frac{1}{2}$" dia. red buttons, 28" of $\frac{1}{4}$"w red grosgrain ribbon, $20\frac{1}{2}$" of $\frac{1}{2}$"w flat lace, and a 6" x 18" piece of bleached muslin for hanging sleeve.

Note: Refer to **Embroidery Stitches**, page 188, and **Stitch Key**, page 40, and use two strands of floss for all embroidery stitches.

1. Mix 1 tablespoon vinegar in 8 ounces of clear water. Soak floss in mixture to release excess dye. Allow to air dry.
2. Cut doilies in half; discard one piece.
3. Matching raw edges, fuse 18" x 20" muslin pieces together.

4. Use transfer pencil to trace alphabet, page 45; Santa, bell, ball, and stocking ornaments without borders, page 41; bow and leaves and bow only onto tracing paper. For borders, trace long border pattern, page 43, repeating as necessary to make two $13\frac{1}{2}$" top/bottom borders and two $15\frac{3}{4}$" side borders.
5. For sampler, arrange patterns on muslin. Follow pencil manufacturer's instructions to transfer patterns to sampler. Place sampler in hoop. Embroider designs. Remove from hoop; press. Repeat to embroider bow and leaves on one doily piece.
6. Trim edges of sampler to $\frac{1}{4}$" from border.
7. For backing, fuse web tape to wrong side of ticking along all edges; do not remove paper backing. Press edges $\frac{1}{2}$" to wrong side; unfold and remove paper backing. Refold and fuse short, then long edges in place.
8. Center sampler on right side of backing; pin in place. Using a narrow zigzag stitch, sew sampler to backing. Overlapping ends, topstitch lace around edges of sampler.

9. Sew one button at each corner of sampler. Tie a bow at center of ribbon. Sew bow to sampler; arrange streamers and tack in place
10. Fuse $\frac{1}{4}$"w web tape to wrong side of backing along bottom edge; remove paper backing. Overlapping to fit along bottom edge of backing and with stitched doily at center, arrange and fuse raw edges of doily pieces to wrong side of backing.
11. Topstitch $\frac{1}{2}$"w lace to doily pieces just below bottom edge of backing.
12. For hanging sleeve, press short edges of 6" x 18" muslin piece $\frac{1}{4}$" to wrong side twice; stitch in place. Matching right sides, sew long edges together to form tube. Turn sleeve right side out; press flat. Center one long edge of sleeve along top edge of back of sampler. Being careful not to sew through front, hand sew long edges of tube to sampler.

BOW AND LEAVES

REDWORK PILLOWCASES

(Shown on page 38)

You will need vinegar, red iron-on transfer pencil, tracing paper, pair of purchased pillowcases (we used white pillowcases with red-and-white striped trims), embroidery hoop, red embroidery floss, sharp needle, two $^1/_2$" dia. red buttons, and two 41" lengths of $^3/_4$ "w lace.

Note: Refer to **Embroidery Stitches**, page 188, and **Stitch Key**, page 40, and use two strands of floss for all embroidery stitches.

1. Mix 1 tablespoon vinegar in 8 ounces of clear water. Soak floss in mixture to release excess dye. Allow to air dry.
2. For each pillowcase, use transfer pencil to trace two short borders and two Santa patterns, page 41, (one of each in reverse) and ". . .And to all a Good Night" onto tracing paper. Arrange patterns on pillowcase above trim. Follow pencil manufacturer's instructions to transfer patterns to pillowcase.
3. Place pillowcase in hoop. Embroider designs; remove from hoop.
4. Sew button on border. Overlapping ends at back, topstitch lace around pillowcase at inside seam of trim.

SHORT BORDER

LONG BORDER

Merry Christmas to all ...

ABCDE
FGHIJ
KLMN
OPQR
STUV
WXYZ

KEEP CHRISTMAS IN YOUR HEART

Hearts abound in this collection, which gets its cheery look from a palette of vibrant color. Trimmed in a garland of white picket fences, the fun, folksy tree plays host to a multitude of winsome ornaments — from painted canvas characters and fabric-covered hearts to festive stars. And of course, we've included an angel to top the tree! Heartwarming messages embellish our framed tree trimmers, photo album cover, and greeting cards, and a photo frame reminds us that family is at the heart of Christmas. You'll also find some great ideas for decorating gift bags, furniture, and more. Instructions begin on page 52.

Keep holiday memories close at hand with this festive **Appliquéd Photo Album** *(page 52)*. Embroidered using simple running stitches, the sentimental message is enhanced by a homey scene.

Love is at the center of our **Keep Christmas in Your Heart Tree** *(page 52)*, which heralds the season in a series of **Heartfelt Framed Messages** *(page 54)*, **Puffed Heart Ornaments** *(page 52)*, and **Cardboard and Fabric Heart Ornaments** *(page 58)*. Foam **Star Ornaments** *(page 55)* and "tapers" fashioned from clip-on lights and sheets of beeswax add to the brilliance of the tree, and painted **Canvas Characters** *(page 56)* include angels, snowmen, and Santas. *(Opposite)* A star-studded frame showcases our **Angel Tree Topper** *(page 56)*, and our **Starry Heart Frame** *(page 54)* recognizes the importance of family. The collection wraps up with a selection of easy-to-assemble **Homey Gift Bags** *(page 57)*.

Our **Santa Picket** *(page 58)* does a stand-up job of spreading Christmas cheer. A wooden heart shows his kind, gentle spirit. *(Opposite)* These easy-to-fashion **Christmas Cards** *(page 55)* will leave you plenty of time to shop for the perfect gift! Designed to nurture your creative possibilities, our **Happy Heart Chairs** *(page 57)* reflect the collection's lively color scheme.

KEEP CHRISTMAS IN YOUR HEART TREE
(Shown on page 47)

You'll have a fun and folksy Christmas when this lovable country tree sets the theme. The 7¹/₂-foot weeping mountain pine looks anything but sad! It's bedecked with happy hearts from its angel-topped tip to its plaid fabric-skirted bottom.

Star Ornaments hang here and there, while stuffed Canvas Characters (page 56) help spread seasonal cheer. These fun-loving Santas, angels, and snowmen add a playful touch. For the Angel Tree Topper (page 56) one of the angel characters keeps a watchful eye over the festivities from a crafty frame.

Heartfelt Framed Messages (page 54) are friendly reminders of the spirit of Christmas. Cardboard and Fabric Heart Ornaments (page 58) and Puffed Heart Ornaments further brighten the boughs and help make your heart merry.

Glowing "tapers" are a snap to make by wrapping sheets of honeycomb beeswax around clip-on candle light strings.

Adding whimsy and a familiar touch of yesteryear, purchased garlands of picket fences and popcorn wind through the branches.

PUFFED HEART ORNAMENTS
(Shown on page 48)

For each ornament, you will need tracing paper, corrugated cardboard, red acrylic paint, paintbrush, 12" shoestring, wood-tone spray, hot glue gun, 3"w puffed wooden heart, ³/₄" dia. red button, and a hole punch.

Note: Allow paint and wood-tone spray to dry after each application.

1. Trace heart F, page 59, onto tracing paper; cut out. Using pattern, cut heart from cardboard. Paint corrugated side of cardboard heart red. Spray shoestring with wood-tone spray.
2. Center and glue wooden heart on cardboard heart. Glue button to wooden heart. For handle, punch two holes at top of cardboard heart. Thread ends of shoestring through holes; knot ends at front.

APPLIQUÉD PHOTO ALBUM (Shown on page 46)

You will need an 11" x 13" photo album with center rings; fabric to cover album; hot glue gun; poster board; fabric to line album; paper-backed fusible web; green print fabric for bow; pinking shears; one yd. of 1"w red grosgrain ribbon; hot glue gun, fabric marking pencil, 9¹/₂" x 11¹/₂" piece of green felt; yellow, red, green, brown, and black print fabrics for appliqués; tracing paper; transfer paper; yellow, red, and black embroidery floss; decorative-edge craft scissors; and lightweight corrugated cardboard.

Note: Follow **Embroidery Stitches**, page 188, and use six strands of floss for all embroidery stitches.

1. To cover album, draw around open album on wrong side of fabric. Cut out fabric 2" outside drawn line.
2. Center open album on wrong side of fabric piece. Fold corners of fabric diagonally over corners of album; glue in place. Fold edges of fabric over edges of cover, trimming fabric to fit under album hardware; glue in place.
3. To line inside of album, cut two pieces of poster board 1" smaller than front of album. Cut two pieces of fabric 2" larger than poster board pieces.
4. Center one poster board piece on one side of one fabric piece. Fold corners of fabric piece diagonally over corners of poster board; glue in place. Fold edges of fabric over edges of poster board; glue in place. Repeat with remaining poster board and fabric.
5. Glue covered poster board to inside covers.

6. For bow, fuse web to wrong side of green fabric. Use pinking shears to cut a ³/₄" x 1 yd.-length of green fabric. Center and fuse strip to ribbon; cut ribbon in half. Glue one end of each ribbon to outside opening edge of front and back covers.
7. Use fabric marking pencil and refer to album sections diagram to mark sections on felt piece.
8. Using fabrics for appliqués and patterns, pages 53 and 59, follow **Making Appliqués**, page 186, to make one each of heart A, heart L, tree trunk, ³/₄" x 1 ¹/₄" door, ³/₄" square chimney, roof, roof side, 2 ¹/₂" x 3 ⁵/₈" house front, 1 ¹/₂" x 2 ¹/₂" house side, and 1" x 6 ¹/₂" checkerboard base; three each of heart M and heart C appliqués; and five ³/₄" square windows and thirteen ¹/₂" square red checkerboard appliqués. Arrange and fuse appliqués to felt.
9. Trace "All Hearts Come Home For Christmas", page 53, onto tracing paper. Using transfer paper, transfer words to felt. Using red floss, work Running Stitches and Cross Stitches along section lines. Using yellow floss, work Running Stitches over words. Using black floss, work Running Stitches to outline appliqués and words and to make chimney smoke.
10. Use craft scissors to cut a 10¹/₄" x 12 ¹/₂" piece of cardboard. Fuse web to back of felt. Fuse felt to cardboard. Glue cardboard to front of album.

DIAGRAM

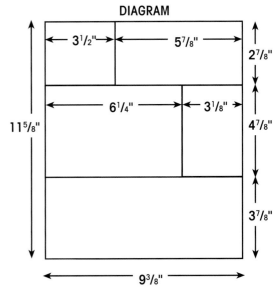

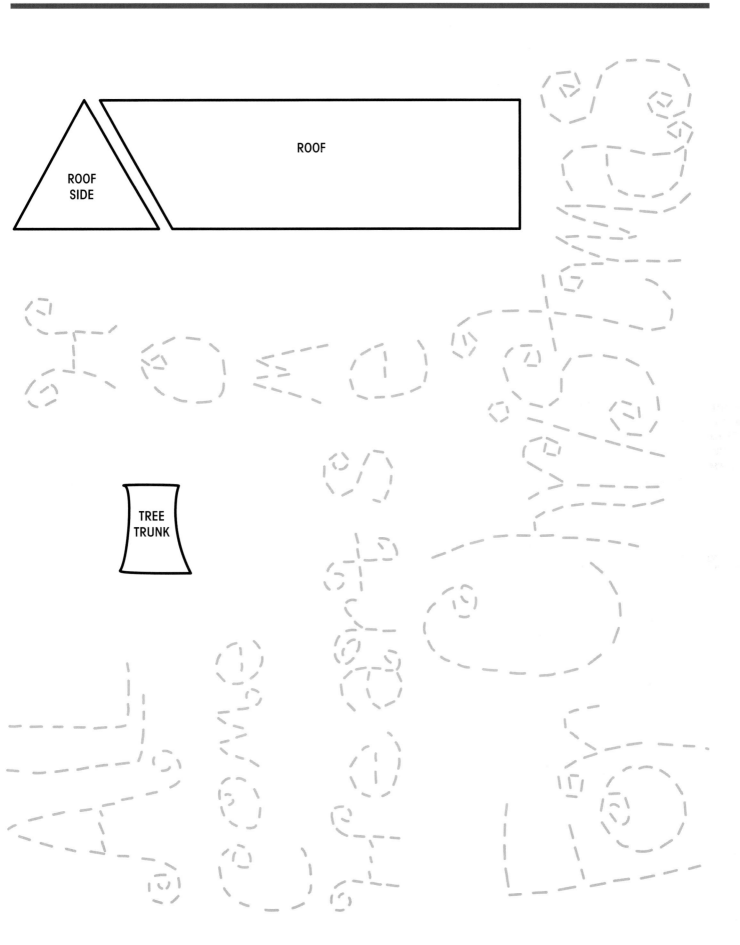

ROOF

ROOF
SIDE

TREE
TRUNK

"KEEP CHRISTMAS" FRAMED MESSAGE

You will need foam core board; craft knife; cutting mat; tracing paper; ultra-thin craft steel; decorative-edge craft scissors; paper crimping tool; red, light green, green, and beige acrylic paint; paintbrush; hot glue gun; crackle medium; clear acrylic spray sealer; black permanent fine-point marker; transfer paper; white card stock; red colored pencil; black permanent medium-point marker; and 10" of 20-gauge black craft wire.

Note: Use craft knife to cut foam core board. Allow paint, crackle medium, and sealer to dry after each application.

1. For back of frame, cut a 5" x 6" piece from foam core board. For front of frame, cut a 4" x 5" piece from foam core board with a 3" x 4" opening.
2. Trace heart J and heart K, page 59, onto tracing paper; cut out. Using patterns, cut one heart K from foam core board and one heart J from steel.
3. Use craft scissors to cut a 4 1/2" x 5 1/2" piece from steel. Use crimping tool to corrugate steel pieces. Paint foam core board heart red. Glue steel heart to foam core board heart.
4. Paint back of frame green. Follow manufacturer's instructions to apply crackle medium to back of frame. Paint back of frame beige. Apply sealer to back of frame. Alternating red and light green, paint stripes on front of frame. Use fine-point marker to draw lines between stripes.
5. Trace design onto tracing paper. Use transfer paper to transfer design onto card stock. Use colored pencil to color heart. Use medium-point marker to draw over message and heart. Trim design to 3 3/4" x 4 3/4".
6. Center and glue steel rectangle on back of frame, card stock on steel, and frame on card stock.
7. For hanger, centering foam core board heart on wire, thread wire through heart. Bend wire into a "U" shape. Apply glue to ends of wire. Insert ends into top of frame.

"SHARING" FRAMED MESSAGE

You will need foam core board, craft knife, cutting mat, tracing paper, ultra-thin craft steel, paper crimping tool, red and light green acrylic paint, paintbrush, crackle medium, clear acrylic spray sealer, transfer paper, white card stock, red colored pencil, hot glue gun, and 9" of 20-gauge black craft wire.

Note: Use craft knife to cut foam core board. Allow paint, crackle medium, and sealer to dry after each application.

1. For frame, cut a 5" square from foam core board with a 4" x 4" opening. Trace heart J and heart K, page 59, onto tracing paper; cut out. Using heart K pattern, cut four hearts from foam core board. Using heart J pattern, cut four hearts from steel. Use crimping tool to corrugate steel hearts.
2. Paint frame and foam core board hearts red. Follow manufacturer's instructions to apply crackle medium to frame. Paint frame light green. Apply sealer to frame.
3. Trace design onto tracing paper. Use transfer paper to transfer design onto card stock. Use colored pencil to color heart. Use medium-point marker to draw over message and heart. Trim design to 4 1/2" square.
4. Center and glue frame over design. Glue steel hearts to foam core board hearts. Glue hearts to corners of frame.
5. For hanger, wrap center of wire around a pencil. Bend wire into a "U" shape. Apply glue to ends of wire; insert ends into top of frame.

"HOME IS WHERE..." FRAMED MESSAGE

You will need foam core board; craft knife; cutting mat; tracing paper; red, green, and beige acrylic paint; paintbrush; crackle medium; black permanent medium-point marker; clear acrylic spray sealer; 5" of 20-gauge black craft wire; green raffia; hot glue gun; paper crimping tool; and ultra-thin craft steel.

Note: Use craft knife to cut foam core board. Allow paint, crackle medium, and sealer to dry after each application.

1. For front of frame, cut a 5" square from foam core board with a 3" square opening. For border, cut a 4" square from foam core board with a 3" square opening.
2. Trace heart N, page 59, onto tracing paper; cut out. Using pattern, cut heart from foam core board.
3. Paint border and heart beige. Paint front of frame green. Follow manufacturer's instructions to apply crackle medium to base and heart. Paint front of frame and heart red.
4. Use marker to write "Home is where you hang your heart" around border. Apply sealer to foam pieces.
5. Shape one end of wire into a heart. Insert straight end through top of front of frame and into top of heart. Tie raffia into a bow. Glue bow to heart. Glue border to front of frame.
6. Use crimping tool to corrugate a piece of steel large enough to cover opening in front of frame. Glue steel to back of base.

STARRY HEART FRAME
(Shown on page 49)

You will need gold, red, and green acrylic paint; paintbrushes; 11 1/4" square wooden frame; three 1 1/2"w and four 1 7/8"w wooden stars; crackle medium; clear acrylic spray sealer; tracing paper; decorative-edge craft scissors; ultra-thin craft steel; paper crimping tool; transfer paper; white card stock; red colored pencil; hot glue gun; 3 1/2"w wooden heart; two 3/4" x 10" and two 3/4" x 8 1/2" strips of green corrugated paper; assorted white buttons; and wood-tone spray.

Note: Allow paint, crackle medium, sealer, and wood-tone spray to dry after each application.

1. Paint frame green and stars gold. Follow manufacturer's instructions to apply crackle medium to frame. Paint front of frame red. Apply sealer to frame.
2. Trace heart D and heart E, page 59, onto tracing paper; cut out. Using heart E pattern and craft scissors, cut heart from steel. Use crimping tool to corrugate steel heart.
3. Trace design onto tracing paper. Use transfer paper to transfer design onto card stock. Use colored pencil to color heart in design. Use medium-point marker to draw over message and heart. Using heart D pattern cut design from card stock.
4. Center and glue card stock heart on wooden heart. Glue wooden heart on steel heart.
5. Glue paper strips to frame. Lightly spray stars and buttons with wood-tone. Glue steel heart to top of frame. Arrange and glue stars and buttons on frame.

CHRISTMAS CARDS (Shown on page 50)

"KEEP CHRISTMAS" CARD

You will need a 7" x 10" piece of red card stock, 5 1/4" x 7 1/4" natural-colored envelope, paper-backed fusible web, red and green print fabric, paper crimping tool, ultra-thin craft steel, tracing paper, transfer paper, white card stock, red colored pencil, black permanent medium-point and fine-point markers, hot glue gun, sewing thread, and assorted buttons.

Note: If mailing card, envelope should be marked "HAND CANCEL."

1. For card, match short edges to fold red card stock in half. Draw around flap of envelope and front of card on paper side of web. Fuse web to wrong side of fabric. Cut out flap along drawn line and card fabric 1/4" inside drawn lines. Fuse fabric to outside of envelope flap.
2. Use crimping tool to corrugate steel. Cut steel 1/2" smaller on all sides than card fabric.
3. Trace design onto tracing paper. Use transfer paper to transfer design onto card stock. Use colored pencil to color heart. Use medium-point marker to draw over message and heart. Trim design to 3"h x 4"w. Use fine-point marker to add a dot in each corner and a wavy line between each dot.
4. Center and glue message on steel. Center and glue steel on fabric. Wrap thread through holes in buttons and knot at back to secure. Glue a button to steel at each side of message.

"SHARING" CARD

You will need a 3" x 7 1/4" and a 7" x 10" piece of red card stock, 1/4" x 7 1/4" natural-colored envelope, hot glue gun, tracing paper, transfer paper, white card stock, red colored pencil, black permanent medium-point and fine-point markers, green corrugated paper, buttons, and green raffia.

Note: If mailing card, envelope should be marked "HAND CANCEL."

1. For card, match short edges to fold 7" x 10" piece of card stock in half. Draw around flap of envelope on remaining piece of red card stock. Cut out flap along drawn line. Glue card stock flap to outside of envelope flap.
2. Trace design onto tracing paper. Use transfer paper to transfer design onto card stock. Use colored pencil to color heart. Use medium-point marker to draw over message and heart. Trim design to 3"h x 5"w. Use fine-point marker to add a dot in each corner and a wavy line between each dot.
3. For card, cut two 1/2" x 4 1/2" and two 1/2" x 6 1/2" strips from corrugated paper; glue to card. For envelope flap, measure edges of flap; cut strips 1/2"w by the determined measurements. Glue strips to flap.
4. Glue buttons to corners of card and flap. Tie raffia into a bow. Glue bow to card.

STAR ORNAMENTS
(Shown on page 48)

For each ornament, you will need tracing paper, craft knife, cutting mat, foam core board, gold acrylic paint, paintbrush, wood-tone spray, hot glue gun, 3/4" dia. green button, and a 6" length of floral wire.

Note: Allow paint and wood-tone spray to dry after each application.

1. Trace star C, page 58, onto tracing paper; cut out. Using pattern and craft knife, cut star from foam core board.
2. Paint star gold. Spray star with wood-tone. Glue button to star. For hanger, glue one end of wire to back of star. Bend opposite end to form hook.

ANGEL TREE TOPPER
(Shown on page 49)

You will need foam core board; craft knife; cutting mat; beige, gold, and red acrylic paint; paintbrushes; assorted wooden stars; crackle medium; green corrugated paper; hot glue gun; assorted white buttons; one 6" and five 12" lengths of 20-gauge black craft wire; wood-tone spray; clear acrylic spray sealer; and a canvas angel without hanger.

Note: Allow paint, crackle medium, wood-tone spray, and sealer to dry after each application.

1. For frame, cut a 9" x 10$\frac{1}{2}$" piece from foam core board with an 8" x 9$\frac{1}{2}$" opening.
2. Paint stars gold and frame beige. Follow manufacturer's instructions to apply crackle medium to frame. Paint frame red.
3. Cut two $\frac{1}{2}$" x 8" strips and two $\frac{1}{2}$" x 9$\frac{1}{2}$" strips from corrugated paper. Center and glue short strips to top and bottom of frame and long strips to sides of frame. Glue stars and buttons to frame.
4. Wrap one 12" length of wire around a pencil; remove pencil. Repeat for remaining 12" lengths. Insert one end of each curled wire into top of frame. Glue one star to each remaining end. Lightly spray frame with wood-tone spray. Spray frame with sealer.
5. With 1" of wire extending above angel, center and glue 6" length of wire to back of angel. Center and insert wire extending above angel into top of frame.

CANVAS CHARACTERS (Shown on page 48)

For each character, you will need tracing paper; two 10" squares of cotton canvas fabric; one 10" square of batting; sewing thread; gesso; paintbrushes; transfer paper; pink, red, and black acrylic paint; black permanent fine-point marker; $\frac{3}{8}$" dia. white buttons; hot glue gun; wood-tone spray; clear acrylic spray sealer; 2"w wooden heart; fabric for heart; spray adhesive; and 10" of floral wire.
For snowman, you will **also** need orange acrylic paint.
For angel, you will **also** need white and green acrylic paint, corrugated cardboard, and household sponge.

Note: Allow gesso, paint, sealer, and wood-tone spray to dry after each application.

1. Trace patterns for desired character onto tracing paper; cut out. Draw around arm and leg or boot patterns twice and beard or body patterns once on one piece of canvas.

2. With drawn side on top, place batting between canvas pieces. Sew directly on drawn lines. Cutting close to stitching, cut out shapes. Paint one side of each piece with gesso. Use transfer paper to transfer detail lines to gesso side of pieces.
3. Paint pieces. Use marker to draw over detail lines. Sew one button to each boot or leg and arm.
4. Glue beard, arms, boots or legs to body. Apply wood-tone spray to character. Spray character with sealer.
5. For angel, trace wings pattern onto tracing paper, cut out. Draw around wings pattern on cardboard, cut out. Follow **Sponge Painting**, page 189, to lightly paint corrugated side of wings white. Glue wings to angel.
6. Draw around heart on wrong side of fabric; cut out just inside drawn line. Apply spray adhesive to wrong side of fabric heart; smooth onto wooden heart.
7. Glue arms to heart. For hanger, bend wire in half; glue ends to back of character.

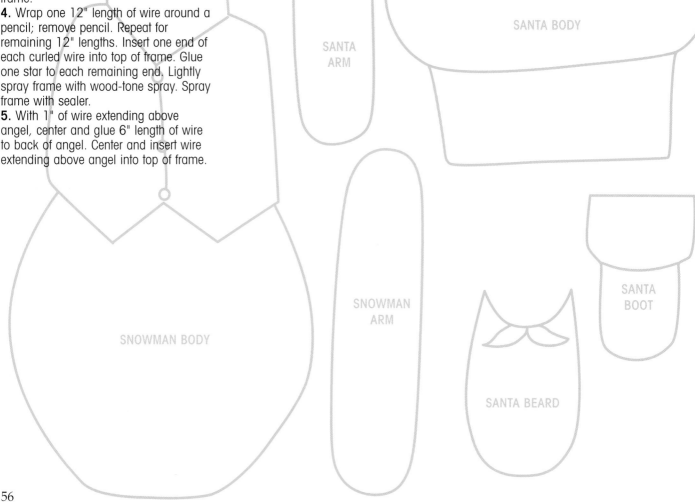

SANTA ARM

SANTA BODY

SANTA BOOT

SNOWMAN ARM

SANTA BEARD

SNOWMAN BODY

HOMEY GIFT BAGS (Shown on page 49)

BOW-TIED BAG
You will need a brown paper shopping bag, paper-backed fusible web, red-and-green print fabric, decorative-edge craft scissors, hole punch, green raffia, hot glue gun, and a 1" dia. button.

1. Measure width and height of front of bag; subtract $^1/_2$" from each measurement. Cut a piece of web the determined measurement.
2. Fuse web to wrong side of fabric; do not remove paper backing. Cut out fabric along edges of web. Center and fuse fabric to front of bag.
3. Use craft scissors to trim top edge of bag. Place gift in bag. Fold top of bag 2$^3/_4$" to front. Punch two holes 1" apart through folded part of bag. Thread several lengths of raffia through holes; tie into a bow on front of bag. Glue button to bow.

PUFFED HEART BAG
You will need paper-backed fusible web, green print fabric, kraft paper, decorative-edge craft scissors, 8" x 10" brown paper gift bag with handles, and a Puffed Heart Ornament (page 52).

1. Cut an 8" x 10" piece each of web, fabric, and kraft paper. Fuse web to wrong side of fabric; fuse fabric to kraft paper. Use craft scissors to trim short edges of rectangle.
2. Matching short edges, fold rectangle in half. Cut a slit along center of fold to fit over handles of bag. Place gift in bag. Place rectangle and ornament over handles.

STAR BAG
You will need a drawing compass, paper-backed fusible web, red print fabric, kraft paper, decorative-edge craft scissors, 8" x 10" gift bag with handles, hot glue gun, and a Star Ornament (page 55) without hanger.

1. Using compass, draw an 8" dia. circle on paper side of web; cut out. Fuse web to wrong side of fabric. Cut out fabric circle along edges of web. Fuse fabric to kraft paper. Use craft scissors to cut out circle.
2. Fold circle in half. Cut a slit along center of fold to fit over handles of bag. Place gift in bag. Place circle over handle. Glue ornament to circle and bag.

LARGE GIFT BAG
You will need large brown paper grocery bag, paper-backed fusible web, red and green print fabrics to cover bag, hot glue gun, jute twine, craft wire, wire cutters, six $^3/_8$" and four 1" buttons, tracing paper, kraft paper, black permanent fine-point marker, and a Cardboard and Fabric Heart Ornament (page 58).

1. Carefully pull bag apart at seams.
2. Measure height of bag; subtract 5". Measure width of bag. Cut a piece of fusible web and one piece of red fabric the determined measurements. Fuse web to wrong side of fabric. Aligning bottom of bag with one long edge of fabric, fuse fabric to bag.
3. Measure width of bag. Cut one piece of fusible web and one piece of green fabric 10" by the determined measurement. Fuse web to wrong side of fabric. Do not remove paper backing. Matching long edges, press fabric in half; unfold. Remove paper backing. Refold fabric over top of bag. Fuse fabric to inside and outside of bag.
4. Trimming to fit, glue twine to bag between red and green fabrics. Reassemble bag.
5. For handles, cut one $^3/_4$" x 32" piece each of green fabric and fusible web. Fuse web to wrong side of fabric. Cut fabric into four equal lengths. Cut two 8" lengths of wire. Center each wire between wrong sides of two fabric strips. Fuse fabric strips together. Glue handles to outside of bag. Glue 1" buttons to ends of handles.
6. Trace heart B pattern, page 59, onto tracing paper; cut out. Using heart B pattern and red fabric, follow **Making Appliqués**, page 186, to make six heart B appliqués. Fuse appliqués to kraft paper. Cut out hearts $^1/_4$" outside edges of fabric. Use marker to draw "stitches" around hearts.
7. Glue heart appliqués to front of bag. Glue $^3/_8$" buttons to hearts. Glue ornament to front of bag.

HAPPY HEART CHAIRS
(Shown on page 50)

MINI CHAIR
You will need a hot glue gun, one Cardboard and Fabric Heart Ornament without hanger (page 58), 5"w flat wooden heart, and a child's chair (we used a red-stained chair with a woven seat).

Note: For decorative use only.

1. Glue ornament to heart.
2. Glue heart to back of chair.

LARGE CHAIR
You will need tracing paper, craft knife, cutting mat, foam core board, ultra-thin craft steel, paper crimping tool, assorted colors of acrylic paint (we used white, yellow, red, and green), paintbrushes, hot glue gun, two 10" lengths of 20-gauge craft wire, large marker (to shape wire), two thumbtacks, ladder-back chair with a removable woven seat, fine-grit sandpaper, tack cloth, spray primer, black permanent medium-point marker, and clear acrylic spray sealer.

Note: Allow primer, paint, and sealer to dry between applications.

1. Trace heart J, heart K, page 59, star A, and star B patterns, page 58, onto tracing paper; cut out. Using patterns and craft knife, cut one heart K and one star B from foam core. Using patterns, cut one heart J and one star A from steel.
2. Use crimping tool to corrugate steel shapes. Paint foam heart and star desired colors. Glue steel shapes to foam shapes.
3. Wrap a length of wire around large marker; remove marker. Repeat with remaining wire. Insert one end of each wire into a foam shape. Wrap remaining end of each wire around a thumbtack. Insert thumbtacks into top of chair uprights.
4. Remove seat. Lightly sand chair. Wipe chair with tack cloth. Spray chair with primer. Paint desired base coats on chair.
5. Use a pencil to draw designs on chair (we drew squares, circles, hearts, and wavy lines). Paint designs. Use medium-point marker to write "Live each day with a happy ♥" on top rung of chair back. Apply two to three coats of sealer to chair. Replace seat.

WING

ANGEL ARM

ANGEL BODY

ANGEL LEG

SANTA PICKET (Shown on page 51)

You will need a handsaw; 6-ft. wooden fence picket; ⁷/₈" dia. wooden ball for nose; white, flesh, pink, red, brown, and black acrylic paint; paintbrushes; 1 ¹/₈" square piece of household sponge; black permanent medium-point marker; 14" x 25" piece of red striped fabric for hat; hot glue gun; red sewing thread; 1 ³/₈" dia. jingle bell; natural raffia; two green print fabrics for patches; paper-backed fusible web; tub and tile caulk; soft cloth; 12" long greenery branch; and a Puffed Heart Ornament (page 52).

Note: Allow paint to dry after each application.

1. Use handsaw to cut 15" from top of picket. Paint picket and nose red.
2. Refer to **Fig. 1** to paint sections on picket.

Fig. 1

3. Follow **Sponge Painting**, page 189, to sponge white squares in a checkerboard pattern on shirt and pants. Use white paint to highlight boots. Paint cheeks pink and eyes black; use marker to add details.
4. Aligning short end of fabric with top of face and overlapping long edges at back, glue fabric for hat to picket. Glue long edges of hat together to secure.
5. Leaving 6" thread ends, work **Running Stitch**, page 189, around top of hat. Pull thread ends to gather top of hat; knot ends to secure. Sew bell to top of hat. Tie raffia into a bow around bell.
6. For patches, use green fabrics and follow **Making Appliqués**, page 186, to make four 2" to 2¹/₂" square appliqués. Fuse two appliqués to front of hat. Fuse remaining appliqués to front of Santa.
7. Referring to **Fig. 1** for placement, apply caulk for pants cuff, hair, eyebrows, mustache, beard, and fur trim on hat. Push nose into caulk to secure. Allow caulk to dry for 24 hours in a warm, dry room.
8. To stain caulk, mix one part brown paint with two parts water. Brush thinned paint over a small area of caulk; use cloth to wipe off excess paint. Continue staining and wiping small areas of caulk until all caulk is covered, allow to dry.
9. Tie raffia into a bow around branch. Glue branch to picket. Hang ornament over branch. Glue side of hat to side of picket.

CARDBOARD AND FABRIC HEART ORNAMENTS
(Shown on page 48)

For each ornament, you will need 1"w wooden heart, gold and brown acrylic paint, paintbrush, crackle medium, soft cloth, clear acrylic spray sealer, tracing paper, decorative-edge craft scissors, corrugated cardboard, two 5" squares each of red and green print fabrics and paper-backed fusible web, pinking shears, 10" of ¹/₈"w green silk ribbon, hot glue gun, hole punch, and natural raffia.

Note: Allow paint and crackle medium to dry between applications.

1. Paint wooden heart gold. Follow manufacturer's instructions to apply crackle medium to wooden heart. For antiquing solution, mix one part brown paint with one part water. Paint heart with solution; use cloth to wipe off excess. Spray heart with sealer.
2. Trace heart I, page 59, onto tracing paper; cut out. Using pattern and craft scissors, cut heart from cardboard.
3. For appliqués, trace heart G and heart H, page 59, onto paper side of web. Using heart G and heart H patterns, and using pinking shears to cut out heart H, follow **Making Appliqués**, page 186, to make one each of heart G and heart H appliqués from fabrics. Fuse heart H to cardboard heart, then heart G to heart H.
4. Tie ribbon into a bow. Glue wooden heart and bow to ornament. For hanger, punch a hole in top of ornament. Thread raffia through hole; knot ends to secure.

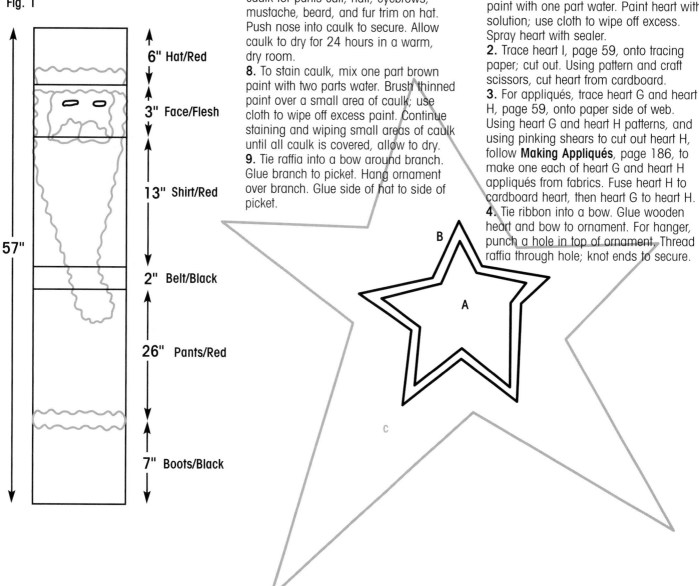

57"

6" Hat/Red
3" Face/Flesh
13" Shirt/Red
2" Belt/Black
26" Pants/Red
7" Boots/Black

B

A

C

"BEARY" SWEET NATIVITY

Here's a whimsical re-creation custom-made for teddy bear collectors — the coming of the Christ Child is depicted with cute, cuddly teddy bears dressed up as the Holy Family! Soft felt robes and traditional headcloths adorn Mary and Joseph, and the sweet face of Baby Jesus peeks out from cozy swaddling clothes tied up with raffia. You won't be able to resist making this "beary" sweet trio!

HOLY FAMILY

MARY

You will need tracing paper, 18" x 21 1/2" piece of blue felt, pinking shears, 12"h jointed teddy bear, hot glue gun, 1 yd. of 1"w blue wired ribbon, blue fabric dye, white tea towel with Battenberg lace edging, straight pins, and 18" of 1/2"w blue picot-edged satin ribbon.

1. For robe pattern, cut a 9" x 10 3/4" piece from tracing paper. Refer to **Fig. 1** to draw pattern on tracing paper; cut out.

Fig. 1

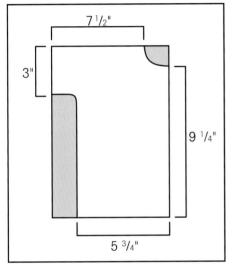

2. Matching short edges, fold felt in half from top to bottom. Fold again from right to left. Refer to **Fig. 2** for pattern placement. Cut out sides and underarms. Use pinking shears to cut out neck and trim sleeves and bottom edges of robe.

Fig. 2

3. Use a 1/4" seam allowance to sew each side seam from ends of sleeves to bottom edges of robe. Turn robe right side out. Use pinking shears to cut robe down center front from neck to bottom edge (**Fig. 3**).

Fig. 3

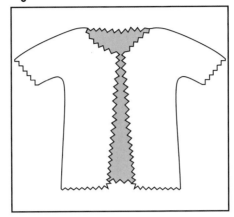

4. Fold sleeves 1 1/2" to right side for cuffs. Press one opening edge of robe 1/2" to right side. Place robe on bear. Overlapping left side over right side, glue robe front closed.

5. Wrap wired ribbon around bear and knot at back. Bring ribbon ends around bear and knot in front.

6. For headcloth, follow manufacturer's instructions to dye towel; press. Measuring from lace edge, cut towel to 12" long. Press cut edge 1/4" to wrong side; press 1/4" to wrong side again. Stitch in place.

7. Drape headcloth over bear's head with lace edge on top. Pull ears through openings in lace; pin to secure. Gather lace edge of headcloth at neck; pin to secure. Knotting at back of head, tie satin ribbon around ears.

JOSEPH

You will need tracing paper, pinking shears, 18" x 21 1/2" piece of green felt, 12"h jointed teddy bear, hot glue gun, 1 yd. of 2"w green moiré ribbon, one 14" square each of white fabric and green print fabric, craft knife, cutting mat, 18" of 1/4" dia. green twisted cord, and round box or can for stand (we used a 3 7/8" dia. x 4 5/8"h papier-mâché box).

1. Using green felt, follow Steps 1 - 3 of Mary to make robe.

2. Fold sleeves 1 1/2" to right side for cuffs. Press one opening edge of robe 3/4" to right side. Place robe on bear. Overlapping left side over right side, glue robe front closed.

3. Using moiré ribbon, follow Step 5 of Mary to tie ribbon around bear.

4. For headcloth, matching right sides and leaving an opening for turning, use a 1/4" seam allowance to sew fabric squares together. Turn right side out. Hand sew opening closed; press.

5. Place headcloth on bear and mark position of ears. Remove headcloth. Use craft knife to cut a slit for each ear. Inserting bear's ears through slits, replace headcloth. Knotting cord ends together at back and gluing to secure, wrap cord around ears.

6. Place Joseph's feet in box or can.

BABY JESUS

You will need pinking shears, 16" square of cotton batting, 6"h teddy bear, and natural raffia.

1. Use pinking shears to trim edges of batting. Place bear right side up on batting with head 4" from one corner.

2. Wrap remaining three corners tightly around bear. Crisscrossing raffia several times before knotting, wrap raffia around bear and batting; knot to secure. Tuck top corner of batting under bear's head.

A FESTIVAL OF WREATHS

Adorned with a wealth of characters and colors, our festive wreaths graciously convey seasonal goodwill. Stylings from this eclectic collection, which range from elegant to whimsical, add beauty and warmth to home and hearth. Including designs with special appeal for lovers of nature, music, and cooking, our versatile wreaths offer handsome ways to deck your halls, doors, and walls. Whatever your fancy, you'll find an enchanting way to spread Christmas joy in our Festival of Wreaths! Instructions for the projects shown here and on the following pages begin on page 66.

Glowing with Yuletide grandeur, the **Elegant Angel and Roses Wreath** *(page 66)* is a gilded fantasy of gold-tipped roses and grape leaves, gold mesh bows, and a paper twist angel dressed in damask.

A delicious inspiration, the **Gingerbread Kitchen Wreath** *(page 67)* is a perfect place to display your favorite tools of the cooking trade. This treasure is all done up in vintage kitchen utensils, spice-trimmed gingerbread men, peppermint candies, and a sprightly gingham bow.

Capable of carrying your thoughts to a mountainside retreat, our **Lively Cardinal Wreath** *(page 67)* is all aflutter with jaunty redbirds, snow-frosted pinecones, red-berried holly, golden jingle bells, and a perky plaid bow.

Add a nostalgic touch to your Christmas trimmings with our **Fabric Poinsettia Wreath** *(page 66)*. A peppermint-striped bow highlights this wintry warmer, which is accented with fused fabric and felt poinsettias, flocked branches, and glittery garlands.

Enter the holiday season on a high note with our golden-tone "**Note-able**" **Nutcracker Wreath** *(page 67)* featuring a parade of nutcrackers in assorted colors and sizes. Delightful drums, antiqued sheet music, a red crinkle bow, and gilded musical notations complete the harmonious arrangement.

ELEGANT ANGEL AND ROSES WREATH (Shown on page 62)

You will need a 20" dia. flocked artificial wreath, 10 gold artificial grape leaves, 2" dia. plastic foam egg, cream and peach paper twist, two 6" lengths of $^1/_8$" dia. wooden dowel, gold angel fleece for hair, 24" of 2$^1/_4$"w gold and white damask wired ribbon, 2 yds. of $^5/_8$"w gold mesh wired ribbon, 3$^1/_2$ yds. of 2"w gold mesh wired ribbon, 3 yds. of 1$^1/_2$"w gold-edged sheer wired ribbon, 6" of gold wired cord, floral wire, wire cutters, three cream **Paper Twist Rose** centers (page 187) for buds, eight cream **Paper Twist Roses** (page 187), tracing paper, metallic gold acrylic paint, paintbrush, 2" wooden star, 2$^2/_3$ yds. of gold bead garland, and a hot glue gun.

1. For angel head, cut foam egg in half lengthwise. Cut a 6" square from peach paper twist; untwist and flatten. Gluing edges of paper twist to flat side of one foam piece, cover head with paper twist. Glue flat side of head to one end of one dowel. Arrange and glue fleece to head for hair.
2. For angel dress, cut a 28" length of cream paper twist; untwist and flatten. Matching short edges, fold paper twist in half. Matching short edges, fold damask ribbon in half. Matching folded edges, place damask ribbon on top of paper twist. For waist, pinch ribbon and paper twist together 2$^1/_2$" below folds; secure

with floral wire. Arrange and glue dress to dowel below head. Tie a 24" length of $^5/_8$"w ribbon into a bow around waist. Trim ribbon and paper twist ends as desired. Glue two gold leaves below bow.
3. For arms, cut a 12" length from 2"w gold mesh ribbon. Thread ribbon through paper twist twist at top of dress. Fold each end of arm 1$^1/_2$" to back. For wrists, knot a length of $^5/_8$"w ribbon around each arm 1" from folded end; trim ends close to knots.
4. For halo, use gold cord to form a 2" dia. circle with a 2" stem; twist to secure. Glue stem to back of head.
5. For wings, cut a 15" length of cream paper twist twist; untwist and flatten. Matching short ends, fold in half. Trim ends diagonally and unfold. Pinch wings at center and secure with floral wire.
6. Use gold paint to paint star, remaining dowel, and highlights on wings, rosebuds, and roses; allow to dry.
7. Glue star to one end of dowel. Glue remaining end of dowel to one hand, wings to back of angel, and grape leaves to bases of roses.
8. For each bow, cut one 24" length each from sheer ribbon and 2"w gold mesh ribbon. Tie ribbon lengths together into a bow. Notch each ribbon end. Repeat to make a total of four bows.
9. Arrange bead garland, bows, angel, and roses on wreath; glue to secure.

FABRIC POINSETTIA WREATH
(Shown on page 64)

You will need a 24" dia. flocked artificial pine wreath, six 18" and six 8" squares of paper-backed fusible web, two 18" squares each of three different red print fabrics, two 8" squares each of three different green print fabrics, three 18" and three 8" squares of white felt, tracing paper, twenty-two 8" lengths of floral wire, 3 yds. of 2$^1/_2$"w red and white striped wired ribbon with gold backing, 4 yds. of 2$^3/_4$"w red taffeta ribbon, 2$^1/_2$ yds. each of metallic red rope garland and clear iridescent bead garland, twelve 15mm gold beads, white flocked branches, garden clippers, and a hot glue gun.

1. Fuse web to wrong side of each fabric square. Fuse matching fabric squares to front and back of each felt square.
2. Trace leaf and poinsettia petal sections A, B, and C separately onto tracing paper; cut out. Use patterns to cut four each A, B, and C petal sections from red fabric-covered felt squares. Cut sixteen leaves from green fabric-covered felt squares.
3. For each poinsettia, layer petal sections from largest to smallest, rotating petals. Bend one length of floral wire in half. Insert wire ends through front center of poinsettia; twist to secure. For each leaf, insert one length of wire between fabric layers for stem. Arrange and glue four leaves to back of each poinsettia. Glue three beads to center of each poinsettia, covering wire.
4. Using striped ribbon, follow **Making a Bow**, page 187, to make a bow with eight 10" loops and two 5" streamers. Using taffeta ribbon, make a bow with six 14" loops and two 20" streamers. Glue striped bow to center of taffeta bow.
5. Cut flocked branches to desired lengths; insert and glue in wreath.
6. Arrange rope and bead garlands in wreath. Arranging as desired, wire bow and poinsettias to wreath.

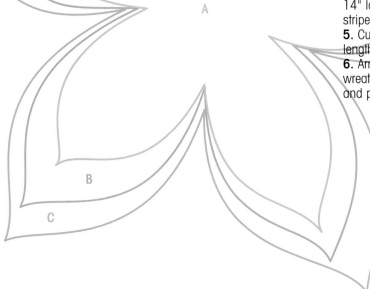

66

GINGERBREAD KITCHEN WREATH

(Shown on page 63)

You will need an 18" dia. artificial pine wreath, tracing paper, yellow foam food trays, craft knife, floral wood tone spray, red and white paint pens, black permanent fine-point marker, whole allspice, whole cloves, floral wire, wire cutters, assorted kitchen utensils, 1 1/4 yds. of 2"w red and white checked wired ribbon, six artificial holly sprigs, peppermint disk candies, cinnamon sticks, and a hot glue gun.

Note: Allow wood tone spray and paint to dry after each application.

1. Trace gingerbread man pattern onto tracing paper; cut out. Draw around pattern three times on wrong side of foam trays. Use knife to cut out gingerbread men. Spray right side of each gingerbread man with wood tone spray.
2. For each gingerbread man, use red paint pen to paint feet, heart, and swirls for cheeks. Use white paint pen to paint a zigzag line across each arm. Use marker to draw "stitches" on each heart.
3. Glue allspice to each gingerbread man for eyes and buttons. For mouth, insert stems of cloves through foam; glue to secure.
4. Arrange utensils on wreath; wire in place. Tie ribbon into a bow. Arrange bow, gingerbread men, holly sprigs, cinnamon sticks, and candies on wreath; glue in place.

GINGERBREAD MAN

"NOTE-ABLE" NUTCRACKER WREATH

(Shown on page 65)

You will need a 24" dia. artificial pine wreath with a foam base, red and green plaid and solid red wrapping paper, sheet music, wood tone spray, gold acrylic paint, paintbrush, floral pins, 4 1/2 yds. of 2 1/2"w red crinkle satin wired ribbon with gold trim, spool of floral wire, 4" long floral picks, wire cutters, six 2 1/4" dia. gold jingle bells, three 3" dia. drum ornaments, five 6"h and three 9"h nutcrackers, six gold musical symbol ornaments, and a hot glue gun.

1. Lightly spray wrapping paper and sheet music with wood tone spray; allow to dry. Tear twenty-five 4" squares each from wrapping paper and sheet music. Lightly brush gold paint along edges of solid red and sheet-music squares; allow to dry.
2. To make each paper cluster, layer one sheet-music square on top of one or two wrapping paper squares. Insert a floral pin through center of layered papers. Loosely wrapping papers around thumb, push floral pin into foam base of wreath. Spacing evenly, repeat to add desired number of paper clusters to wreath.
3. For each bell, thread wire through loop of bell and center of one wrapping paper square; wire to floral pick.
4. Using wired ribbon, follow **Making a Bow**, page 187, to make a bow with ten 12" loops and two 10" streamers. Wire bow and drums to floral picks.
5. Using a length of wire to secure large nutcrackers to wreath and inserting floral picks into foam, arrange drums, bells, large nutcrackers, and bow on wreath.
6. Arrange and glue musical symbols and small nutcrackers around wreath.

LIVELY CARDINAL WREATH

(Shown on page 63)

You will need a 24" dia. artificial pine wreath, tracing paper, red felt, black fabric scraps, gold fabric scraps, black embroidery floss, five 2 1/2" dia. gold jingle bells, 1 2/3 yds. of 3/4"w plaid ribbon, two 2 1/2 yd. lengths of 2 1/2"w plaid wired ribbon with gold backing, four 1" dia. gold glass ornaments, sixteen artificial holly sprigs, floral wire, wire cutters, seven flocked pinecones, gold glitter twigs, fabric glue, and a hot glue gun.

Note: Use hot glue for all gluing, unless otherwise indicated.

1. Trace cardinal patterns onto tracing paper; cut out. Use patterns to cut ten cardinal bodies and sixteen wings from red felt, five beaks from gold fabric, and five masks from black fabric.
2. For each body or wing, match edges of two felt pieces and use six strands of floss to work **Blanket Stitch**, page 189, to join edges.
3. For each bird, determine direction bird will face on wreath. Use fabric glue to glue mask, beak, and one wing to front of bird. For three birds, glue a second wing to back of bird.
4. Cut 3/4"w ribbon into five 12" lengths. Thread one length of ribbon through loop at top of each bell and tie into bow.
5. Using one length of 2 1/2"w ribbon, follow **Making a Bow**, page 187, to tie a bow with a 6" center loop, six 10" loops, and two 9" streamers. Arrange remaining ribbon length on wreath; glue in place.
6. Arrange and wire bow and bells to wreath. Arrange birds, ornaments, pinecones, holly sprigs, and gold twigs on wreath; glue to secure.

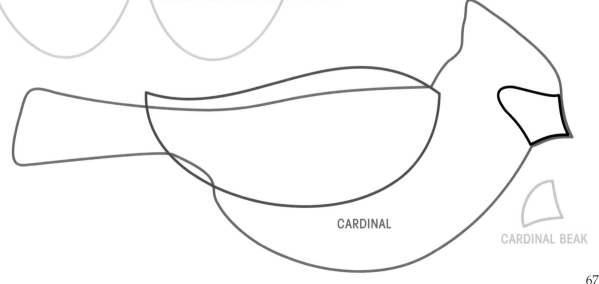

CARDINAL

CARDINAL BEAK

YULETIDE MEMORIES

*T*he coming together of family and friends at Christmastime creates memories that last a lifetime. This festive collection is full of ways to capture those cherished moments so they may be enjoyed again and again. For decorating the tree, you'll find creative photograph ornaments and hand-painted baubles, as well as a merry memento tin. For truly timeless reminders of your loved ones, there are precious keepsakes such as a memory album and a personalized Christmas quilt. Instructions for the projects shown here and on the following pages begin on page 72.

A charming quilt square and cheery bow adorn our fabric-covered **Yuletide Memories Album** *(page 76)*. The **Memory Album Pages** *(page 76)* are decorated with jolly motifs to accent your favorite photographs. *(Opposite)* Wrap someone special in holiday spirit with a **Yuletide Memories Quilt** *(page 72)*. Each block contains a loved one's signature that is stitched over with embroidery floss.

(Top left) Remember the holidays with our charming dated **Quilt-Block Ornament** *(page 76)* made from remnants of holiday fabric or show off a picture of someone sweet in this **Candy Cane Heart Ornament** *(page 79)*. **Starry Glass Ornaments** *(page 77)* are easy to decorate using paint pens. *(Top right)* Leave lasting impressions of a child's touch on these **Handprint Ornaments** *(page 78)*. They're created from fabric-covered poster board shapes stamped with handprints. *(Above)* These **Stocking Photo Ornaments** *(page 75)*, fashioned from painted canvas and "stuffed" with photographs, make fun and festive decorations for the mantel or tree.

Store your precious remembrances in a colorful **Holiday Keepsake Tin** (*page 74*). We accented a spray-painted can with simple Christmas designs and topped it with a fabric-covered lid.

These decorations are even more festive when they're sporting the faces of your favorite folks! To make our adorable **Star Photo Ornaments** (*page 75*), **Snow Folk Ornaments** (*page 77*), **Bearded Santa Ornaments** (*page 79*), and **Gingerbread Photo Ornaments** (*page 78*), simple holiday shapes are cut from felt.

YULETIDE MEMORIES QUILT (Shown on page 69)

Block size: 14 1/4" x 14 1/4"
Quilt size: 75" x 91"

Note: Fabric yardage is based on 45"w fabric. All fabrics should be washed, dried, and pressed before beginning project.

You will need 3 5/8 yds. of green print fabric, 3 3/4 yds. of white print fabric, 2 3/8 yds. of red print fabric, rotary cutter, rotary cutting ruler, cutting mat, sewing thread, quilter's silver pencil, embroidery floss, embroidery needle, embroidery hoop (optional), stencil plastic, craft knife, 81" x 96" fabric (pieced as necessary) for quilt backing, masking tape, 81" x 96" batting, quilting hoop or frame, quilting needle, quilting thread, thimble, and 1 yd. of fabric for binding.

CUTTING OUT THE PIECES

Note: All measurements include a 1/4" seam allowance. Strips are cut from selvage to selvage across the width of the fabric. To cut strips, fold fabric, matching selvages. Aligning ruler at a right angle to fold of fabric, cut one edge to even fabric. Continue cutting strips from evened edge. Use rotary cutter, rotary cutting ruler, and cutting mat for all cutting.

1. From green print:
- Cut 12 **strips** 2 7/8"w.
- Cut 2 lengthwise **side borders** 4" x 83 3/4".
- Cut 2 lengthwise **top/bottom borders** 4" x 74 1/2".

2. From white print:
- Cut 12 **strips** 2 7/8"w.
- Cut 3 strips 14 3/4"w. From these strips, cut 49 **sashing strips** 2 1/2" x 14 3/4".
- Cut 6 strips 5 1/4"w. From these strips, cut 80 **rectangles** 2 7/8" x 5 1/4".
- Cut 3 strips 5 1/4"w. From these strips, cut 20 **large squares** 5 1/4" x 5 1/4".

3. From red print:
- Cut 6 strips 5 1/4"w. From these strips, cut 80 **rectangles** 2 7/8" x 5 1/4".
- Cut 12 strips 2 7/8"w. From these strips, cut 160 **squares** 2 7/8" x 2 7/8".
- Cut 2 strips 2 1/2"w. From these strips, cut 30 **sashing squares** 2 1/2" x 2 1/2".

ASSEMBLING THE QUILT TOP

Note: Unless otherwise indicated, match right sides and raw edges and use a 1/4" seam allowance and sewing thread for all sewing. Press seam allowances to one side (toward darker fabric when possible).

1. Sew 1 white and 1 green **strip** together to make **Strip Set**. Make 12 **Strip Sets**. Cut across **Strip Sets** at 2 7/8" intervals to make 160 **Unit 1's**.

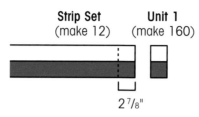

Strip Set (make 12)   Unit 1 (make 160)

2 7/8"

2. Sew 2 **Unit 1's** together to make **Unit 2**. Make 80 **Unit 2's**.

Unit 2 (make 80)

3. Place 1 red **square** on 1 white **rectangle** and stitch diagonally as shown in **Fig. 1**. Trim 1/4" from stitching line as shown in **Fig. 2**. Press open, pressing seam allowance toward darker fabric.

Fig. 1   **Fig. 2**

4. Place 1 red **square** on opposite end of **rectangle**. Stitch diagonally, as shown in **Fig. 3**. Trim 1/4" from stitching line as shown in **Fig. 4**. Press open, pressing seam allowance toward darker fabric, to make **Unit 3**.

Fig. 3   **Fig. 4**

Unit 3

5. Using remaining red **squares** and white **rectangles**, repeat Steps 3 and 4 to make a total of 80 **Unit 3's**.
6. Sew 1 **Unit 3** and 1 red **rectangle** together to make **Unit 4**. Make 80 **Unit 4's**.

Unit 4 (make 80)

7. Sew 2 **Unit 2's** and 1 **Unit 4** together to make **Unit 5**. Make 40 **Unit 5's**.

Unit 5 (make 40)

8. Sew 2 **Unit 4's** and 1 **large square** together to make **Unit 6**. Make 20 **Unit 6's**.

Unit 6 (make 20)

9. Sew 2 **Unit 5's** and 1 **Unit 6** together to make **Block**. Make 20 **Blocks**.

Block (make 20)

10. Sew 5 **sashing squares** and 4 **sashing strips** together to make **Sashing Row**. Make 6 **Sashing Rows**.

Sashing Row (make 6)

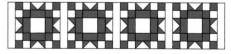

11. Sew 5 **sashing strips** and 4 **Blocks** together to make **Block Row**. Make 5 **Block Rows**.

Block Row (make 5)

12. Referring to **Quilt Top Diagram**, sew **Sashing Rows** and **Block Rows** together to make center section of quilt top.
13. Sew **side**, then **top** and **bottom** borders to center section of quilt top.

COMPLETING THE QUILT

14. For embellishment, have family members use silver pencil to write names and messages on center squares of quilt blocks. Use embroidery floss to work **Stem Stitch**, page 189, over penciled messages.

15. Using quilting patterns, this page and page 74, follow **Making Patterns**, page 186, to trace patterns onto stencil plastic. Use craft knife to cut narrow segments along traced lines. Referring to **Quilting Diagram**, use stencils and silver pencil to mark quilting lines on quilt top.

16. To layer quilt, place quilt backing wrong side up on a large, flat surface. Use masking tape to tape edges in place. Center batting on backing. Center quilt top right side up on batting. Beginning at center of quilt and smoothing fullness toward outer edges, baste quilt layers together (use long stitches and place basting lines 3" to 4" apart).

17. Secure quilt in a quilting hoop or frame. Thread quilting needle with an 18" to 20" length of quilting thread; knot one end. Using a thimble, insert needle into quilt top $1/2$" from where you wish to begin quilting. Bring needle back up at desired beginning point. When knot catches on quilt top, give thread a quick, short pull to "pop" knot through fabric into batting. Using a short **Running Stitch**, page 189, through all fabric layers, quilt along all marked lines. At end of each thread length, knot thread close to fabric and "pop" knot into batting. Clip thread close to fabric.

18. Cutting binding strips $2 1/2$"w, follow **Binding**, page 186, to bind quilt.

QUILT TOP DIAGRAM

QUILTING DIAGRAM

HOLIDAY KEEPSAKE TIN (Shown on page 71)

You will need a large tin (we used a 10" dia. x 11"h tin); white spray primer; white spray paint; medium-weight batting; white solid, red and green print, and red striped fabrics; paper-backed fusible web; ³/₈ "w red print and ³/₄ "w green grosgrain ribbon; ³/₄" iron-on letters; green and red felt; tracing paper; pinking shears; fabric glue; and a hot glue gun.

Note: Use hot glue for all gluing unless otherwise indicated.

1. Remove lid from tin. Allowing to dry between applications, paint outside of tin with primer, then white paint.

2. Trace around lid on batting, white fabric, and wrong side of red print fabric. Cut out batting along drawn line. Cut out print fabric ³/₄" outside drawn line. Use pinking shears to cut out white fabric 1¹/₂" inside drawn line.

3. Glue batting to top of lid. Center and glue print fabric circle over batting. Make ¹/₂" clips in fabric around lid. Glue edges of fabric to side of lid. Trim fabric even with bottom edge of lid if necessary.

4. Measure around lid; add ¹/₂". Cut a length of each ribbon the determined measurement. Overlapping ends at back, glue ³/₄", then ³/₈" ribbons around lid. Repeat to add ribbon around bottom of tin.

5. Use fabric glue to glue white circle to green felt. Using pinking shears and leaving a ¹/₈" felt border, cut out circle. Follow manufacturer's instructions to fuse letters to circle. Using fabric glue, center and glue circle to lid.

6. Using patterns, pages 116 and 117, follow **Making Appliqués**, page 186, to make one each tree, gingerbread boy, large star, and heart appliqués from desired fabrics.

7. Cut four 5" x 7¹/₄" rectangles each from white fabric and web. Cut one 4" x 7¹/₄" rectangle each from striped fabric and web. Cut one 4" x 5" rectangle each from striped fabric and web. Fuse web to wrong side of each fabric piece. Cut 4" x 7¹/₄" rectangle into eight ¹/₂" x 7¹/₄" strips. Cut 4" x 5" rectangle into eight ¹/₂" x 5" strips.

8. Use pinking shears to cut two 5¹/₂" x 7³/₄" rectangles each from red and green felt. Center and fuse one white rectangle to each felt rectangle. Center and fuse one appliqué to each rectangle. Fuse long, then short strips along edges of each white rectangle.

9. Spacing evenly, glue rectangles to side of tin.

QUILTING PATTERN

STOCKING PHOTO ORNAMENTS (Shown on page 70)

For each ornament, you will need tracing paper; canvas fabric; gesso; transfer paper; white, red, and green acrylic paint; paintbrushes; black permanent medium-point marker; white paper; craft glue; photograph; poster board; craft stick; hot glue gun; 4" of grosgrain ribbon; and a button.

Note: Use hot glue for all gluing unless otherwise indicated. Allow gesso, paint, and glue to dry after each application.

1. Trace stocking pattern, including detail lines, onto tracing paper. Use pattern to cut two stocking shapes from canvas.
2. Matching edges and leaving top edge open, use a $1/4$" seam allowance to sew stocking pieces together. Trim seam allowance to $1/8$".

3. Paint stocking with gesso. Use transfer paper to transfer cuff, toe, and heel lines onto stocking. Use acrylic paints to paint cuff white and stocking, heel, and toe desired colors. If desired, transfer small star and "stitches" to stocking. Paint details on stocking. Use marker to write desired message on white paper; cut out. Use craft glue to glue message on cuff.
4. Use craft glue to glue photograph on poster board; cut out as desired. Glue craft stick to back of poster board. Insert craft stick in stocking; glue to secure.
5. For hanging loop, glue ends of ribbon inside stocking. Glue button to front of stocking below hanger.

STAR PHOTO ORNAMENTS
(Shown on page 71)

For each ornament, you will need one 6" square each of white felt and poster board, craft glue, green print fabric scrap, red print fabric scrap, paper-backed fusible web, green felt, pinking shears, tracing paper, photograph, hot glue gun, 12" of $1/8$"w gold braid, black permanent fine-point marker, five 5mm gold jingle bells, and clear thread.

Note: Use craft glue for all gluing unless otherwise indicated. Allow glue to dry after each application.

1. Glue white felt to poster board.
2. Using heart and large star patterns, follow **Making Appliqués**, page 186, to make heart appliqué from green fabric and star appliqué from red fabric. Fuse star to felt-covered poster board. Leaving a $1/4$" white border, cut out star. Glue star to green felt. Using pinking shears and leaving a $1/4$" green border, cut out star. Fuse heart to center of red star.
3. Trace star photo pattern onto tracing paper. Use pattern to cut face from photograph. Glue photograph to center of heart. Beginning at top, hot glue braid around photograph. Tie remaining braid into a bow. Hot glue bow above photograph.
4. Use marker to draw "stitches" around heart and along edges of red star. Hot glue a jingle bell to each point of red star.
5. For hanger, use a needle to thread 8" of clear thread through top of ornament; knot ends together 3" above ornament and trim ends.

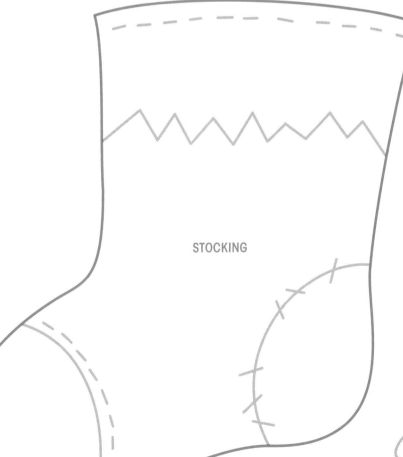

LARGE STAR

STOCKING

SMALL STAR

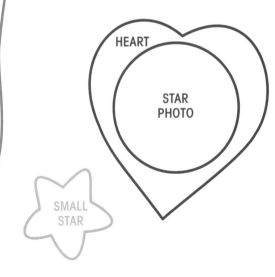

HEART

STAR PHOTO

YULETIDE MEMORIES ALBUM
(Shown on page 68)

You will need a photo album with acid-free pages and aluminum post-and-screw binders; batting; red striped fabric to cover album; red, green, and white print fabrics; paper-backed fusible web; hot glue gun, 8" of 60"w green felt; decorative-edge craft scissors; poster board; one Quilt-Block Ornament without buttons, bow, and hanger; 16" length of 1"w satin ribbon; and a 1" dia. button.

1. Draw around closed album twice on poster board and batting. Cut out batting pieces along drawn lines and poster board pieces $^1/4$" inside drawn lines. Glue one batting piece each to front and back covers. Remove covers from album. With stripes positioned vertically on album, draw around entire front cover on wrong side of fabric. Cut out 4" outside drawn lines. Repeat for back cover.
2. Center album front batting side down on wrong side of one fabric piece. Fold corners of fabric piece diagonally over corners of cover; glue in place. Fold edges of fabric over edges of cover; glue in place. Make clips in fabric at holes for posts. Repeat for back cover. Replace covers on album.
3. Measure height of album; add 3". Cut one piece 7"w by the determined measurement each from red fabric and web. Fuse web to wrong side of fabric. Fuse fabric to green felt. Using craft scissors and leaving a $^3/8$" felt edge, trim edges of fabric piece. Centering fabric piece on front cover, wrap and glue short ends to inside of cover.
4. With stripes positioned vertically on poster board piece, draw around poster board piece on wrong side of fabric. Cut out 2" outside drawn lines. Center poster board on wrong side of fabric. Fold corners of fabric piece diagonally over corners of poster board; glue in place. Fold edges of fabric over edges of poster board; glue in place. Center and glue fabric-covered poster board inside front cover. Repeat for back cover.
5. Center and glue ornament on front of album.
6. Tie ribbon into a bow. Glue button and bow at top of quilt square.

MEMORY ALBUM PAGES
(Shown on page 68)

You will need tracing paper; 8 $^1/2$" x 11" sheets of acid-free paper in solids and prints; colored pencils; green, brown, and black permanent medium-point markers; photographs; glue stick; decorative-edge craft scissors; and acid-free album pages.

GINGERBREAD BOY PAGE
1. Trace gingerbread boy pattern, page 116, onto tracing paper; cut out. For each gingerbread boy, use brown marker to draw around pattern on right side of acid-free paper; cut out just outside drawn lines. Use black marker to add face and buttons to gingerbread boy. Use brown pencil to shade edges of gingerbread boy. Use white pencil to draw zigzags across arms and legs.
2. For each photo, glue photo to desired paper for border. Using craft scissors and leaving a $^1/4$" border, cut out photo. Arrange photos and gingerbread boys on desired paper for background; glue in place. Use markers and colored pencils to freehand greenery and berry details on page as desired. Glue photo page to album page.

TREE PAGE
1. Trace tree and trunk patterns, page 116, onto tracing paper; cut out. Draw around patterns on wrong side of acid-free paper; cut out.
2. For each photo, glue photo to desired paper for border. Using craft scissors and leaving a $^1/4$" border, cut out photo. Use green pencil to add line and dot details along edges of border. Arrange photos, trunk, and tree on desired background paper; glue in place. Use white pencil to add snowflakes and dots to background paper. Glue photo page to album page.

QUILT-BLOCK ORNAMENTS
(Shown on page 70)

For each ornament, you will need one 4 $^1/2$" square each of white print fabric, poster board, and paper-backed fusible web; red and green print fabric scraps; paper-backed fusible web; craft glue; green felt; pinking shears; 12" of 1"w red satin polka-dot ribbon; four $^3/8$" dia. white buttons; black permanent fine-point marker; and clear thread.

1. Fuse web square to white fabric square. Fuse fabric to poster board.
2. Using patterns A and B, follow **Making Appliqués**, page 186, to make four A appliqués from red fabric and eight B appliqués from green fabric.
3. Arrange appliqués on fabric-covered poster board and fuse in place.
4. Glue quilt block to green felt. Using pinking shears and leaving a $^1/4$" green border, cut out quilt block.
5. Tie ribbon into a bow; glue bow and buttons to ornament.
6. Use marker to write date across center of ornament.
7. For hanger, use a needle to thread 8" of clear thread through top of ornament; knot ends together 3" above ornament and trim ends.

SNOW FOLK ORNAMENTS (Shown on page 71)

For each ornament, you will need one 4" x 6" piece each of white felt and poster board, craft glue, tracing paper, assorted colors of felt scraps, photograph for face, buttons, small artificial holly with berries, and clear thread.

Note: Allow glue to dry after each application.

1. Glue white felt to poster board.
2. Trace snowman photo, body, hat or bonnet, and shawl or scarf patterns onto tracing paper; cut out.

3. Use body pattern to cut body from felt-covered poster board. Use snowman photo pattern to cut face from photograph. Cut remaining pieces from desired colors of felt scraps.
4. Glue photograph, felt pieces, and buttons to body. Glue holly to hat.
5. For hanger, use a needle to thread 8" of clear thread through top of ornament; knot ends together 3" above ornament and trim ends.

STARRY GLASS ORNAMENTS
(Shown on page 70)

For each ornament, you will need a red frosted glass ornament, pencil, and white and green paint pens.

1. Use pencil to draw desired designs on ornament.
2. Use paint pens to draw over designs; allow to dry.

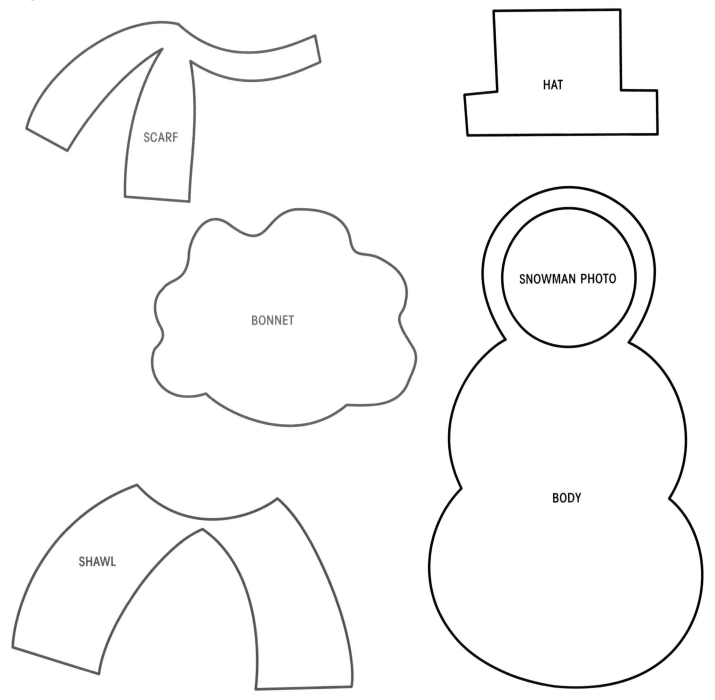

HANDPRINT ORNAMENTS (Shown on page 70)

For each ornament, you will need paper-backed fusible web, green gingham fabric, poster board, red acrylic paint, foam plate, tracing paper, white fabric, transfer paper, black permanent fine-point marker, red and green dimensional paint, $1/8$"w red braided trim, 8" length of $1/8$"w red satin ribbon, and a hot glue gun.

1. Fuse web to wrong side of fabrics. Fuse gingham fabric to poster board.
2. Pour acrylic paint onto plate. Place child's hand palm down in paint. Stamp handprint on gingham.
3. Follow **Making Patterns**, page 186, to make mitten and cuff patterns; cut out.
4. Centering palm prints on mitten, draw around pattern. Cut out mitten.
5. Use cuff pattern to cut cuff from white fabric. Use transfer paper to transfer holly design to cuff. Fuse cuff to mitten. Use marker to write year on cuff. Use dimensional paint to add name and paint holly leaves and berries.
6. Wrapping ends to wrong side, glue trim along lower edge of cuff. Forming a 1" loop at center of ribbon, knot ends together. Glue knot of loop to corner of cuff.

GINGERBREAD PHOTO ORNAMENTS

(Shown on page 71)

For each ornament, you will need one 7" square each of tan felt and poster board, tracing paper, photograph for face, craft glue, white baby rickrack, 8" of $1/8$"w red satin polka-dot ribbon, three buttons, and clear thread.

Note: Allow glue to dry after each application.

1. Glue felt to poster board.
2. Trace gingerbread man and photo patterns onto tracing paper; cut out.
3. Use gingerbread man pattern to cut body from felt-covered poster board. Use photo pattern to cut face from photograph. Glue face to body.
4. Overlapping ends, glue rickrack along edges of body. Tie ribbon into a bow. Glue bow to neck and buttons to body.
5. For hanger, use a needle to thread 8" of clear thread through top of ornament; knot ends together 3" above ornament and trim ends.

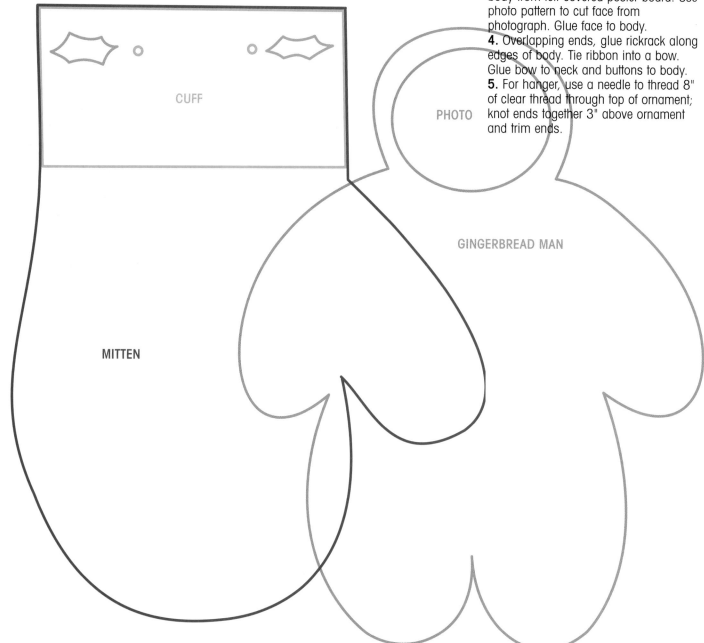

CUFF

PHOTO

GINGERBREAD MAN

MITTEN

CANDY CANE HEART ORNAMENTS (Shown on page 70)

For each ornament, you will need tracing paper, aluminum foil, cookie sheet, white polymer clay, 1" of craft wire, red acrylic paint, paintbrush, 2 $1/4$"w wooden heart, black permanent fine-point marker, hot glue gun, spray matte sealer, 9" of $3/8$"w green satin ribbon, craft glue, poster board, photograph, 14" of $1/8$"w green satin polka-dot ribbon, and a $1/2$" dia. gold jingle bell.

Note: Use hot glue for all gluing unless otherwise indicated. Allow paint and sealer to dry after each application.

1. Trace heart pattern onto tracing paper. Place a piece of aluminum foil larger than pattern on cookie sheet. Trace over pattern on aluminum foil. Roll an 18" long $1/4$" dia. piece of clay. Place clay on pattern, trimming ends as necessary. Bend wire and insert ends into point of heart. Follow manufacturer's instructions to bake clay. Allow to cool.

2. Use red paint to paint wooden heart and stripes on candy canes. Use marker to write name and date on wooden heart. Glue wooden heart between tops of candy canes. Spray frame with sealer.

3. Fold 9" ribbon length in half. Glue ends to back of wooden heart.

4. Use craft glue to glue photograph to poster board; allow to dry. Draw around heart frame on tracing paper. Cut out pattern $1/8$" inside drawn lines. Use pattern to cut out photograph. Hot glue photo to back of frame.

5. Thread remaining ribbon length through bell and wire loop at bottom of heart. Tie ribbon into a bow.

BEARDED SANTA ORNAMENTS
(Shown on page 71)

For each ornament, you will need a 1"w wooden star, yellow acrylic paint, paintbrush, one 4 $1/2$" x 6" piece each of white felt and poster board, craft glue, tracing paper, red and white fabric scraps, photograph for face, brown and black permanent fine-point markers, and clear thread.

Note: Allow paint and glue to dry after each application.

1. Paint wooden star yellow. Glue felt to poster board.

2. Trace hat, hat trim, mustache, and beard onto tracing paper. Use patterns to cut hat trim, mustache, and beard from white fabric and hat from red fabric.

3. Center and glue beard and hat on felt-covered poster board. Leaving a $1/8$" felt border, cut out ornament.

4. Cut out face from photograph; center and glue on ornament. Glue hat trim and mustache over photograph. Use brown marker to draw "stitches" along edges of hat trim and beard. Use black marker to draw "stitches" along edges of star. Glue star to hat trim.

5. For hanger, use a needle to thread 8" of clear thread through top of ornament; knot ends together 3" above ornament and trim ends.

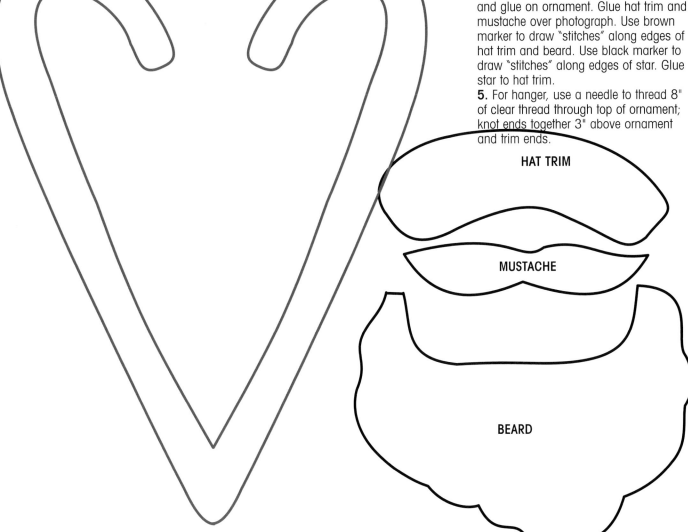

HAT

HAT TRIM

MUSTACHE

BEARD

79

SNOWMAN FROLIC

*B*lanket your home with the lighthearted charm of these lovable snow fellows! Covered with
a blizzard of tube-sock snowmen, wintry white mitten ornaments, and miniature buckets of
5-cent "snowballs," our captivating evergreen gives a carefree, cuddly appeal to your holiday
decor. Fun-loving snow people decked out with top hats, ice skates, and other fanciful flourishes
add to the mischievous mood. Carry the fun outdoors with a one-of-a-kind snowman tree
(complete with galoshes!) and a measuring stick friend to gauge snowfall. Indoors or out,
our easy-to-make snow folk will make sure your holidays are full of merriment! Instructions
for the projects shown here and on the following pages begin on page 86.

No matter what the weather, our cheerful **Snow Buddy Pillow** *(page 89)* will melt your heart and warm your spirit.
This happy-faced threesome sports cozy stocking hats on their stuffed tube-sock bodies. Buttons, jingle bells, and a
pom-pom add clever accents.

From **Mini Snowball Buckets** *(page 86)* to **Cozy Mitten Ornaments** *(page 86)*, our **Snowman Frolic Tree** *(page 86)* is a frosty delight! Clever **Nordic Sock Ornaments** *(page 86)*, hand-painted **Heartwarming Ornaments** *(page 86)*, lovable **Snow Buddy Ornaments** *(page 89)*, and whimsical **Juggling Snowmen** *(page 87)* and **Top-Hat Snowmen** ornaments *(page 89)* add to the merriment. Nestled among the branches are purchased icicles, snowflakes, white ball fringe, and garlands of wooden beads and ice crystals. We also placed a glistening snowflake atop the tree.

Display festive treats, favors, or cards in a sprightly basket escorted by a pair of jolly snow characters. This **Snow Buddy Basket** *(page 89)* makes a useful and eye-catching centerpiece.

Our quick-and-easy **Snowball Tree Skirt** *(page 86)*, featuring white ball fringe and pom-pom "snowballs" in assorted sizes, echoes the tree's spirit of wintry fun.

Let your favorite people know how much you care with our **Heartwarming Ornaments** *(page 86)*. These painted iridescent glass balls are terrific as package accents, great little gifts, or glistening touches on your own evergreen.

Put smiles on the faces of all your holiday visitors with our **Whimsical Snow Buddy Tree** *(page 88).* Decked out in wintry garb, from top hat and scarf to galoshes, this "tree-man" has irresistible appeal!

Show your love for wintertime fun by planting our **Snowfall Gauge** *(page 88)* in your yard. This measuring stick is an outdoor decoration with a purpose — youngsters can keep track of the local snowfall while declaring a love for snowy days.

Although they're dressed for frosty weather, our snow characters are quite comfortable indoors on your mantel, table, or bookshelf! Our **Skating Snow Lady** *(page 87)* is ready to take a twirl on the ice with darling "skates" — doll shoes fitted with craft steel "blades." The **Juggling Snowman** *(page 87)* and **Top-Hat Snowman** *(page 89)* are her cuddly companions. For a cute accent that's a snap to make, whip up some **Mini Snowball Buckets** *(page 86)* filled with stuffed felt "snowballs."

SNOWMAN FROLIC TREE
(Shown on page 81)

"Let it snow! Let it snow! Let it snow!" Our frolicsome snowmen bring merriment and joy to our seven-foot-tall fir tree. Their mission is to keep you in good spirits through the Christmas season.

For whimsical fancies, we draped white ball fringe, red and green wooden bead garland, and acrylic ice crystal garland on the branches of our Snowman Frolic Tree. We purchased a majestic snowflake tree topper, acrylic icicles, and a blizzard of frosted snowflakes.

Mini Snowball Buckets are suspended from the evergreen boughs, while Heartwarming Ornaments carry a message for a special someone.

Can you believe the Nordic Sock Ornaments, Cozy Mitten Ornaments, and Snow Buddy Ornaments (page 89) began as ordinary socks? Clad in red and green, our Juggling Snowmen and Top-Hat Snowmen (page 89) are bursting with personality and ready to bring your holiday festivities to life.

To complete the effect, we used bright red felt, white pom-poms, and white ball fringe for a Snowball Tree Skirt to catch any snowballs that might fall from our flurry of fun.

COZY MITTEN ORNAMENTS
(Shown on page 82)

For each mitten, you will need tracing paper, two 6" x 7 $\frac{1}{2}$" pieces of white tube sock, stencil plastic, craft knife, cutting mat, red acrylic paint, stencil brush, child-size striped sock, white and red yarn, hot glue gun, and a $\frac{1}{2}$" dia. button.

1. Trace mitten pattern, page 78, onto tracing paper. Using pattern and leaving wrist open, follow **Sewing Shapes**, page 186, to make mitten from sock.
2. Trace snowflake pattern onto stencil plastic. Use craft knife to cut out stencil. Place stencil on mitten and use stencil brush to paint snowflake red. Remove stencil and allow to dry.
3. For cuff, cut a 2 $\frac{1}{2}$" tube from child-size sock. Matching wrong sides and raw edges, fold tube in half. Matching raw edges, insert cuff in mitten; pin in place. Use a $\frac{1}{4}$" seam allowance to sew cuff to mitten. Fold cuff out over mitten.
4. For yarn bow, cut several 3" lengths of white and red yarn. Knot a 10" length of yarn around center of 3" lengths, then knot ends together. Glue bow and button to mitten.

SNOWBALL TREE SKIRT
(Shown on page 83)

You will need string, thumbtack, pencil, 60" square of red felt, 5 yds. of white ball fringe, white pom-poms in assorted sizes, and fabric glue.

1. Using a 2" measurement for inside cutting line and a 28" measurement for outside cutting line, follow **Cutting a Fabric Circle**, page 186, to cut skirt from red felt square.
2. For opening, match edges and fold skirt in half. Cut along one fold from center to outer edge.
3. Unfold tree skirt. With $\frac{1}{2}$" of fringe end extending beyond one opening edge, glue fringe along outer edge of skirt. Trim remaining fringe end $\frac{1}{2}$" past edge. Fold fringe ends to wrong side of skirt and glue in place. Glue pom-poms randomly to tree skirt. Allow to dry.

HEARTWARMING ORNAMENTS
(Shown on page 84)

HEART

For each ornament, you will need an iridescent white glass ornament; red, green, and black paint pens; tracing paper; and transfer paper.

1. Use green paint pen to write "You melt my" on ornament.
2. Trace heart pattern onto tracing paper.
3. Use transfer paper to transfer heart to ornament.
4. Use red paint pen to paint heart. Use black paint pen to outline heart and freehand paint snowflakes and heart rays as desired.

SNOWFLAKE

MINI SNOWBALL BUCKETS
(Shown on page 82)

For each bucket, you will need a 9-oz. red plastic cup, craft knife, hot glue gun, 2 $\frac{1}{2}$" dia. plastic foam ball, 2 $\frac{1}{4}$" x 3 $\frac{1}{2}$" piece of tan paper, black permanent fine-point marker, 5" twig, white felt, drawing compass, white thread, polyester fiberfill, $\frac{1}{8}$" dia. hole punch, green chenille stem, craft glue, paintbrush, and artificial snow.

Note: Use hot glue for all gluing unless otherwise indicated.

1. Draw around cup 1 $\frac{1}{4}$" from bottom. Cut away bottom just above drawn line. Glue foam ball in bucket.
2. Use marker to write "Snowballs 5¢" and draw border on tan paper. Glue sign to one end of twig and insert opposite end into foam ball.
3. For snowballs, use compass to draw five 3" circles on felt; cut out. Baste $\frac{1}{8}$" from edge around each felt circle. Stuff circles with fiberfill while gathering basting threads. Tie basting threads to secure.
4. Punch a hole on each side of cup for handle. Thread one end of chenille stem through each hole; bend stem ends to secure. Glue snowballs in bucket. Lightly brush craft glue on snowballs; sprinkle with snow and allow to dry.

NORDIC SOCK ORNAMENTS
(Shown on page 82)

For two ornaments, you will need one ladies' knee-high red and white patterned sock, sewing needle and thread, two 4" dia. plastic foam balls, rubber band, two 18" lengths of $\frac{3}{8}$"w green satin ribbon, hot glue gun, two 1" dia. jingle bells, and clear thread.

1. Cut toe from sock. Matching ends, fold sock in half; cut sock along fold. Turn tubes wrong side out. Use needle and thread to tightly gather one end of each tube. Turn tubes right side out. Place one foam ball inside each tube. Gather sock over top of ball; secure with rubber band.
2. Tie one ribbon length into a bow around rubber band on each ornament. Glue one bell to knot of each bow.
3. For hanger, use a needle to thread 8" of clear thread through top of ornament; knot ends together 3" above ornament and trim ends.

SKATING SNOW LADY (Shown on page 85)

You will need one adult-size white tube sock; polyester fiberfill; white, brown, and black embroidery floss; white and red thread; 3 1/2" x 11", 11" x 34", and 1/4" x 3" pieces of red checked flannel; drawing compass; tracing paper; 1 1/2" x 14" red felt strip for muffler; red and black felt; pinking shears; 2" x 3" piece of white felt; hot glue gun, orange bugle bead; small artificial holly sprig; 1" twig; ultra-thin craft steel; removable tape; sandpaper; and a pair of 2" doll shoes.

Note: Use a 1/4" seam allowance for all sewing. Refer to **Embroidery Stitches**, page 188, and use three strands of floss for all embroidery stitches.

1. Stuff toe section of tube sock with fiberfill up to beginning of ribbed cuff. Tightly knot a length of floss 2" below toe of sock for neck. For legs, cut cuff in half from opening edge to stuffing. Use sewing thread to stitch long edges together, forming legs. Stuff each leg with fiberfill and sew ends closed.
2. For arms, match right sides and long edges of 3 1/2" x 11" flannel piece. Sew long edges together. Turn arms right side out and stuff with fiberfill. Tack center of arms to back of body.
3. Use compass to draw a 2 3/4" dia. and a 9" dia. circle on tracing paper for hand and hat patterns. For each hand, use pattern to cut one 2 3/4" dia. circle from red felt. Baste 1/2" inside edge of circle. Stuff with fiberfill while pulling thread ends to gather; knot thread ends to secure. Insert gathered end into arms; sew arm to hand.
4. For dress, match right sides and short edges of 11" x 34" flannel piece. Sew short edges together and turn right side out. Baste around top of dress 1/4" from edge. For armholes, position seam at center back and cut a 3/4" vertical slit 1"

below top edge on each side of dress. Place dress on doll. Pull thread ends to gather dress around neck; knot thread ends. For fringe on muffler, make 1/2" cuts 1/8" apart on each end of red felt strip.
5. Follow **Making Patterns**, page 186, to trace jacket, eye, and blade patterns onto tracing paper. Fold 29" black felt square in half. Aligning shoulders of jacket pattern with fold of felt, use pinking shears to cut out jacket. Sew along side seams. Use pinking shears to cut jacket open down center front; turn right side out.
6. For snowman on jacket, trace snowman pattern onto tracing paper. Use pattern to cut snowman from white felt. Using black floss, stitch French Knots for eyes. Sew bead to face for nose. Wrap 1/4" x 3" strip of flannel around neck. Glue snowman to jacket front. Using brown floss, work Straight Stitch for twig arms.
7. Using white floss, stitch a 3/4" and a 3/8" Cross Stitch for each large snowflake on opposite side of jacket front. Work a French Knot at each end of 3/4" cross stitch. Work additional French Knots on jacket front as desired. Place jacket on snow lady.
8. Using 9" dia. circle pattern and pinking shears, cut one circle from black felt. Using black floss, baste around circle 1" inside edge. Stuff with fiberfill while pulling thread ends to loosely gather; knot thread ends to secure. Glue hat to head. Glue holly to hat.
9. Use patterns to cut two eyes from black felt. Glue eyes to face. Make a small clip in sock for nose. Apply glue to one end of twig and insert 1/4" of glued end into hole. Using black floss and Running Stitch, stitch mouth. Work a French Knot at each end of mouth.
10. For each skate, tape blade pattern on craft steel; cut out. Sand edges smooth. Fold blade posts to a 90° angle as indicated by dashed lines on pattern. Glue blade to bottom of shoe. Glue leg in skate.

JUGGLING SNOWMEN
(Shown on page 85)

For each ornament, you will need 2 1/4" wooden heart, black acrylic paint, paintbrush, white child-size tube sock, polyester fiberfill, rubber band, white thread, two 10" lengths of white thread-covered floral wire, hot glue gun, orange and black felt, black embroidery floss, red colored pencil, one striped child-size crew sock, 4" twigs for arms, four 1/2" dia. pom-poms, and one green child-size crew sock.

1. Paint heart black; allow to dry.
2. Stuff toe section of tube sock with fiberfill up to beginning of ribbed cuff. Gather sock over fiberfill; secure with rubber band. Roll cuff over rubber band.
3. Divide body into three equal sections by knotting a length of thread around body in two places.
4. Fold one length of wire in half. Push wire into body for support. Glue wooden heart to cuff for feet.
5. Cut two circles from black felt for eyes and one triangle from orange felt for nose; glue to face. Use three strands of black floss and **Running Stitch**, page 189, to stitch mouth. Use red pencil to color cheeks.
6. Cut a 2 1/2" tube from striped sock. Use thread to baste around one edge of tube. Place tube over snowman; gather and tie thread ends around neck. Stuff front of tube with fiberfill; turn cut edge under.
7. For each arm, cut a 1 1/2" x 3" piece from striped sock. Wrap and glue sock piece around one end of one twig end. Glue sock-covered end of twig to body.
8. Thread three pom-poms onto remaining wire; bend wire into a semicircle. Wrap one end of wire around each arm; glue to secure. Arrange and glue pom-poms as desired.
9. For hat, roll cuff of green sock 1/2" to right side two or three times. Glue hat to head. Glue remaining pom-pom to hat.

SNOWMAN

BLADE

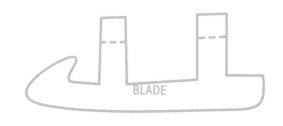

JACKET

EYE

WHIMSICAL SNOW BUDDY TREE (Shown on page 84)

You will need tracing paper; string; thumbtack; pencil; white corrugated plastic; white, orange, pink, red, green, and black craft foam; craft knife; low-temperature hot glue gun; orange, pink, and black markers; two white chenille stems; drawing compass; a pair of galoshes; a 5-foot-tall artificial tree; 2 1/2" dia. and 4" dia. plastic foam balls for snowballs; batting; artificial snow; craft glue; and a 10" x 48" piece of red fleece for muffler.

Note: Use glue gun for all gluing unless otherwise indicated.

1. Using a 6 1/2" measurement for cutting line, follow **Cutting a Fabric Circle**, page 186, to cut head pattern from a 14" square of tracing paper. Use pattern to cut head from corrugated plastic.
2. For hat pattern, cut a 2" x 18" rectangle and a 6" x 10 1/2" rectangle from tracing paper. Center 10 1/2" edge of wide rectangle on one 18" edge of narrow rectangle. Use pattern to cut hat from black foam. For hatband, cut a 2 1/2" x 10 1/2" piece from red foam.
3. Trace star, eye, nose, highlight, and heart patterns onto tracing paper; cut out. Use patterns to cut one nose from orange foam, two eyes from black foam, two highlights from white foam, two hearts from pink foam, and three stars from green foam. Use markers to add shading to nose and hearts.
4. Glue stars to hatband, hatband to hat, and highlights to eyes. Glue eyes, nose, and hearts to face. Use black marker to draw mouth on face.
5. Glue one end of each chenille stem to center back of head. Use chenille stems to fasten head to top of tree.
6. For buttons, use drawing compass to draw three 4" dia. circles on green craft foam and three 5" dia. circles on red craft foam; cut out. Center and glue one green circle on each red circle. Use black marker to draw an "X" in the center of each green circle. Draw dots at outer points of each "X."
7. Place galoshes under tree for feet. For snowballs, cover foam balls with batting; glue in place. Lightly spread craft glue over ball and roll in artificial snow. Tuck 6"w strips of batting into tree branches and sprinkle with artificial snow. Place snowballs in tree limbs. Glue buttons to front of tree.
8. For fringe on muffler, make 4" cuts 1/2" apart on each end of fleece. Loosely tie muffler around tree.

SNOWFALL GAUGE

(Shown on page 85)

You will need tracing paper; string; thumbtack; pencil; white corrugated plastic; craft knife; white, orange, pink, red, green, and black craft foam; orange, pink, and black permanent markers; 1 1/2"w yardstick; 24" square of kraft paper; 17" length of 1/4" x 1" wooden stick; and a low-temperature hot glue gun.

1. Follow Steps 1 - 4 of Whimsical Snow Buddy Tree to make head.
2. For sign, cut a 7" x 10" piece of corrugated plastic. Cut two each 1" x 7" and 1" x 10" strips from black foam for border. Trace border pattern onto tracing paper. Use pattern to cut notches along one long edge of each border strip. Use heart pattern to cut one heart from red foam. Glue heart and border strips to sign. Use black marker to write "I" and "Snow" on sign. Glue sign to wooden stick.
3. Aligning arrows and dotted lines, trace upper arm and hand patterns onto tracing paper; cut out. For full arm pattern, fold kraft paper in half. Matching blue line of pattern to fold of paper, draw around pattern; cut out and unfold. Use full arm pattern to cut arms from corrugated plastic.
4. Glue head to 36-inch end of yardstick. Glue arms to back of yardstick. Glue sign to hand.

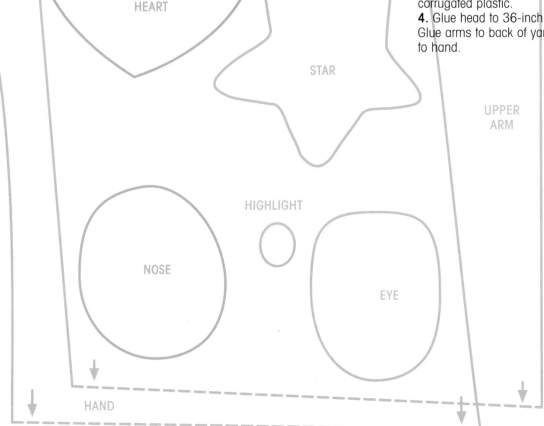

HEART

BORDER

STAR

UPPER ARM

HIGHLIGHT

NOSE

EYE

HAND

SNOW BUDDY ORNAMENTS (Shown on page 82)

For each ornament, you will need one youth-size white tube sock, polyester fiberfill, rubber band, fabric scraps, fabric glue, two $1/4$" dia. black shank buttons for eyes, red and green embroidery floss, assorted buttons for front of body, $3/8$" dia. jingle bell, tracing paper, one pair of infant-size crew socks for arms, white thread, and clear thread.

For white hat buddy, you will **also** need a $1/4$" dia. red shank button for nose and a 1" dia. green pom-pom for hat.

For green or red hat buddy, you will **also** need a child-size green or red crew sock and a $1/4$" dia. red shank button for nose.

For striped hat buddy, you will **also** need a child-size striped crew sock, orange and green felt, and red worsted weight yarn.

Note: Large snow buddies can be made from adult-size tube socks using $1/2$" dia. jingle bells, $1/2$" dia. shank button for nose, and $1 1/2$" dia. pom-poms. Allow glue to dry after each application.

WHITE HAT BUDDY

1. Stuff toe section of tube sock with fiberfill up to beginning of ribbed cuff. Gather sock over fiberfill; secure with rubber band.

2. For hat, fold cuff down over stuffed sock. Fold edge of hat $1/2$" to right side two or three times.

3. Tear 1" squares of fabric for patches. Glue patches and pom-pom to hat.

4. Sew buttons to face for eyes and nose. Use three strands of red floss to work **Stem Stitch**, page 189, for mouth. Use floss to sew buttons and jingle bell to snowman.

5. For muffler, tear a 3" x 12" fabric strip. Tie muffler around neck.

6. Trace heart pattern, page 88, onto tracing paper. Use pattern to cut one heart from fabric; glue to hat.

7. For each arm, cut foot from infant-size sock; stuff toe section with fiberfill. Sew opening closed. Use thread to gather a small amount of sock to form thumb. Sew arms to body.

8. For hanger, use a needle to thread 8" of clear thread through top of ornament; knot ends together 3" above ornament and trim ends.

GREEN OR RED HAT BUDDY

1. Follow Step 1 of White Hat Buddy to make body. Cut off cuff above rubber band.

2. For hat, cut ribbed cuff from red or green sock. Fold finished edge of hat $1/2$" to right side two or three times. Place hat on head. Tie floss into a bow around top of hat.

3. Follow Steps 4 - 8 of White Hat Buddy to finish ornament.

STRIPED HAT BUDDY

1. Follow Step 1 of White Hat Buddy to make body. Cut off cuff above rubber band.

2. For hat, fold cuff of striped sock 1" to right side two or three times. Place hat on head. Glue tip of hat to cuff. Glue bell to tip of hat.

3. Trace nose pattern onto tracing paper. Use pattern to cut nose from orange felt. Roll nose into a cone shape; glue to secure. Glue nose to face. Use three strands of red floss to work **Stem Stitch**, page 189, for mouth. Sew buttons to face for eyes. Use floss to sew buttons to front of snowman.

4. Follow Step 7 of White Hat Buddy to add arms to snowman.

5. Trace mitten pattern onto tracing paper. Use pattern to cut four mittens from green felt. Glue two mittens together over each end of yarn. Knot mittens around body.

6. Trace heart pattern onto tracing paper. Use pattern to cut two hearts from fabric; glue one heart to each mitten.

7. For hanger, use a needle to thread 8" of clear thread through top of ornament; knot ends together 3" above ornament and trim ends.

SNOW BUDDY BASKET

(Shown on page 83)

Make a large White Hat Buddy and a large Green or Red Hat Buddy. Glue one buddy to each side of a handled basket.

SNOW BUDDY PILLOW

(Shown on page 80)

Make one large White Hat Buddy with right arm, one large Green or Red Hat Buddy with left arm, and one large Striped Hat Buddy with no arms. Sew buddies together along sides.

TOP-HAT SNOWMEN

(Shown on page 85)

For one ornament, you will need a $2 1/4$" wooden heart; white, green, and black acrylic paint; paintbrush; child-size white tube sock; polyester fiberfill; rubber band; white, red, and black thread; 10" of floral wire; a hot glue gun; tracing paper; orange, red, green, and black felt; white and black embroidery floss; red colored pencil; 4" twigs for arms; drawing compass; three $3/8$" dia. black buttons; red berry pick; and a 2" wooden tree.

1. Follow steps 1 - 5 of Juggling Snowman, page 87, to make body. For arms, glue one twig to each side of body.

2. Follow **Making Patterns**, page 186, to trace coat pattern onto tracing paper. Use pattern to cut coat from red felt. Beginning between curved edges, cut coat open along center front.

3. Use two strands of white floss to work **Blanket Stitch**, page 189, along front and neck edges of coat. Place coat on snowman. Use red thread to stitch side and sleeve edges together. Fold up sleeves.

4. Use compass to draw a $3 1/2$" dia. and a 5" dia. circle on tracing paper for hat patterns. Use patterns to cut one of each circle from black felt.

5. Use thread to baste $1/8$" inside edge of 5" dia. circle; stuff with fiberfill while pulling thread ends to gather. Fold gathered edges under. Center and glue folds on $3 1/2$" dia. circle.

6. For muffler, cut a $1 1/2$" x 10" piece of green felt. For fringe, make $1/2$" clips in short ends.

7. Glue hat, muffler, and buttons to snowman. Glue berries to hat.

8. Paint tree green; allow to dry. Dot white paint on tree; allow to dry. Glue tree to one arm.

COAT

NOSE

MITTEN

Santa, Look At This!

Christmas is the perfect time to encourage children to be creative, and this collection, designed especially for kids, makes it easy for them to be proud of their accomplishments. With just a little help from a grown-up, youngsters can craft a variety of quick-and-easy projects, from coffee filter angels and cowbell reindeer to painted handprint sweatshirts or a felt stocking. Whether the projects are fashioned at home or at school, children will be having fun, developing skills, and learning that "I can do it!" Instructions begin on page 94.

These cute projects encourage "hands on" experience! There are two **Handprint Sweatshirts** *(page 95)* — the Santa is simply a trio of painted palm prints finished with fingerprint eyes and pom-poms. A cluster of palm prints form the Christmas tree, which is trimmed with a garland of dimensional paint and jewel stones. *(Opposite, inset)* Youngsters can create our **Handprint Santa Ornament** *(page 94)* from a plain papier-mâché ball. For a fun finish, thumbprints were used in the "Ho Ho Ho," and pinky finger prints dot Santa's eyes.

(Clockwise from top left) Holiday shapes cut from craft foam deck a painted **Message Chalkboard** *(page 97)* with cheer. Dressed in a black felt top hat, our **Peppermint Stick Man** *(page 97)* is a festive fashion star. The lacy **Paper Bag Angel** *(page 96)* is simply a plain white lunch sack embellished with paper doilies and a poster board head. Made from a "recycled" baby food container, our **Santa Candy Jar** *(page 96)* is a sweet little keepsake or gift. The **Pinecone Santas** *(page 96)* are natural tree trimmers, especially when peppermint candies are added for color.

(Clockwise from top left) Kids can create a dozen **Cookie Cutter Ornaments** *(page 95)* like our candy cane and Christmas tree in no time at all. **Coffee Filter Angel Ornaments** *(page 97)* are great little projects for preschool or Sunday school classes. Fashioned from felt, our **Pom-Pom Snowman Stocking** *(page 95)* features a snowman juggling "snowballs." The main things needed to build **Snowman Sock Ornaments** *(page 94)* are some socks, buttons, and a jingle bell. Freehand drawings add charm to a **Photo Frame Ornament** *(page 94)*, which gets its shine from aluminum foil. Ring in the holidays with our whimsical **Cowbell Reindeer** *(page 96)*. He's quick to make with just a few trims.

PHOTO FRAME ORNAMENT

(Shown on page 93)

You will need two 4" x 5" pieces of craft foam, two 6" x 7" pieces of aluminum foil, low-temperature glue gun, photo to fit 2" x 3" opening, 9" of silver tinsel stem, black fine-point marker, and four 7mm red acrylic jewels.

Note: Adult supervision required.

1. Cut a 2" x 3" opening in center of one foam piece for frame front.
2. For frame front and frame back, center foam piece on dull side of foil. Fold corners of foil diagonally over corners of foam; glue in place. Fold edges of foil over edges of foam; glue in place. Refer to **Fig. 1** to cut foil in frame front opening 1" from edges of opening. Fold flaps of foil over edges of opening; glue to secure.

Fig. 1

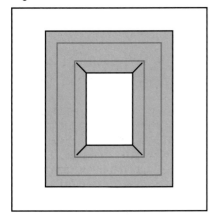

3. Center and glue photo in opening of frame front. Glue frame front and frame back together.
4. For hanger, insert ends of tinsel stem through top corners of frame; bend and twist to secure.
5. Have child draw designs around edge of frame with marker (we drew hearts, snowflakes, and trees).
6. Glue jewels to front of frame.

SNOWMAN SOCK ORNAMENT

(Shown on page 93)

You will need utility scissors, a craft stick, orange acrylic paint, paintbrush, 3" dia. plastic foam ball, one white and one red child-size sock, rubber band, craft glue, 10" of $1/8$"w green ribbon, $1/2$" dia. jingle bell, red thread, two $1/2$" dia. black shank buttons for eyes, and assorted buttons for mouth.

Note: Adult supervision required.

1. For nose, use utility scissors to cut a 2" length from craft stick. Cut each end of stick at an angle. Paint nose orange; allow to dry.
2. For head, place ball in toe of white sock. Gather sock at top of ball; secure with rubber band. Cut off cuff above rubber band.
3. For hat, fold cuff of red sock up 1". Place hat on head over gathers; glue to secure. Tie ribbon into a bow through eye of bell. Sew bell to tip of hat.
4. Glue buttons to head for eyes and mouth. Insert nose in head.

HANDPRINT SANTA ORNAMENT

(Shown on page 91)

You will need white, flesh, red, and brown acrylic paint; paintbrushes; 4" dia. papier-mâché ornament with hanger; black permanent medium-point marker; two $1/2$" dia. white pom-poms; $3/8$" dia. red wooden bead; and craft glue.

Note: Adult supervision required.

1. For each stamp, refer to **Fig. 1** to apply paint to child's hand. With fingers together, stamp hand on two sides of ornament; allow to dry.

Fig. 1

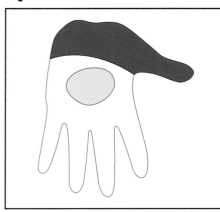

2. For eyes, apply brown paint to tip of child's smallest finger. Stamp eyes on Santa faces; allow to dry. Apply brown paint to tip of child's thumb. Leaving spaces for "H's", stamp three thumbprints above each Santa; allow to dry.
3. Use marker to draw "H's" and dots. Glue pom-poms to Santa hats; allow to dry. Thread hanger through bead; glue bead to ball and allow to dry.

COOKIE CUTTER ORNAMENTS

(Shown on page 93)

Note: Adult supervision required.

CANDY CANE

You will need one 5" x 8" piece each of paper-backed fusible web, red-and-white striped fabric, and cardboard; 6"h candy cane cookie cutter; craft glue; eight 7mm red acrylic jewels; assorted white and red buttons; and 6" of gold cord.

1. Fuse web to wrong side of fabric. Remove paper backing; fuse fabric to cardboard.
2. Draw around cookie cutter on fused cardboard; cut out along drawn line.
3. Arrange and glue jewels and buttons on candy cane; allow to dry.
4. For hanger, glue ends of cord to back of ornament; allow to dry.

CHRISTMAS TREE

For each ornament, you will need one 5" x 7" piece each of paper-backed fusible web, green fabric, and cardboard; 5 1/2 "h tree cookie cutter; craft glue; red baby rickrack; one 1/2 "w gold star acrylic jewel; assorted gold and red acrylic jewels; and 6" of gold cord.

1. Fuse web to wrong side of fabric. Remove paper backing; fuse fabric to cardboard.
2. Draw around cookie cutter on fused cardboard; cut out along drawn line.
3. Glue rickrack and jewels on tree; allow to dry.
4. For hanger, glue ends of cord to back of ornament; allow to dry.

HANDPRINT SWEATSHIRTS

(Shown on page 90)

Note: Adult supervision required.

TREE SWEATSHIRT

You will need a child-size white sweatshirt; green and brown acrylic paint; freezer-paper or T-shirt form; paintbrush; gold dimensional fabric paint; 16mm gold, red, and blue acrylic jewels; and a 20mm gold acrylic jewel.

1. Refer to **Painting Techniques**, page 189, to prepare sweatshirt.
2. Use brown paint to paint a 23"h tree trunk above center of waistband; allow to dry.
3. For each stamp, paint child's hand green. Beginning at bottom, stamp handprints in rows to form tree shape; allow to dry.
4. Use dimensional paint to paint garland. To attach each jewel, squeeze a dot of dimensional paint slightly smaller than jewel onto sweatshirt. Press jewel into paint; allow to dry.
5. Use dimensional paint to draw snowflakes on sweatshirt. Dot dimensional paint over tree and front of sweatshirt; allow to dry.

SANTA SWEATSHIRT

You will need a child-size grey sweatshirt; white, flesh, red, and brown acrylic paint; freezer paper or T-shirt form; paintbrush; fabric glue; and three 1/2 " dia. white pom-poms.

1. Refer to **Painting Techniques**, page 189, to prepare sweatshirt.
2. For each stamp, refer to **Fig. 1** of Handprint Santa Ornament to apply paint to child's hand. Stamp hand three times across front of sweatshirt; allow to dry.
3. For eyes, apply brown paint to tip of child's smallest finger. Stamp eyes on Santa faces; allow to dry. Glue one pom-pom to each Santa hat; allow to dry.

POM-POM SNOWMAN STOCKING

(Shown on page 93)

You will need tracing paper; two 10" x 13" pieces of red felt; white and black sport weight yarn; large-eye needle; craft glue; two 1" dia., nine 3/8 " dia., and four 3/4 " dia. white pom-poms; and two 3mm black pom-poms for eyes.

Note: Adult supervision required.

1. Aligning dotted lines and arrows, trace stocking top A and stocking bottom onto tracing paper; cut out. Using pattern, cut two stocking pieces from felt.
2. Use white yarn to work **Running Stitches**, page 189, to outline heel and toe areas on front of stocking.
3. Matching wrong sides, place stocking front and back together. Leaving top open, use white yarn to work **Overcast Stitches**, page 189, along edges of stocking to sew stocking pieces together.
4. For mouth, tie two knots 3/4 " apart in a length of black yarn; trim ends close to knots. Glue eyes and mouth to one 3/4 " dia. pom-pom. For arms, knot ends of a 3" length of black yarn; trim ends close to knots.
5. For snowman, glue arms, head, and 1" dia. pom-poms on stocking; allow to dry. For snowballs, glue six 3/8 " dia. pom-poms in an arch above head.
6. Glue remaining pom-poms along top edge of stocking. Tie 21" of black yarn into a bow. Glue bow to corner of stocking; allow to dry.

STOCKING BOTTOM

STOCKING TOP B

STOCKING TOP A

PAPER BAG ANGEL

(Shown on page 92)

For each angel, you will need a lunch-size white paper bag, craft glue, two 8" dia. paper doilies, transparent tape, tracing paper, poster board, black permanent fine-point marker, pink colored pencil, natural raffia, $^1/_{28}$"w gold ribbon, and an 18mm star sequin.

Note: Adult supervision required. Allow glue to dry after each application.

1. Fold top corners of bag to back to form point; glue to secure.
2. For dress, wrap one doily around point of bag; glue edges of doily to back of bag. For wings, gather center of remaining doily; tape to secure. Glue wings to back of bag.
3. Trace head pattern onto tracing paper; cut out. Using pattern, cut head from poster board. Use marker and colored pencil to draw face. For hair, glue 5$^1/_2$" lengths of raffia around face. For halo, form a 5" length of ribbon into a circle; glue ends to back of head.
4. Glue head to bag. Tie a 7" length of ribbon into a bow. Glue bow and sequin at neck.

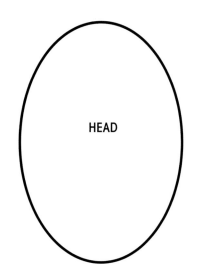

HEAD

COWBELL REINDEER

(Shown on page 93)

You will need a low-temperature glue gun, 20mm oval wiggle eyes, 1" dia. brown pom-pom for nose, 3"h cowbell, black permanent medium-point marker, 4" lengths of natural raffia, two 12" brown chenille stems, and 12" of $^3/_4$"w red polka-dot ribbon.

Note: Adult supervision required.

1. Glue eyes and nose to one side of bell. Use marker to draw mouth and eyebrows. For hair, fold raffia in half; glue to top of bell.
2. For antlers, cut each stem into 5" and 7" lengths. Twist one end of each 7" length around handle. Twist one 5" length around each 7" length; shape antlers. Tie ribbon into a bow around handle.

SANTA CANDY JAR

(Shown on page 92)

You will need tracing paper; tape; large baby food jar with lid; white, red, and black acrylic paint; paintbrushes; black permanent medium-point marker; flesh-colored candy; green yarn; $^3/_4$" dia. white button; low-temperature glue gun; and a child-size red sock.

Note: Adult supervision required. Allow paint to dry after each application.

1. Trace Santa pattern onto tracing paper. Tape pattern inside jar. Use white paint to paint eyebrows, mustache, and area below mustache for beard. Use red paint to paint nose and mouth. Use marker to color eyes and outline mustache and eyebrows. Remove pattern. Fill jar with candy; place lid on jar.
2. For hat, thread 6" of yarn through button; tie into a bow. Glue button to toe of sock. Fold cuff of sock $^3/_4$" to right side. Place hat on jar.

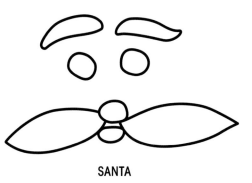

SANTA

PINECONE SANTAS

(Shown on page 92)

Note: Adult supervision required.

PEPPERMINT SANTA

For each ornament, you will need a 3"h plastic foam egg, flesh-colored acrylic paint, paintbrush, two straight pins with black heads, low-temperature glue gun, one 5mm red pom-pom, polyester fiberfill, child-size red sock, thread, one $^3/_4$" dia. white pom-pom, straight pins with red heads, large pinecone with flat bottom, and wrapped round peppermint candies.

1. For head, paint egg flesh; allow to dry. Insert black pins into head for eyes. Glue red pom-pom to head for nose. Arrange and glue fiberfill on head for hair, beard, and mustache.
2. For hat, cut cuff from sock; discard toe. Knot thread around cut edge of cuff to gather. Glue white pom-pom to gathered end. Fold cuff of hat $^1/_2$" to right side twice. Place hat on head; secure with pins between cuff and hat.
3. Glue head to pinecone. Insert candies in pinecone.

HANGING ORNAMENT

For each ornament, you will need flesh-colored acrylic paint, paintbrush, 2"h plastic foam egg, two straight pins with black heads, low-temperature glue gun, 5mm red pom-pom, polyester fiberfill, child-size red sock, thread, $^3/_4$" dia. white pom-pom, straight pins with red heads, 6" narrow pinecone, and 12" of $^1/_{24}$"w red satin ribbon.

1. For head, paint egg flesh; allow to dry. Insert black pins into head for eyes. Glue red pom-pom to head for nose. Arrange and glue fiberfill on head for hair, beard, and mustache.
2. For hat, cut cuff from sock; discard toe. Knot thread around cut edge of cuff to gather. Glue white pom-pom to gathered end. Fold cuff of hat $^1/_2$" to right side twice. Place hat on head; secure with pins.
3. Glue head to pinecone. Pin ribbon ends to back of head for hanger.

MESSAGE CHALKBOARD

(Shown on page 92)

You will need white and red acrylic paint; paintbrush; 6 1/2" x 8 1/2" chalkboard with wooden frame; tracing paper; white, yellow, red, blue, and green craft foam; black permanent fine-point marker; 1/4" dia. hole punch; low-temperature glue gun; 13" of 5/8"w green grosgrain ribbon; 15" of 1"w red striped grosgrain ribbon; and chalk.

Note: Adult supervision required.

1. Paint chalkboard frame white; allow to dry. Paint red stripes along short ends of frame; allow to dry.
2. Trace tree, star, stocking, and cuff patterns onto tracing paper; cut out. Using patterns, cut shapes from craft foam. Use marker to draw "stitches" along edges of foam pieces and each white area on frame.
3. For ornaments on tree, punch holes from assorted colors of craft foam. Glue ornaments to tree. Glue cuff to stocking. Glue shapes to frame.
4. For hanger, glue one end of green ribbon to each top back corner of frame. Tie striped ribbon into a bow around hanger.
5. Use chalk to write message on chalkboard.

COFFEE FILTER ANGEL ORNAMENT

(Shown on page 93)

You will need two coffee filters, craft glue, flesh colored pencil, drawing compass, poster board, black permanent fine-point marker, curly doll hair, gold tinsel stem, assorted buttons, and white embroidery floss.

Note: Adult supervision required. Allow glue to dry after each application.

1. For dress, fold one filter in half. Overlap folded edges to make a cone shape; glue to secure. With glued edges at back, flatten cone.
2. For wings, cut remaining filter in half. Fold each piece in half; fold in half again. Glue wings to back of dress.
3. For head, use compass to draw a 1 1/2" dia. circle on poster board; cut out. Use pencil to color circle. Use marker to draw eyes and mouth. Glue doll hair to head. For halo, twist ends of a 3 1/2" length of chenille stem together to form a circle; glue to head.
4. Glue head and buttons to dress. For hanger, glue ends of a 7" length of floss to back of head.

PEPPERMINT STICK MAN

(Shown on page 92)

You will need white, yellow, and red acrylic paint; paintbrush; jumbo craft stick; two 1 1/2"w wooden stars; 1"w wooden heart; black permanent fine-point marker; tracing paper, black felt; low-temperature glue gun; 1" dia. wrapped peppermint candy stick, red and green chenille stems; and two 3/4" dia. wiggle eyes.

Note: For decorative purposes only. Adult supervision required. Allow paint and glue to dry after each application.

1. Paint craft stick white, stars yellow, and heart red. Use tip of paintbrush handle to add white dots to heart.
2. Use marker to draw "stitches" along edges of stars.
3. Trace hat, hat brim, and hat top patterns onto tracing paper; cut out. Using patterns, cut hat pieces from felt. Glue hat top to one end of candy stick. Overlapping ends, glue hat around same end of candy stick. Place hat brim on candy stick; glue to bottom edge of crown. Glue 4" of green chenille stem around hat for hat trim.
4. Glue eyes to a 1 1/2" length of red chenille stem. For mouth, bend 2 1/2" of red chenille stem into a "U" shape. Glue stem ends to back of eyes. Glue face to candy stick.
5. For arms, glue stars to each end of craft stick. Glue arms to back and heart to front of candy stick.

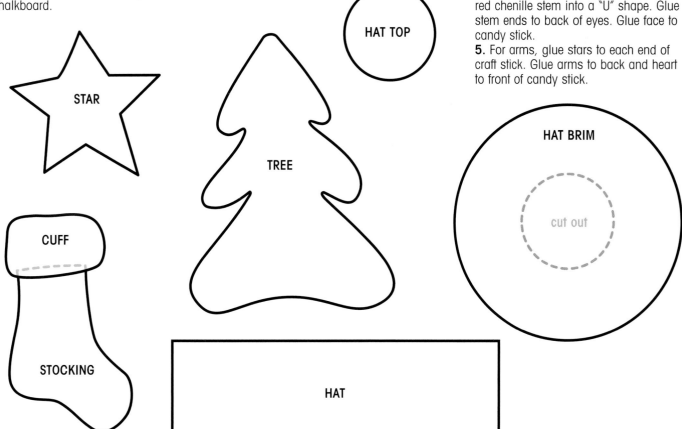

STAR

HAT TOP

TREE

CUFF

STOCKING

HAT

HAT BRIM

cut out

HEARTFELT GIFTS

Get into the true spirit of giving with handmade gifts! We've got great ideas for everyone on your list: festive apparel, memory keepers, decorative accents, and more. It's oh-so-easy to add holiday appliqués to a little girl's ready-made dress, or transform a ladies' sweatshirt into a festive vest. You can also add cheery accents to glass plates, make scented bath accessories in a friend's favorite fragrance, or cross stitch a frosty friendship sampler … just turn the page to get started!

Fashion a festive **Seasonal Sweatshirt Vest** *(page 117)* from an ordinary fleece top and fabric appliqués and present it to a deserving lady on your list.

Keep a buddy warm and toasty with our **Fleecy Winter Wear** *(page 118)*, decorated with felt and fabric appliqués.

A little miss will look especially charming in our **Appliquéd Knit Dress** *(page 116).* It's easy to make by fusing a few fabric cutouts onto a cotton knit dress and adding a plaid ruffle and trim.

Wrap a bundle of joy in this **Sweet Baby Set** *(page 117).* The ensemble features a cotton knit gown and blanket that are decorated with fabric appliqués and rickrack trim.

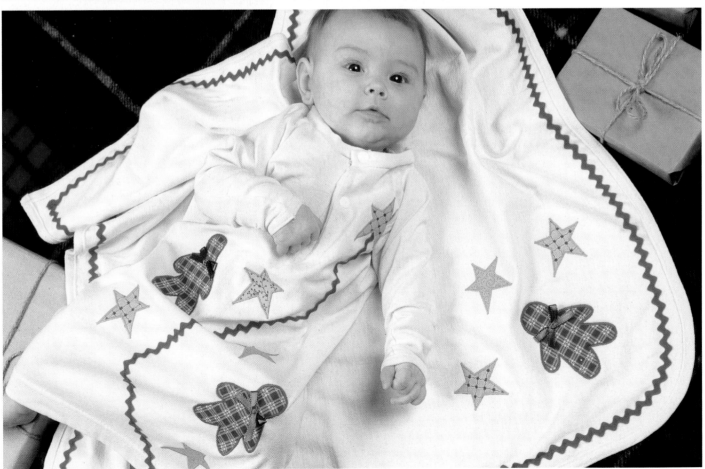

Rock-a-bye Santa, it's Christmas Eve! Dress baby in holiday style with a sweet cross-stitched **Santa Patch** *(page 127)*. Sew the quick-to-stitch "patch" on a little one's romper, or add festive fun to a diaper bag or blanket.

To create this clever **Snowman Dress** *(page 122)*, just add an appliquéd felt skirt to a ready-made T-shirt. A young miss will love wearing the frosty party dress!

Santa Claus is coming to town! Use your imagination — and our colorful cross-stitched **Santa Patches** *(page 127)* — to add a Christmasy touch to a variety of ready-to-wear items such as the overalls and shirt shown here. Your creativity will be a hit with all ages.

Whether the mood is subtle chic or vibrant cheer, this reversible **Crocheted Vest** *(page 130)* makes a fashionable statement! The vest is worked entirely in simple single crochet stitches, so it's easy enough for even a beginning crocheter to make.

Everyone will think you found this luxurious **Covered Album** *(page 129)* at an exclusive gift shop! It's actually affordable to create by covering a plain photo album with tapestry fabric.

Handsomely attired in stock-market style, our **Masculine Desk Set** *(page 126)* will please a business-minded gentleman. The decoupaged photo frame, pencil holder, and storage box are trimmed with buttons and cording in neutral tones.

Our attractive **Hand-Painted Holiday Tableware** *(page 114)* is surprisingly easy to make. You just paint festive motifs on clear gold-rimmed glass dinnerware.

Treat a friend to selections from our **Luxurious Bath Set** *(page 119)*. The collection includes rich bath oils, refreshing bath gel, and relaxing bath salts, all packaged in prettily adorned bottles.

Easy-to-mix **Fragrant Bath Tea Bags** *(page 116)* possess the soothing and invigorating qualities of dried chamomile blossoms, mint leaves, and lavender.

This cozy **Crocheted Angel Afghan** *(page 120)* is made of cloud-soft brushed acrylic yarn. Each block portrays an angel with popcorn-stitch wings.

Perfect for a parent or grandparent, this decorative **Memory Plate** (*page 131*) showcases decoupaged photographs of loved ones.

Sewn from richly colored fabric and trimmed in gold, a set of **Ornament Place Mats** (*page 126*) will bring an elegant look to a friend's dining table.

Wrapped with plaid ribbon, a ready-made pillow becomes a festive "package." The jewel-like blossom on our **Poinsettia Pillow** *(page 131)* is easy to craft from lengths of wired ribbon.

More ribbon flowers transform a store-bought chenille throw into a stunning **Poinsettia Afghan** *(page 131)*.

Fill a basket with folksy appliquéd **Heart Coasters** *(page 124) to* please a country-loving friend! Pull your favorite fabrics out of the scrap box to make the fused-on hearts; finish with basic embroidery stitches.

Share down-home holiday cheer with this **"Warm Wishes" Card Holder** *(page 124)*. The wall hanging is easy to make with no machine-sewing involved — just fuse together and add embroidered embellishments.

Displayed on the front door, our hand-painted **Skating Santa Sled** *(page 128)* offers a whimsical greeting to all. What a great gift for a special family!

Layering simple appliqués makes our cheery handmade **Snowman Pillow** (*page 114*) a quick and festive decoration.

In no time, you can cross stitch these cute **Winter Warmer Mugs and Towels** (*page 123*) to share with special friends.

Jolly Yuletide symbols unite to make this **Winter Warmer Wall Hanging** *(page 122)* a delightful offering for someone dear. Use motifs from this piece to cross stitch the mugs and towels on the facing page.

SNOWMAN PILLOW (Shown on page 112)

You will need paper-backed fusible web; white, red, green, and black fabric scraps for appliqués; two 12 1/2" squares of red checked flannel for pillow; stabilizer; clear thread; white and black embroidery floss; small silk holly leaf; one red and three black 3/8" dia. buttons; red colored pencil; 2 yds. of 5"w red checked fabric for ruffle (pieced as necessary); 1 1/2" x 50" bias strip of green checked fabric for welting (pieced as necessary); 50" of 1/4" dia. cord; polyester fiberfill; tracing paper; orange and black felt scraps; and fabric glue.

Note: Use a 1/4" seam allowance for all sewing. Use three strands of floss and follow **Embroidery Stitches**, page 188, for all embroidery stitches unless otherwise indicated.

1. Trace nose and eye patterns, page 115, onto tracing paper; cut out. Use patterns to cut pieces from felt.
2. Follow **Making Appliqués**, page 186, to make remaining snowman appliqués from fabric scraps.
3. For pillow front, arrange appliqués on right side of one flannel square, overlapping as necessary; fuse in place. Using clear thread, follow **Machine Appliqué**, page 186, to sew over raw edges of each appliqué. Glue eyes and nose to snowman; allow to dry.
4. Using white floss, stitch a 3/4" and a 3/8" Cross Stitch for each snowflake on pillow front. Work a French Knot at each end of 3/4" cross stitch. Using Stem Stitch and black floss, stitch snowman's mouth. Sew holly leaf and red button to hat and black buttons to snowman. Use red pencil to shade cheeks on snowman.

5. For welting, press one end of bias strip 1/2" to wrong side. Beginning 1/2" from folded end, center cord on wrong side of strip. Fold strip over cord. Beginning 1/2" from folded end, use a zipper foot to baste close to cord along length of strip. Trim seam allowance to 1/4".
6. Matching raw edges and beginning with pressed end at center bottom of pillow front, pin welting to right side of pillow front. Trimming welting to fit, insert unfinished end of welting into folded end. Sewing as close to welting as possible, use a zipper foot to baste welting to pillow top.
7. Matching right sides, sew short edges of ruffle piece together; press seam open. Matching wrong sides and long edges, fold ruffle in half. Baste long raw edges of ruffle together. Pull basting thread, gathering ruffle to fit pillow top. Matching raw edges, pin ruffle to right side of pillow top.
8. Leaving an opening for stuffing and stitching as close to welting as possible, use zipper foot to sew right sides of pillow front and back together. Clip curves, turn right side out, and press. Stuff pillow with fiberfill; sew opening closed.

HAND-PAINTED HOLIDAY TABLEWARE
(Shown on page 106)

For each place setting, you will need gold-rimmed clear glass dinner plate, salad plate, stemware, and rose bowl; red, green, and gold permanent enamel glass paint; tracing paper; removable tape; and small paintbrushes.

Note: Follow manufacturer's instructions to apply paints.

ROSE BOWL AND STEMWARE
1. Trace holly pattern onto tracing paper.
2. Tape pattern on inside of glass. Working on outside of glass, paint leaves green and berries red. Remove pattern.
3. Use gold paint to paint veins on leaves and highlights on berries.

PLATES
1. Trace holly or gift pattern onto tracing paper. With traced side down, tape pattern on front of plate.
2. Painting on wrong side of plate, paint gold highlights, red areas, then green areas.
3. Remove tape and pattern. Repeat for desired number of designs.

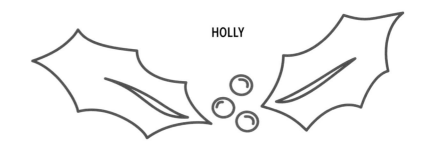

HOLLY

GIFT

SNOWMAN

APPLIQUÉD KNIT DRESS (Shown on page 101)

You will need a girl's cotton knit dress; black, green print, and plaid fabrics; $\frac{1}{2}$" dia. red shank button; clear thread; assorted buttons; paper-backed fusible web; stabilizer; and red thread for sewing buttons.

Note: Use a $\frac{1}{4}$" seam allowance for all sewing unless otherwise indicated.

1. Make a 3" vertical cut at center back of neck of dress. Measure around bottom edge of neckband, add 10". Cut a bias strip $1\frac{1}{2}$"w by the determined measurement from plaid fabric. Press edges of strip $\frac{1}{2}$" to wrong side. Matching wrong sides and long edges, press strip in half.

2. For ruffle, measure around bottom edge of neckband. Cut a length of bias strip the determined measurement. Multiply measurement by $1\frac{1}{2}$ and cut a piece of plaid fabric $3\frac{1}{4}$"w by the determined measurement. Press short ends $\frac{1}{4}$" to wrong side; press $\frac{1}{4}$" to wrong side again. Repeat for one long edge. Baste along long raw edge. Pull basting threads to gather fabric to fit bias strip. Adjusting gathers as necessary, insert gathered edge of ruffle into fold of bias strip. Stitch edges of strip together, catching ruffle in stitching. Pin ruffle along bottom edge of neckband; top stitch in place.

3. For back closure of dress, cut a 7" length from bias strip. Unfold strip and press ends $\frac{1}{2}$" to wrong side; refold strip. Pin strip over cut edge and sew in place. Cut a $2\frac{1}{2}$" length from bias strip. Unfold strip and press ends $\frac{1}{2}$" to wrong side; refold strip. Sew along long edges. Matching short ends, fold strip in half. Sew short ends of loop to inside left edge of neckband at opening. Sew shank button to outside right edge of neckband.

4. For skirt border, measure around skirt 2" above bottom edge; add $1\frac{1}{2}$". Cut a bias strip $1\frac{1}{4}$"w by the determined measurement. Press long edges $\frac{1}{4}$" to wrong side. Press one end $\frac{1}{2}$" to wrong side. Beginning with raw end, pin strip around dress 2" above bottom edge, overlapping ends at back. Top stitch in place.

5. Follow **Making Appliqués**, page 186, to make three tree and three trunk appliqués. Arrange appliqués on front of dress, overlapping as necessary; fuse in place. Using clear thread, follow **Machine Appliqué**, page 186, to sew over edges of appliqués. Sew buttons to trees as desired.

FRAGRANT BATH TEA BAGS
(Shown on page 107)

For tea bags, you will need dried chamomile blossoms, $\frac{1}{4}$"w flat gold trim, 12" squares of gold tulle and sheer organza, and dried mint leaves for invigorating bath tea **or** dried lavender for soothing bath tea.

1. Using equal parts, mix chamomile blossoms with mint leaves or lavender.
2. For each tea bag, center one square of organza over one square of tulle. Place $\frac{1}{4}$ cup of desired tea mixture in center of squares. Gather edges of squares around tea. Wrap an 8" length of trim several times around gathers. Knot ends to secure.
3. To use: Place one bag in bathtub under warm running water.

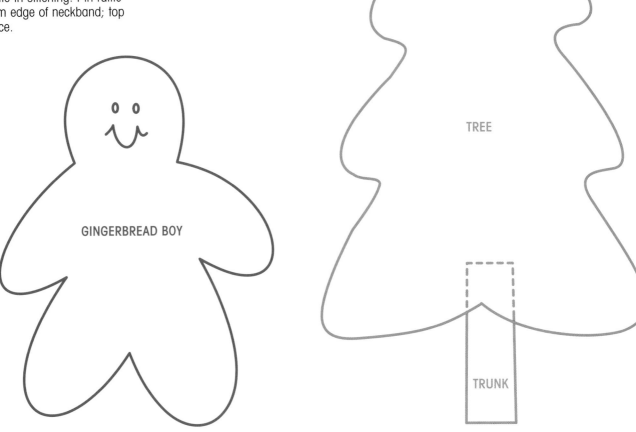

TREE

GINGERBREAD BOY

TRUNK

SEASONAL SWEATSHIRT VEST (Shown on page 100)

You will need a women's sweatshirt (we used an extra large), seam ripper, tailor's chalk, plaid fabric for binding and elastic casing, assorted print fabrics for appliqués, paper-backed fusible web, stabilizer, clear thread, black permanent fine-point marker, red fabric paint, small paintbrush, 6" length of $1/16$"w green satin ribbon, assorted buttons, 6" of $1/2$"w elastic, and a safety pin.

For background appliqués, you will **also** need one 5" x 8" fabric rectangle for tree; $4^1/2$" x $5^1/2$" fabric rectangle, 1" x $5^1/2$" fabric strip, and 1" x 6" fabric strip for gingerbread boy; two $3^1/2$" x $4^1/2$" fabric rectangles and one $1^3/4$" x $4^1/2$" fabric strip for hearts; and one $3^3/4$" x $6^1/2$" fabric rectangle and two 1" x $6^1/2$" fabric strips for ornaments.

Note: Match wrong sides of fabric pieces and use a $1/4$" seam allowance for all sewing unless otherwise indicated.

1. Use seam ripper to remove neckband, sleeves, and bottom ribbing from sweatshirt. If desired, shorten length of shirt. Cut shirt open vertically down center front.
2. Use chalk to mark 11" below neck on both sides of front opening. Draw a line from each mark to shoulder seam (**Fig. 1**); cut along drawn lines.

Fig. 1

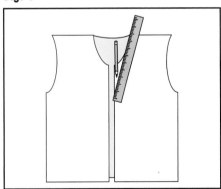

3. To enlarge armholes, mark shoulder seams $4^1/2$" from neck edge. Following the curves of armhole openings, draw tapering lines from shoulder marks to bottoms of armholes (**Fig. 2**). Cut along drawn lines.

Fig. 2

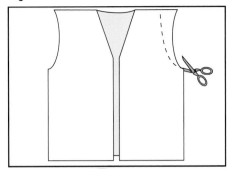

4. Stay-stitch along all edges of vest. Using $2^1/2$"w bias strip, follow **Binding**, page 186, to bind raw edges of vest.
5. Follow **Making Appliqués**, page 186, to make five large star; three each small star, ornament, and cap; two heart; and one each tree, trunk, and gingerbread boy appliqués.
6. For gingerbread boy background, sew 5" strip to 5" edge of rectangle. Sew 6" strip to right side of rectangle. For heart background, sew one $4^1/2$" edge of each rectangle to each $4^1/2$" side of strip. For ornament background, sew one 6" strip to each 6" side of rectangle. Press edges of each background $1/4$" to wrong side.
7. Arrange appliqués on backgrounds, overlapping as necessary; fuse in place. Using clear thread, follow **Machine Appliqué**, page 186, to sew over edges of appliqués. Use permanent marker to draw face on gingerbread boy. Thin red paint with water, paint cheeks on gingerbread boy. Tie ribbon into a bow; tack bow to gingerbread boy.
8. Arrange backgrounds on vest; top stitch in place. Arrange star appliqués on vest; fuse in place. Machine Appliqué over edges of stars. Sew buttons to vest as desired.
9. For elastic casing in back, cut a $1^1/2$" x 9" strip from fabric. Press ends, then long edges $1/4$" to wrong side. Mark $8^1/2$" across center back 6" from bottom edge. Center strip over marked line. Sewing close to pressed edges, top stitch long edges in place. Use safety pin to thread elastic through casing. Catching one end of elastic in stitches, sew a button over one end of casing. Repeat to catch remaining end of elastic at opposite end of casing.

SWEET BABY SET
(Shown on page 101)

You will need red rickrack, infant's cotton knit gown, cotton knit receiving blanket, assorted red and gold fabric scraps for appliqués, paper-backed fusible web, stabilizer, thread to match fabrics, and three 10" lengths of $1/4$"w green satin ribbon.

1. Arrange and pin rickrack down front of gown. Cut rickrack 1" below hem. Fold rickrack $1/4$" to wrong side and around bottom edge of hem; pin in place. Beginning at hem, sew rickrack to front of gown.
2. Beginning and ending at one corner, folding ends $1/2$" to wrong side, and placing rickrack 1" from edges, pin rickrack along edges of blanket. Sew rickrack to blanket.
3. Follow **Making Appliqués**, page 186, to make eight small star and three gingerbread boy appliqués. Arrange two gingerbread boys and five small stars on gown and one gingerbread boy and three stars on one corner of blanket; fuse in place.
4. Follow **Machine Appliqué**, page 186, to stitch over edges of appliqués.
5. Tie ribbons into bows. Tack one bow to each gingerbread boy.

SMALL STAR

LARGE STAR

HEART

ORNAMENT

CAP

You will need 1 yd. of 60"w red fleece, tracing paper, green and gold felt, pinking shears, plaid fabric, gold embroidery floss, sixteen $^5/_8$" dia. buttons, and eight $^3/_8$" dia. jingle bells. **For mittens**, you will **also** need 15" of $^1/_2$"w elastic and a safety pin.

Note: Using three strands of floss, follow **Embroidery Stitches**, page 188, for all embroidery stitches. Use a $^1/_4$" seam allowance for all sewing unless otherwise indicated.

MUFFLER

1. Cut a 12" x 50" piece of fleece. Follow **Making Patterns**, page 186, to make star and border patterns. Use border pattern to cut two pieces from green felt. Use pinking shears to trim long straight edge of each border piece. Use star pattern to cut six stars from gold felt.

2. Cut two 2 $^1/_2$" x 13" pieces of plaid fabric. Press long, then short edges of each fabric piece $^1/_2$" to wrong side.

3. For each end of muffler, place border across short edge of muffler with pointed edge of border 1 $^1/_4$" from short end of muffler. Work Running Stitch along pointed edges of border through both layers. Use Straight Stitch to make a vertical stitch at each point.

4. Arrange three stars above border piece. Work Straight Stitch and French Knots as indicated on star pattern to stitch stars to muffler. For each star burst, stitch a 1" vertical Straight Stitch, a Cross Stitch across center of Straight Stitch, and a French Knot at each end of one stitch of cross stitch.

5. Place one fabric strip across border pieces $^1/_4$" below pinked edge. Work Running Stitch along each long edge of fabric strip through all layers.

6. For fringe, make 1" clips $^1/_4$" apart along short edge.

7. Sew buttons above Straight Stitches at points of border. Sew bells to points of border.

MITTENS

1. Trace mitten and star patterns onto tracing paper; cut out. Leaving mittens open at wrist, follow **Sewing Shapes**, page 186, to make two mittens. Use star pattern to cut two stars from gold felt. Use pinking shears to cut two 2 $^3/_4$" squares from green felt.

2. For each mitten, center star on square. Work Straight Stitch and French Knots as indicated on star pattern to stitch star to square.

3. Work one Cross Stitch and two French Knots to secure corners of square to mitten top.

4. Fold $^1/_4$" of straight edge of mitten to wrong side, fold $^1/_4$" to wrong side again; sew in place.

5. For elastic casing, cut a 1 $^1/_4$" x 11" piece of plaid fabric. Press long, then short edges of fabric strip $^1/_4$" to wrong side. Beginning at thumb seam, pin strip around mitten 1 $^1/_4$" from bottom edge. Work Running Stitch along long edges of fabric strip to sew strip to mitten.

6. Use safety pin to insert elastic in casing. Overlap elastic ends $^1/_4$"; sew ends together. Hand sew casing closed.

HAT

1. Cut a 12" x 25" piece of fleece. Matching short edges, fold fleece in half. Sew short edges together.

2. Refer to **Fig. 1** to stitch curved seams across top corners of cap. Trim corners $^1/_2$" from curved seams. With seam at center back, fold hat flat. Refer to **Fig. 2** to sew $^1/_2$" x 3" darts at top of side folds.

Fig. 1

Fig. 2

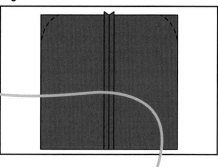

3. Matching darts and top edge, baste across top of hat from back seam to front curve. Pull basting thread to gather top edge of hat. Sew top edge of hat along gathers. Remove basting thread.

4. Using dotted line as bottom of pattern, follow **Making Patterns**, page 186, to make border pattern. Use pattern to cut border from a 28" strip of green felt. Use pinking shears to trim long straight edge of border.

5. Beginning with short edge at back seam and matching wrong sides and long edges, pin border around hat. Use Running Stitch to sew border to hat along points and pinked edge. Use Straight Stitch to make vertical stitches at points of border. Sew buttons above straight stitches at points of border. Turn hat right side out. Fold edge of hat up.

6. For pom-pom, cut a 3" x 3 $^1/_2$" piece of fleece. Make 1 $^1/_2$" cuts $^1/_4$" apart along short edges of piece. Matching long edges, fold fleece in half, fold in half again. Stitch center of pom-pom to top of hat.

STAR

MITTEN

BORDER

LUXURIOUS BATH SET (Shown on page 106)

WAX-SEALED BOTTLE
You will need a small glass bottle with cork stopper, wax crystals, gold crayon with paper removed, large can, saucepan, and a letter seal.

1. Follow recipe to prepare and fill bottle with Exotic Bath Salts, Sparkling Bath Gel, **or** Silky Bath Oil; cork bottle tightly.
2. Follow **Working with Wax**, this page, to melt wax and crayon to a depth of 2". Dip cork and rim of bottle in melted wax until completely coated. Allowing wax to cool slightly, repeat until desired thickness is achieved. If desired, stamp letter seal in warm wax on top of cork; allow wax to harden.

GOLD-SEALED BOTTLE
You will need a small glass bottle with cork stopper, 9" length of $1/2$"w gold mesh ribbon, gold sealing wax, and desired letter seal.

1. Follow recipe to prepare and fill bottle with Exotic Bath Salts, Sparkling Bath Gel, **or** Silky Bath Oil; cork bottle tightly.
2. Tie gold mesh ribbon into a knot around neck of bottle. Trim or notch ribbon ends.
3. (**Note:** Follow manufacturer's instructions to use gold sealing wax and letter seal.) Leaving $1/2$" of ribbon ends free, stamp seal on ribbon streamers and bottle.

HEART-STAMPED BOTTLE
You will need a small glass bottle with cork stopper to fit a $1 1/2$" x $2 1/4$" design, gold leaf, gold spray paint, $1 1/2$" x $1 3/4$" rectangle of screen wire, 1" dia. heart-shaped rubber stamp, gold ink pad, $1 1/4$" square of decorative paper, $1 1/2$" x $2 1/4$" rectangle of gold wrapping paper, and a hot glue gun.

1. Follow manufacturer's instructions to apply gold leaf to entire bottle.
2. Spray paint screen gold; allow to dry. Stamp heart on decorative paper. Center and glue decorative paper to screen. Center and glue screen to gold wrapping paper; glue to front of bottle.
3. Follow recipe to prepare and fill bottle with Exotic Bath Salts, Sparkling Bath Gel, **or** Silky Bath Oil; cork bottle tightly.

SCREEN-WRAPPED BOTTLE
You will need a small glass bottle with cork stopper, screen wire, gold spray paint, gold cord, hot glue gun, wax crystals, gold crayon with paper removed, large can, and saucepan.

1. Follow recipe to prepare and fill bottle with Exotic Bath Salts, Sparkling Bath Gel, **or** Silky Bath Oil; cork bottle tightly.
2. Measure around bottle; add 1". Measure height of bottle; subtract $1/2$". Cut a piece of screen the determined measurement. Spray paint screen gold; allow to dry.
3. Overlapping ends at back, wrap screen around bottle; glue to secure.
4. Follow Step 2 of Wax-Sealed Bottle to coat cork and rim with melted wax.
5. Tie cord into a bow around neck of bottle.

GOLD CORD-WRAPPED BOTTLE
You will need a small glass bottle with cork stopper, gold cord, gold charm, and a hot glue gun.

1. Follow recipe to prepare and fill bottle with Exotic Bath Salts, Sparkling Bath Gel, **or** Silky Bath Oil; cork bottle tightly.
2. Beginning and ending at back of bottle, glue one end of cord at top of bottle neck. Wrap cord closely around bottle neck until desired amount of neck is covered. Trim end and glue to secure.
3. Cut a length of cord to drape around bottle. Spot glue center of cord length at center back of bottle. Bring ends to front of bottle. Glue charm to bottle over cord to secure ends together.

STAR-SPANGLED BOTTLE
You will need a small glass bottle with cork stopper, gold glitter dimensional paint, wax crystals, gold crayon with paper removed, large can, saucepan, gold tassel, flat gold trim, and a hot glue gun.

1. Follow recipe to prepare and fill bottle with Exotic Bath Salts, Sparkling Bath Gel, **or** Silky Bath Oil; cork bottle tightly.
2. Use dimensional paint to paint stars on bottle; allow to dry.
3. Follow Step 2 of Wax-Sealed Bottle to coat cork and rim with melted wax.
4. Beginning and ending at back of bottle and working through hanging loop of tassel, glue one end of trim at top of bottle neck. Wrap trim around bottle neck three or four times. Trim end and glue to secure.

EXOTIC BATH SALTS
You will need $1/2$ cup rock salt, skin-safe essential oil, and a funnel.

1. Combine rock salt with ten drops of essential oil.
2. Use funnel to pour salt mixture into bottle; cork bottle tightly.

SPARKLING BATH GEL
For bath gel, you will need $1 1/3$ cups aloe vera gel, 1 teaspoon lanolin, fine gold glitter, and a funnel.

1. Mix gel and lanolin with a small amount of glitter.
2. Use funnel to pour mixture into bottle; cork bottle tightly.

SILKY BATH OIL
You will need 16 oz. of almond oil, $1/2$ oz. of skin-safe essential oil, dried flowers and greenery (we used small dried rosebuds, dried Queen Anne's lace, and thin dried leaves), and a funnel.

1. Mix oils together.
2. Place desired dried items in bottle. (**Note:** If using a bottle with a narrow neck, soak dried items in oil mixture before placing them in bottle.)
3. Pour oil mixture into bottle; cork bottle tightly.

WORKING WITH WAX

MELTING WAX
Caution: Do not melt wax over an open flame or in a pan placed directly on burner.
1. Cover work area with newspaper.
2. Heat 1" of water in a saucepan to boiling. Add water as necessary.
3. Place wax in a large can. If pouring wax, pinch top rim of can to form a spout. If dipping candles, use a can 2" taller than height of candle to be dipped.
4. To melt wax, place can in boiling water, reduce heat to simmer. If desired, melt crayon pieces in wax for color. Use a craft stick to stir, if necessary.

CROCHETED ANGEL AFGHAN (Shown on page 107)

Finished Size: 46" x 61"

You will need, 46 ounces (1,310 grams, 1,330 yards) of worsted weight brushed acrylic yarn, and size G (4.00 mm) crochet hook **or** size needed for gauge

Note: Refer to **Crochet**, page 188, for abbreviations and general instructions.

GAUGE: Each Square =15"
Gauge Swatch: 2³/₄" Square
Work same as Square through Rnd 2.

STITCH GUIDE
POPCORN
4 dc in st or sp indicated, drop loop from hook, insert hook in first dc of 4-dc group, hook dropped loop and draw through.

REVERSE SINGLE CROCHET
Working from **left** to **right**, ★ insert hook in st or sp to right of hook (**Fig. 1**), YO and draw through, under and to left of loop on hook (2 loops on hook) (**Fig. 2**), YO and draw through both loops on hook (**Fig. 3**) (**Reverse Single Crochet made, Fig. 4**); repeat from ★ around.

Fig. 1

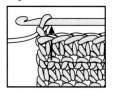

Fig. 2

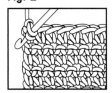

Fig. 3

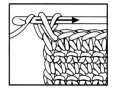

Fig. 4

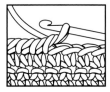

SQUARE (Make 12)
Ch 6; join with sl st to form a ring.

Rnd 1: (Right side): Ch 3 **(counts as first dc, now and throughout)**, 2 dc in ring, (ch 3, 3 dc in ring) 3 times, ch 2, sc in first dc to form last ch-3 sp: 12 dc and 4 ch-3 sps.
Note: Loop a short piece of yarn around any stitch to mark Rnd 1 as **right** side.

Rnd 2: Ch 3, dc in same sp and in next 3 dc, (2 dc, ch 3, dc) in next ch-3 sp, ch 1, dc in next dc, work Popcorn in next dc, dc in next dc, ch 1, (dc, ch 3, dc) in next ch-3 sp, ch 1, dc in next dc, ch 1, skip next dc, dc in next dc, ch 1, (dc, ch 3, dc) in next ch-3 sp, ch 1, dc in next dc, work Popcorn in next dc, dc in next dc, ch 1, dc in same sp as first dc, ch 2, sc in first dc to form last ch-3 sp: 19 dc, 2 Popcorns, and 11 sps.

Rnd 3: Ch 3, dc in same sp and in next dc, ch 1, skip next 2 dc, (dc, ch 3, dc) in next dc, ch 1, skip next 2 dc, dc in next dc, (2 dc, ch 3, dc) in next ch-3 sp, † ch 1, dc in next dc, work Popcorn in next ch-1 sp, dc in next dc, ch 1, dc in next dc, work Popcorn in next ch-1 sp, dc in next dc, ch 1 †, (dc, ch 3, dc) in next ch-3 sp, ch 1, dc in next dc, skip next ch-1 sp, 5 dc in next ch-1 sp, skip next dc, dc in next dc, ch 1, (dc, ch 3, dc) in next ch-3 sp, repeat from † to † once, dc in same sp as first dc, ch 2, sc in first dc to form last ch-3 sp: 29 dc and 15 sps.

Rnd 4: Ch 3, dc in same sp and in next dc, ch 1, skip next 2 dc, dc in next dc, 9 dc in next ch-3 sp, dc in next dc, ch 1, skip next 2 dc, dc in next dc, (2 dc, ch 3, dc) in next ch-3 sp, ch 1, † dc in next dc, work Popcorn in next ch-1 sp, dc in next dc, ch 1 †, repeat from † to † 2 times **more**, (dc, ch 3, dc) in next ch-3 sp, (ch 1, dc in next dc) twice, skip next 2 dc, 5 dc in next dc, skip next 2 dc, (dc in next dc, ch 1) twice, (dc, ch 3, dc) in next ch-3 sp, ch 1, repeat from † to † 3 times, dc in same sp as first dc, ch 2, sc in first dc to form last ch-3 sp: 44 dc and 18 sps.

Rnd 5: Ch 4 **(counts as first dc plus ch 1, now and throughout)**, dc in next 3 dc, ch 1, hdc in next 5 dc, 2 hdc in next dc, hdc in next 5 dc, ch 1, dc in next 3 dc, ch 1, (dc, ch 3, dc) in next ch-3 sp, ch 1, † dc in next dc, work Popcorn in next ch-1 sp, dc in next dc, ch 1 †, repeat from † to † 3 times **more**, (dc, ch 3, dc) in next ch-3 sp, ch 1, (dc in next dc, ch 1) 3 times, skip next 2 dc, 5 dc in next dc, ch 1, skip next 2 dc, (dc in next dc, ch 1) 3 times, (dc, ch 3, dc) in next ch-3 sp, ch 1, repeat from † to † 4 times, dc in same sp as first dc, ch 2, sc in first dc to form last ch-3 sp: 41 dc and 26 sps.

Rnd 6: Ch 4, dc in next dc, ch 1, dc in next 3 dc, ch 2, skip next 2 hdc, hdc in next 3 hdc, 2 hdc in each of next 2 hdc, hdc in next 3 hdc, ch 2, skip next 2 hdc, dc in next 3 dc, ch 1, dc in next dc, ch 1, (dc, ch 3, dc) in next ch-3 sp, ch 1, † dc in next dc, work Popcorn in next ch-1 sp, dc in next dc, ch 1 †, repeat from † to † 4 times **more**, (dc, ch 3, dc) in next ch-3 sp, ch 1, dc in next dc, skip next ch-1 sp, 5 dc in next ch-1 sp, ch 1, skip next 4 dc, 5 dc in next dc, ch 1, skip next 2 ch-1 sps, 5 dc in next ch-1 sp, skip next dc, dc in next dc, ch 1, (dc, ch 3, dc) in next ch-3 sp, ch 1, repeat from † to † 5 times, dc in same sp as first dc, ch 2, sc in first dc to form last ch-3 sp: 53 dc and 26 sps.

Rnd 7: Ch 4, (dc in next dc, ch 1) 3 times, skip next dc, dc in next dc, 2 dc in next ch-2 sp, ch 2, skip next 2 hdc, sc in next 6 hdc, ch 2, 2 dc in next ch-2 sp, dc in next dc, ch 1, skip next dc, (dc in next dc, ch 1) 3 times, (dc, ch 3, dc) in next ch-3 sp, ch 1, † dc in next dc, work Popcorn in next ch-1 sp, dc in next dc, ch 1 †, repeat from † to † 5 times **more**, (dc, ch 3, dc) in next ch-3 sp, (ch 1, dc in next dc) twice, skip next 2 dc, 5 dc in next dc, ★ ch 1, skip next 4 dc, 5 dc in next dc; repeat from ★ once **more**, skip next 2 dc, (dc in next dc, ch 1) twice, (dc, ch 3, dc) in next ch-3 sp, ch 1, repeat from † to † 6 times, dc in same sp as first dc, ch 2, sc in first dc to form last ch-3 sp: 63 dc and 34 sps.

Rnd 8: Ch 4, (dc in next dc, ch 1)

5 times, skip next dc, dc in next dc, 2 dc in next ch-2 sp, ch 2, skip next 2 sc, sc in next 2 sc, ch 2, 2 dc in next ch-2 sp, dc in next dc, ch 1, skip next dc, (dc in next dc, ch 1) 5 times, (dc, ch 3, dc) in next ch-3 sp, ch 1, † dc in next dc, work Popcorn in next ch-1 sp, dc in next dc, ch 1 †, repeat from † to † 6 times **more**, (dc, ch 3, dc) in next ch-3 sp, ch 1, (dc in next dc, ch 1) 3 times, skip next 2 dc, 5 dc in next dc, ch 1, ★ skip next 4 dc, 5 dc in next dc, ch 1; repeat from ★ once **more**, skip next 2 dc, (dc in next dc, ch 1) 3 times, (dc, ch 3, dc) in next ch-3 sp, ch 1, repeat from † to † 7 times, dc in same sp as first dc, ch 2, sc in first dc to form last ch-3 sp: 73 dc and 44 sps.

Rnd 9: Ch 4, (dc in next dc, ch 1) 7 times, skip next dc, dc in next dc, 2 dc in next ch-2 sp, ch 1, 2 dc in next ch-2 sp, dc in next dc, ch 1, skip next dc, (dc in next dc, ch 1) 7 times, (dc, ch 3, dc) in next ch-3 sp, ch 1, (dc in next dc, ch 1) 16 times, (dc, ch 3, dc) in next ch 3 sp, ch 1, dc in next dc, skip next ch-1 sp, 5 dc in next ch-1 sp, ch 1, ★ skip next 4 dc, 5 dc in next dc, ch 1; repeat from ★ 2 times **more**, skip next 2 ch-1 sps, 5 dc in next ch-1 sp, skip next dc, dc in next dc, ch 1, (dc, ch 3, dc) in next ch-3 sp, ch 1, (dc in next dc, ch 1) 16 times, dc in same sp as first dc, ch 2, sc in first dc to form last ch-3 sp: 87 dc and 61 sps.

Rnd 10: Ch 3, (dc in next dc, ch 1) 9 times, skip next dc, (dc in next dc, ch 1) twice, skip next dc, dc in next dc, (ch 1, dc in next dc) 8 times, (dc, ch 3, dc) in next ch-3 sp, ch 1, (dc in next dc, ch 1) 18 times, (dc, ch 3, dc) in next ch-3 sp, ch 1, (dc in next dc, ch 1) twice, skip next 2 dc, 5 dc in next dc, ch 1, ★ skip next 4 dc, 5 dc in next dc, ch 1; repeat from ★ 3 times **more**, skip next 2 dc, (dc in next dc, ch 1) twice, (dc, ch 3, dc) in next ch-3 sp, ch 1, (dc in next dc, ch 1) 18 times, dc in same sp as first dc, ch 2, sc in first dc to form last ch-3 sp: 93 dc and 71 sps.

Rnd 11: Ch 4, skip next dc, dc in next dc, (dc in next ch-1 sp and in next dc) 19 times, ch 1, skip next dc, (dc, ch 3, dc) in next ch-3 sp, ch 1, dc in next dc, (dc in next ch-1 sp and in next dc) 19 times, ch 1, (dc, ch 3, dc) in next ch-3 sp, ch 1, (dc in next dc, ch 1) 3 times, skip next 2 dc, 5 dc in next dc, ch 1, ★ skip next 4 dc, 5 dc in next dc, ch 1; repeat from ★ 3 times **more**, skip next 2 dc, (dc in next dc, ch 1) 3 times, (dc, ch 3, dc) in next ch-3 sp, ch 1, dc in next dc, (dc in next ch-1 sp and in next dc) 19 times, ch 1, dc in same sp as first dc, ch 2, sc in first dc to form last ch-3 sp: 156 dc and 22 sps.

Rnd 12: Ch 4, dc in next dc and in each ch-1 sp and each dc across to next ch-3 sp, ch 1, (dc, ch 3, dc) in ch-3 sp, ch 1, dc in each dc and in each ch-1 sp across to next ch-3 sp, ch 1, (dc, ch 3, dc) in ch-3 sp, ch 1, (dc in next dc, ch 1) 4 times, skip next 2 dc, 5 dc in next dc, ch 1, ★ skip next 4 dc, 5 dc in next dc, ch 1; repeat from ★ 3 times **more**, skip next 2 dc, (dc in next dc, ch 1) 4 times, (dc, ch 3, dc) in next ch-3 sp, ch 1, dc in each dc and in each ch-1 sp across, ch 1, dc in same sp as first dc, ch 2, sc in first dc to form last ch-3 sp: 170 dc and 24 sps.

Rnd 13: Ch 4, dc in next dc and in each ch-1 sp and each dc across to next ch-3 sp, ch 1, (dc, ch 3, dc) in ch-3 sp, ch 1, dc in next dc and in each ch-1 sp and each dc across to next ch-3 sp, ch 1, (dc, ch 3, dc) in next ch-3 sp, (ch 1, dc in next dc) 5 times, ch 2, skip next 2 dc, sl st in next dc, ch 2, ★ sc in next ch-1 sp, ch 2, skip next 2 dc, sl st in next dc, ch 2; repeat from ★ 3 times **more**, skip next 2 dc, (dc in next dc, ch 1) 5 times, (dc, ch 3, dc) in next ch-3 sp, ch 1, dc in each dc and in each ch-1 sp across, ch 1, dc in same sp as first dc, ch 2, sc in first dc to form last ch-3 sp: 159 dc and 30 sps.

Rnd 14: Ch 4, † (dc in next dc, ch 1) twice, (skip next st, dc in next dc, ch 1) across to next ch-3 sp, (dc, ch 3, dc) in ch-3 sp, ch 1 †, repeat from † to † once **more**, (dc in next dc, ch 1) 6 times, place marker around last dc made to mark bottom edge, skip next ch, dc in next ch, ch 1, skip next sl st, dc in next ch, ch 1, skip next ch, ★ dc in next sc, ch 1, skip next ch, dc in next ch, ch 1, skip next sl st, dc in next ch, ch 1, skip next ch; repeat from ★ 3 times **more**, (dc in next dc, ch 1) 6 times, (dc, ch 3, dc) in next ch-3 sp, ch 1, (dc in next dc, ch 1) twice, (skip next st, dc in next dc, ch 1) across, dc in same sp as first dc, ch 3; join with sl st to first dc, finish off: 112 dc and 112 sps.

ASSEMBLY

Assemble Afghan by forming three vertical strips of four Squares each. Join Squares as follows:
With right sides together, match sps on bottom edge of one Square to top edge of next Square. Working through both thicknesses, join yarn with sl st in first corner ch-3 sp; (ch 1, sl st in next sp) across; finish off.
Join strips together in same manner.

EDGING

With right side facing, join yarn with sl st in any st; working from **left** to **right**, work Reverse Single Crochet in each dc and in each ch-1 sp around, working 3 Reverse Single Crochet in each corner ch-3 sp; join with sl st to first st, finish off.

SNOWMAN DRESS (Shown on page 102)

For a girl's size 5 dress, you will need a size 6-8 black T-shirt, 42" square of white felt, tracing paper, orange and black felt, orange and black embroidery floss, 1/4"w elastic, and 9" x 44" strip of fabric for sash.

1. Press hem of T-shirt 4 1/2" to wrong side. Leaving a small opening along bottom edge of hem to insert elastic, sew close to top and bottom of hem to make casing.
2. Using a 6" measurement for inside cutting line and a 21" measurement for outside cutting line, follow **Cutting a Fabric Circle**, page 186, to cut skirt from white felt.
3. Match inside opening edge of skirt to pressed edge on right side of T-shirt. Easing to fit and using 1/2" seam allowance, sew skirt to T-shirt.

4. Trace face patterns onto tracing paper; cut out. Using patterns, cut one nose from orange felt and two eyes and five mouth pieces from black felt. Use matching color floss and long stitches to sew face pieces to skirt.
5. Measure child's waist; add 1". Cut a length of elastic the determined measurement. Thread elastic through casing. Sew elastic ends together. Sew opening closed.
6. For sash, matching right sides and long edges, fold fabric strip in half. Leaving an opening for turning and using a 1/2" seam allowance, sew raw edges of fabric strip together. Turn sash right side out. Sew opening closed and press.

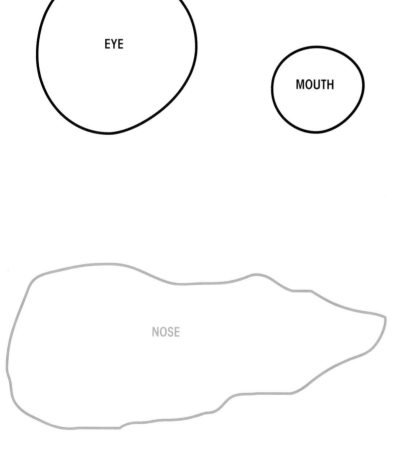

WINTER WARMER WALL HANGING
(Shown on page 113)

You will need an 8" x 14" piece of white Aida (14 ct); embroidery floss (refer to color key); #24 tapestry needle; two each 2 1/4" x 11 3/4" and 2 1/4" x 14 1/4" strips, 7" x 10" piece of fabric for hanging sleeve, and one 11 3/4" x 17 1/2" backing piece of red checked flannel; two each 1 1/2" x 8 1/2" and 1 1/2" x 12" strips of green check fabric; 11 3/4" x 17 1/2" piece of batting; four 1" dia. white buttons; and an 11" length of 1/4" dia. wooden dowel.

Note: Use 1/4" seam allowance for all sewing unless otherwise indicated.

1. Following **Cross Stitch**, page 188, and using three strands of floss for Cross Stitch and one strand of floss for Backstitch and French Knot, work Winter Warmer Wall Hanging design on Aida cloth. Trim finished stitched piece to 6" x 12".
2. For wall hanging front, match right sides and raw edges and sew long green strips to sides of cross-stitched piece. Repeat to sew short green strips to top and bottom of cross-stitched piece.
3. Repeat Step 2 to sew red strips to sides, then top and bottom of wall hanging front. Center batting piece on wrong side of backing. Center wrong side of wall hanging front on batting. Pin front, batting, and backing together. Use three strands of black floss to sew buttons to corners of sampler.
4. Press short edges of hanging sleeve fabric piece 1/4" to wrong side. Press 1/4" to wrong side again; stitch in place. Matching wrong sides and long edges, fold piece in half. Match raw edges to center top back of wall hanging; pin in place. Taking care not to stitch through design, tack folded edge in place.
8. Using a 2"w bias strip, follow **Binding**, page 186, to bind wall hanging.
9. Insert dowel into hanging sleeve.

WINTER WARMER MUGS
(Shown on page 112)

For each mug, you will need one red Crafter's Pride® Stitch-a-Mug™ with 14 ct white Vinyl Weave™ insert, DMC embroidery floss (refer to color key), and a #24 tapestry needle.

1. Centering design 2¹/₂" from short edge of insert, use three strands of floss and follow **Cross Stitch,** page 188, to stitch snowman or snow woman from Winter Warmer Wall Hanging chart. Beginning at one short edge of insert and leaving three unworked threads between border and long edges, stitch red heart border along long edges of insert.
2. Place stitched piece in mug. Remove stitched piece before washing mug.

WINTER WARMER TOWELS
(Shown on page 112)

You will need a white fingertip towel with 14 ct Aida insert, DMC embroidery floss (refer to color key), and #24 tapestry needle.

1. Using three strands of floss, follow **Cross Stitch**, page 188, to stitch tree border or verse of Winter Warmer Wall Hanging chart in center of Aida inserts.
2. Center and stitch red and black border above and below stitched design, repeating as needed to work border to approximately ¹/₂" from towel edges.

Winter Warmer Wall Hanging

X	DMC	B'ST	ANC.	COLOR
▨	310	✓	403	black
⊖	415		398	grey
■	433		358	brown
▬	666		46	red
✳	701		227	green
△	725		305	yellow
★	826		161	blue
▢	827		160	lt blue
◇	3716		25	pink
●	310			French Knot

STITCH COUNT (51w x 137h)

14 count	3³/₄"	x	9⁷/₈"
16 count	3¹/₄"	x	8⁵/₈"
18 count	2⁷/₈"	x	7⁵/₈"
22 count	2³/₈"	x	6¹/₄"

"WARM WISHES" CARD HOLDER (Shown on page 110)

You will need 21 1/2" of 1/2" dia. wooden dowel, green acrylic paint, paintbrush, two 2 1/4"w wooden stars, assorted gold and red print fabrics, fabric glue, paper-backed fusible web, 18" x 40" piece of ecru felt, red and green embroidery floss, three 5" squares of assorted tan print fabrics, pinking shears, tracing paper, transfer paper, 3" x 11" piece of tan felt, 12" x 12" piece of red felt, 5" x 13" piece of green felt, four red 1/2"w buttons, floral wire, wire cutters, and a hot glue gun.

Note: Refer to **Embroidery Stitches**, page 188, and use six strands of green floss for all Running Stitches and three strands of red floss for all Blanket Stitches. Stitch through all layers for all embroidery stitches. Use fabric glue for all gluing unless otherwise indicated.

1. Paint dowel green. Trace around wooden stars on wrong side of gold fabric; cut out. Glue fabric stars to wooden stars.
2. Cut an 18" x 20" piece of web. Matching one 18" edge of ecru felt with one 18" edge of web, fuse web to felt. Remove paper backing and fold unfused side of felt over web; fuse felt layers together. Work Running Stitches along folded edge of felt.
3. For pocket, fold stitched edge 5 1/2" to one side (front). Work Running Stitches along all outer edges of card holder and 6" from each side edge of pocket.
4. Fuse web to wrong side of each tan fabric square. Use pinking shears to trim edges of squares. Fuse squares to pockets.

5. Follow **Making Appliqués**, page 186, to make three heart A appliqués from red felt, three heart B and two heart C appliqués from red fabric, and five star appliqués from gold fabric. Fuse heart B appliqués to heart A appliqués. Work Blanket Stitches around each heart B appliqué. Fuse heart A appliqués to pockets.
6. For sign, trace the words "Warm Wishes" onto tracing paper; transfer words to tan felt. Work Running Stitches over transferred lines. Glue sign to red felt. Leaving a 1/4" red border, use pinking shears to cut out sign.
7. Matching arrows and dotted lines, trace outer border A and outer border B onto tracing paper. Using pattern, cut outer border from green felt. Center and glue sign to outer border. Center and glue outer border to card holder 1 1/2" below top edge. Fuse heart C appliqués and stars to card holder.
8. For hanging loops, cut a 2" x 26" strip of red fabric and a 1" x 26" strip of web. Center and fuse web strip to wrong side of fabric strip. Remove paper backing and fold long edges of fabric 1/2" to wrong side; fuse in place. Use pinking shears to trim ends of strip and cut strip into four 6" lengths; fold each length in half. With ends at front and back of card holder and spacing loops evenly across top, use red floss to sew buttons and loops to card holder.
9. Insert dowel through loops. Hot glue center of a 5" length of wire to back of each wooden star. Wire one star to each end of dowel; hot glue to secure.

HEART COASTERS

(Shown on page 110)

For each coaster, you will need paper-backed fusible web; one 5 1/2" square each of red felt, green felt, and beige print fabric; 4 1/2" square of gold, red, or green print fabric; 2" square of yellow print fabric; red embroidery floss; and pinking shears.

1. Fuse web to wrong side of each fabric square and red felt.
2. Follow **Making Appliqués**, page 186, to make one heart A from red felt, one heart B from gold, red, or green fabric, and one star from yellow fabric.
3. Fuse heart B to heart A. Fuse star to heart B. Using six strands of floss and stitching through both layers, work **Blanket Stitches**, page 189, around edges of heart B. Fuse heart A to beige square.
4. Leaving a 1/4" beige border, use pinking shears to trim edges of beige square. Center and fuse beige square to green felt. Using six strands of floss, work **Running Stitches**, page 189, along edges of beige square.

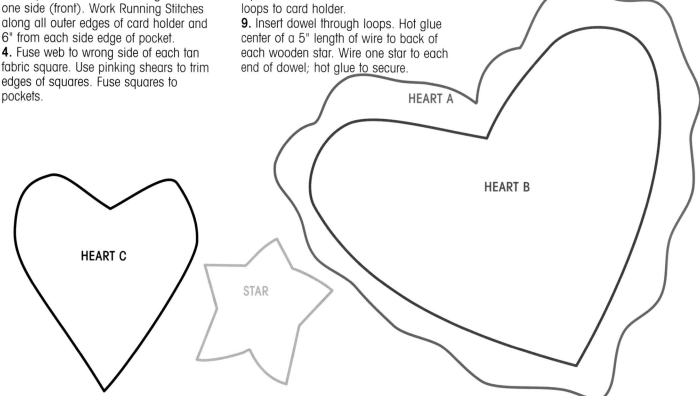

HEART A

HEART B

HEART C

STAR

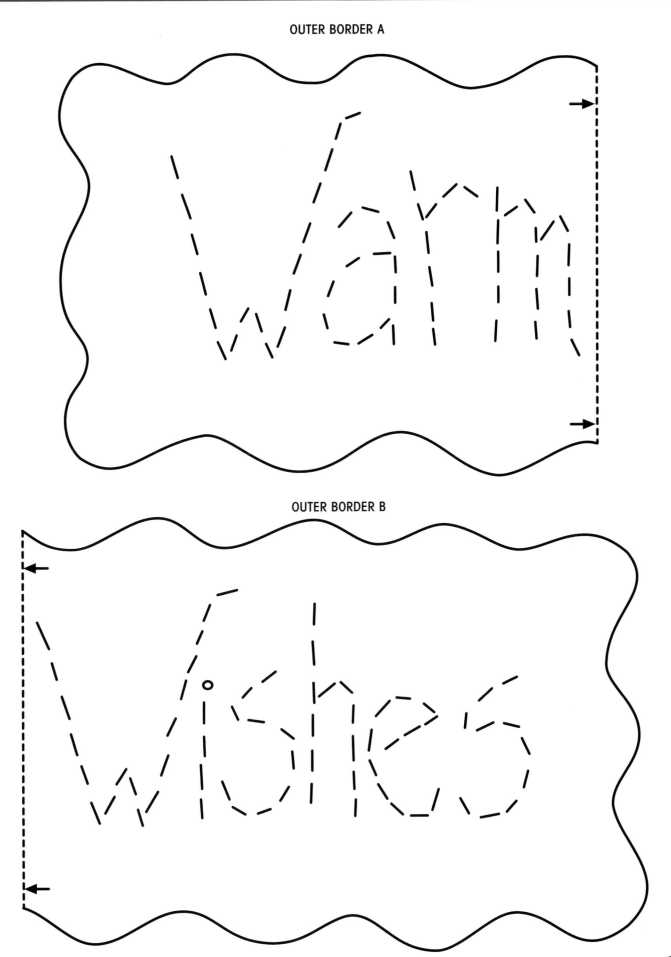

OUTER BORDER B

ORNAMENT PLACE MATS

(Shown on page 108)

For one place mat, you will need tracing paper, two 16" x 20" pieces of fabric for place mat front and backing, one 16" x 20" piece of batting, 20" of 1 1/2"w decorative ribbon with gold edges, 1 1/2 yds. of gold twist cord with lip, and 16" of 1 1/2"w gold mesh wired ribbon.

1. Aligning arrows and dotted lines, trace place mat A and place mat B patterns onto tracing paper; cut out. Using pattern, follow **Making Patterns**, page 186, to make full-size place mat pattern. Cutting 1/2" outside edges of pattern, cut shape from fabrics and batting.
2. Arrange and sew decorative ribbon on right side of place mat front.
3. Beginning at top and matching raw edges, baste lip of cord on right side of place mat front.
4. Place backing fabric right side up on batting. With right sides together, position place mat front on backing. Leaving an opening for turning and using a zipper foot, sew layers together as close as possible to cording. Clip curves and trim seam allowance to 1/4". Turn right side out and sew opening closed.
5. Press place mat. Tie gold ribbon into a bow. Tack bow at top of place mat.

PLACE MAT B

MASCULINE DESK SET (Shown on page 105)

Note: Allow paint, wood-tone spray, and sealer to dry after each application. We used stock market report newsprint to cover projects.

FRAME
You will need a frame with stand, newsprint, spray adhesive, wood-tone spray, clear acrylic spray sealer, hot glue gun, 3/8" dia. brown satin cord, and assorted buttons.

1. Measure length and width of one long side of frame; add 2" to each measurement. Cut two strips of newsprint the determined measurements. Apply spray adhesive to wrong side of strips. Center one strip on one long side of frame. From inside opening of frame, make a clip at each corner. Smooth strip onto sides and around to back of frame. Repeat for opposite side.
2. Measure length and width of one short side of frame; add 2" to width measurement. Cut two strips of newsprint the determined measurements. Apply spray adhesive to wrong side of strips. Center one strip on one short side of frame. Fold short ends of strip diagonally to wrong side to fit frame opening. Smooth strip around sides and onto back of frame. Repeat for opposite side.
3. Apply wood-tone spray, then sealer to frame.
4. Tie a knot in one end of cord. Beginning with knot at center top of frame and trimming to fit, glue cord around sides of frame. Glue buttons to frame.

PENCIL CUP
You will need brown spray paint, clean empty can, newsprint, spray adhesive, wood-tone spray, clear acrylic spray sealer, 3/8" dia. brown satin cord, hot glue gun, and assorted buttons.

1. Spray paint inside and outside of can. Measure around can; add 1/2". Measure height of can between rims. Cut a piece of newsprint the determined measurements. Apply spray adhesive to wrong side of paper. Overlapping ends, smooth paper around can.
2. Apply wood-tone spray, then sealer to can.
3. Tie a knot in one end of cord. Beginning with knot at top front of can and trimming to fit, glue cord around can. Glue buttons to can.

BOX
You will need newsprint, an empty cardboard box with lid, spray adhesive, wood-tone spray, clear acrylic spray sealer, 3/8" dia. brown satin cord, hot glue gun, and assorted buttons.

1. Cut a piece of newsprint large enough to cover box lid. Apply spray adhesive to wrong side of newsprint. Center lid on wrong side of newsprint. Pleating as necessary, smooth newsprint over sides to inside of lid. Repeat to cover bottom of box.
2. Apply wood-tone spray, then sealer to box and lid.
3. Tie a knot in one end of cord. Beginning with knot at center front of lid and trimming to fit, glue cord around top of lid. Glue buttons to box. PLACE MAT A

SANTA PATCHES

(Shown on pages 102 and 103)

For each patch, you will need a 6" square each of white Aida (14 ct) and desired color felt, embroidery floss (see color key), paper-backed fusible web, pinking shears, and purchased garment.

Note: Refer to **Cross Stitch**, page 188, before beginning project. Use 3 strands of floss for Cross Stitch and 1 strand for Backstitch unless otherwise indicated.

1. Center and work desired Santa design on Aida.
2. Fuse web to wrong side of stitched piece. Trim edges of stitched piece to one thread outside Cross Stitch border. Fuse stitched piece to center of felt. Leaving a ¹/₂" felt border, use pinking shears to trim patch.
3. Pin patch to garment. Sewing inside Cross Stitch border, sew patch to garment.

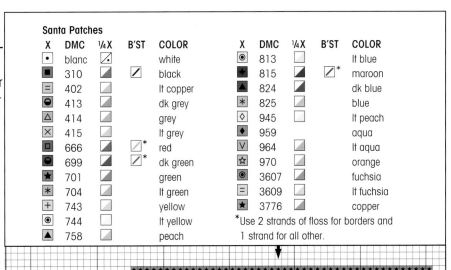

Santa Patches

X	DMC	¼X	B'ST	COLOR		X	DMC	¼X	B'ST	COLOR
•	blanc			white		◉	813			lt blue
■	310		∕	black		✦	815		∕*	maroon
≡	402			lt copper		▲	824			dk blue
◕	413			dk grey		✳	825			blue
△	414			grey		◇	945			lt peach
✕	415			lt grey		◆	959			aqua
▣	666		∕*	red		∨	964			lt aqua
◕	699		∕*	dk green		☆	970			orange
★	701			green		◎	3607			fuchsia
✳	704			lt green		⊟	3609			lt fuchsia
+	743			yellow		★	3776			copper
◉	744			lt yellow		*Use 2 strands of floss for borders and				
▲	758			peach		1 strand for all other.				

46w x 47h

46w x 46h

47w x 47h

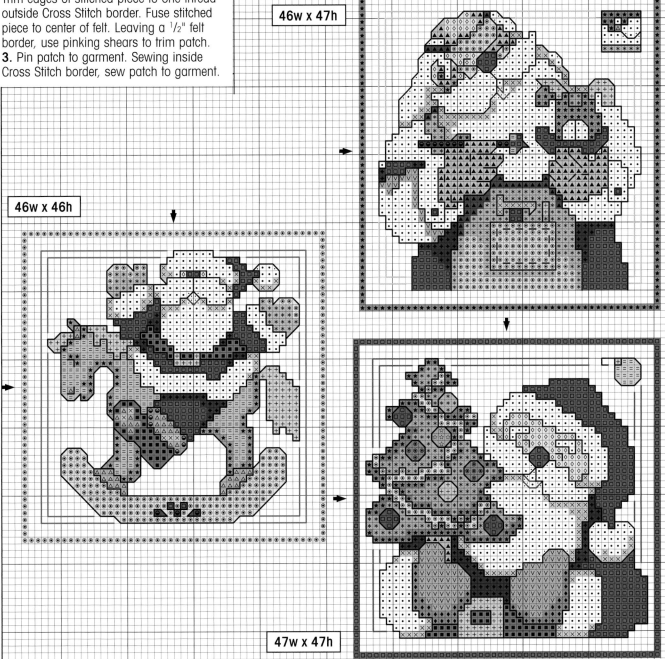

SKATING SANTA SLED (Shown on page 111)

You will need sandpaper; an unfinished wooden sled with an area $8^3/_4$" x $13^1/_2$" or larger for painting; two 2"w wooden stars; tack cloth; clear satin varnish; soft cloth; walnut stain; white, antique white, yellow, dark yellow, flesh, red, grey blue, navy blue, brown, and black acrylic paint; paintbrushes; tracing paper; graphite transfer paper; pencil; kraft paper; tape; old toothbrush; matte acrylic spray sealer; two yds. of $2^1/_2$"w wired ribbon; floral wire; wire cutters; artificial greenery; twigs; hot glue gun; and three pinecones.

Note: Refer to **Painting Techniques**, page 189, before beginning project. Allow stain, varnish, paint, and sealer to dry after each application unless otherwise indicated. To thin paint, mix one part paint to one part water. Use graphite transfer paper when transferring designs.

1. Sand sled and stars. Use tack cloth to remove dust. Apply varnish to sled and stars. Sand again and remove dust. Use soft cloth to apply stain to stars and sled runners.

2. Excluding runners, paint sled red. Paint stars dark yellow.

3. Aligning arrows and dotted lines, trace Sled A and Sled B patterns onto tracing paper. Transfer oval outline to sled and to center of a piece of kraft paper large enough to cover sled. Paint oval on sled navy blue.

SLED A

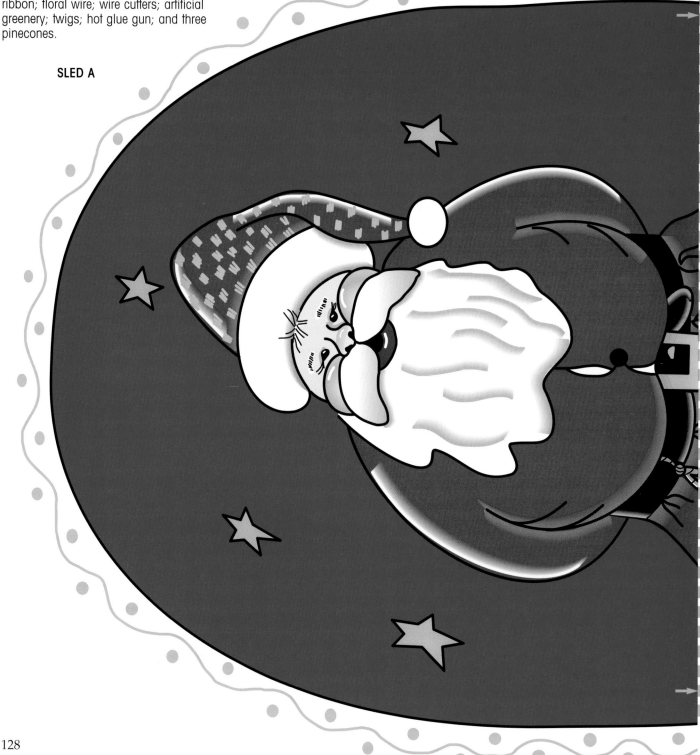

4. Transfer "ice" line to sled. Follow **Painting Techniques** to float thinned white paint across, then down "ice."
5. Transfer remaining design to sled. Refer to photo and follow **Painting Techniques** to paint Santa.
6. Cut transferred oval from kraft paper; discard oval. Covering red background, position opening in kraft paper over painted design; secure with tape. Cover Santa's face with a piece of kraft paper; secure with tape. Use toothbrush to spatter thinned white paint over exposed area of oval. Remove paper. Spatter thinned yellow and brown paint over stars.
7. Paint wavy line and dot border. Spray sled and stars with sealer.
8. Follow **Making a Bow**, page 187, and use ribbon to make a bow with four 8" loops, one 16" streamer, and one 24" streamer. Notch ribbon ends. Wire greenery and twigs to sled. Wire bow to greenery. Glue stars and pinecones to greenery and bow. Glue streamers to runners.

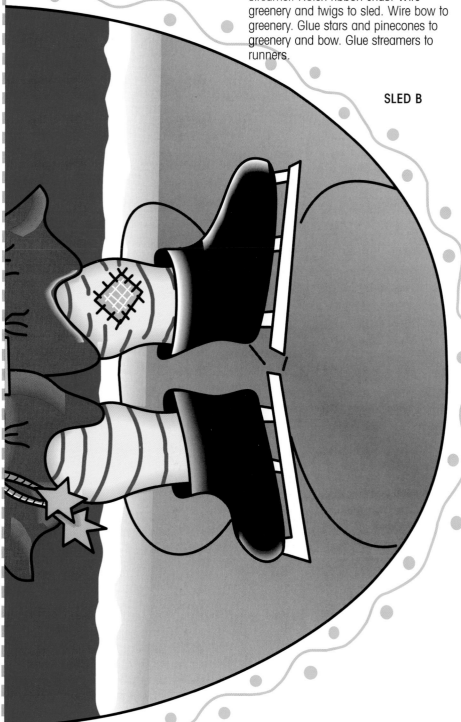

SLED B

COVERED ALBUM
(Shown on page 105)

You will need tapestry fabric to cover album, photo album with center rings, hot glue gun, 1 1/4"w wired ribbon, 1/2"w gold braid, fabric glue, 5/8"w wired ribbon, poster board, fabric for lining, large nail, hammer, and tassel.

Note: Use hot glue for all gluing unless otherwise indicated.

1. Cut a piece of fabric for cover 2" larger on all sides than opened album. Center opened album on wrong side of fabric piece.
2. Fold corners of fabric diagonally over corners of album; glue in place. Fold short edges of fabric over side edges of album; glue in place. Fold long edges of fabric over edges of album, trimming fabric to fit 1/4" under binding hardware; glue in place.
3. Cut two 3"w tapestry fabric strips 1/2" shorter than height of album. Press ends of each strip 1/4" to wrong side. On inside of album, center and glue one strip along each side of binding hardware with one long edge of each strip tucked 1/4" under hardware.
4. Cut one length each of 1 1/4"w ribbon and braid 2" longer than width of open album. Glue braid along center of ribbon.
5. Use fabric glue to glue ribbon around album, gluing ends to inside front and back covers.
6. For ribbon tie closure, cut two 10" lengths of 5/8"w ribbon. Center and glue one end of each ribbon length to inside front and back of album on long opening edge.
7. For liners, cut two pieces of poster board 1" smaller on all sides than front of album. Cut two pieces of fabric for lining 2" larger than poster board pieces. Center one poster board piece on wrong side of one fabric piece. Fold corners of fabric piece diagonally over corners of poster board; glue in place. Fold edges of fabric over edges of poster board; glue in place. Repeat with remaining poster board and fabric. Glue liners to insides of covers.
8. Use hammer and nail to punch a hole through front album cover at center of long opening edge. Insert tassel hanger through hole from inside to outside of album and pull up a loop. Insert tassel through loop and pull tightly.
9. Tie long ribbon ends together into a bow.

CROCHETED VEST (Shown on page 104)

Vest Size	Finished Chest
Small	40"
Medium	44"
Large	48"

Instructions are written for size Small with sizes Medium and Large in braces {}. If only one number is given, it applies to all sizes.

You will need size E crochet hook or size needed for gauge, yarn needle, and sport weight yarn in the following colors and amounts:
Color A (tan) - 6{7-8} ounces
Color B (rust) - 2¹/₂{3-3} ounces
Color C (teal) - 2{2-2¹/₂} ounces

Note: Refer to **Crochet**, page 188, for abbreviations and general instructions. Read **Changing Colors** before beginning the vest and follow **Stripe Sequence** to work vest.

CHANGING COLORS
Change color in the last sc of the row **before** the row which is to be worked in the new color.

To work color change, insert hook in last sc of row, YO and pull up a loop, drop yarn, with new yarn, YO and draw through both loops on hook **(Fig. 1)**. Cut old yarn and work over both ends.
Fig. 1

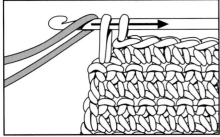

STRIPE SEQUENCE
Sizes small and medium only
Work one row of **each** color: ★ Color A **(Fig. 1)**, Color B, Color A, Color C; repeat from ★ throughout.

Size large only
Work one row of **each** color: Color A **(Fig. 1)**, Color B, Color A, ★ Color C, Color A, Color B, Color A; repeat from ★ throughout.

Gauge: 18 sc and 22 rows = 4"

BODY
Ch 181{199-217} **loosely**.
Row 1 (Right side): Sc in second ch from hook and in each ch across: 180{198-216} sc.
Note: Loop a short piece of yarn around any stitch to mark last row as **right** side.
Rows 2-52: Ch 1, turn; sc in each sc across. Do **not** finish off.

RIGHT FRONT
Row 53: Ch 1, turn; sc in first 38{43-48} sc, leave remaining 142{155-168} sc unworked.
Rows 54 and 55: Ch 1, turn; sc in each sc across to last 2 sc, skip next sc, sc in last sc: 36{41-46} sc.
Row 56: Ch 1, turn; sc in each sc across.
Rows 57-59: Ch 1, turn; sc in each sc across to last 2 sc, skip next sc, sc in last sc: 33{38-43} sc.
Rows 60-63: Repeat Rows 56-59: 30{35-40} sc.
Rows 64 and 65: Ch 1, turn; sc in each sc across.
Row 66: Ch 1, turn; sc in each sc across to last 2 sc, skip next sc, sc in last sc: 29{34-39} sc.
Rows 67-69: Ch 1, turn; sc in each sc across.
Rows 70-89{97-105}: Repeat Rows 66-69, 5{7-9} times: 24{27-30} sc.
Row 90{98-106}: Ch 1, turn; sc in each sc across to last 2 sc, skip next sc, sc in last sc: 23{26-29} sc.
Rows 91{99-107} thru 104{108-111}: Ch 1, turn; sc in each sc across.
Finish off leaving a long end for sewing.

BACK
Row 53: With **right** side facing and working in unworked sc on Row 52, skip first 12 sc from Right Front and join yarn with slip st in next sc; ch 1, sc in same st and in next 79{87-95} sc, leave remaining 50{55-60} sc unworked: 80{88-96} sc.
Row 54: Ch 1, turn; sc in each sc across.
Row 55: Ch 1, turn; skip first sc, sc in next sc and in each sc across to last 2 sc, skip next sc, sc in last sc: 78{86-94} sc.
Rows 56-63: Repeat Rows 54 and 55, 4 times: 70{78-86} sc.
Rows 64-104{108-111}: Ch 1, turn; sc in each sc across.
Finish off.

LEFT FRONT
Row 53: With **right** side facing and working in unworked sc on Row 52, skip first 12 sc from Back and join yarn with slip st in next sc; ch 1, sc in same st and in each sc across: 38{43-48} sc.
Rows 54 and 55: Ch 1, turn; skip first sc, sc in next sc and in each sc across: 36{41-46} sc.
Row 56: Ch 1, turn; sc in each sc across.
Rows 57-59: Ch 1, turn; skip first sc, sc in next sc and in each sc across: 33{38-43} sc.
Rows 60-63: Repeat Rows 56-59: 30{35-40} sc.
Rows 64 and 65: Ch 1, turn; sc in each sc across.
Row 66: Ch 1, turn; skip first sc, sc in next sc and in each sc across: 29{34-39} sc.
Rows 67-69: Ch 1, turn; sc in each sc across.
Rows 70-89{97-105}: Repeat Rows 66-69, 5{7-9} times: 24{27-30} sc.
Row 90{98-106}: Ch 1, turn; skip first sc, sc in next sc and in each sc across: 23{26-29} sc.
Rows 91{99-107} thru 104{108-111}: Ch 1, turn; sc in each sc across.
Finish off leaving a long end for sewing.
Sew shoulder seams **(Fig. 2)**.
Fig. 2

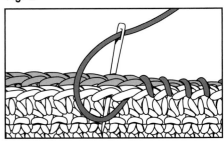

EDGING
Rnd 1: With **right** side facing, join Color A with slip st in any sc at center of Back neck edge; ch 1, sc evenly around working 3 sc in each corner; join with slip st to first sc, finish off.

ARMHOLE EDGING
Rnd 1: With **right** side facing, join Color A with slip st in any sc at underarm; ch 1, sc evenly around; join with slip st to first sc, finish off.

Repeat for second Armhole.

POINSETTIA AFGHAN (Shown on page 109)

You will need straight pins, five 44" lengths of 1 1/2"w red wired ribbon, sewing thread to match ribbons, five 18" lengths of 1/2 "w gold satin ribbon, seven 7" lengths of 1 1/2"w green wired ribbon, and an afghan (we used a 48" square green chenille afghan with fringe).

1. For each poinsettia, use pins to mark one red ribbon length at 2 3/4" intervals (**Fig. 1**).

Fig. 1

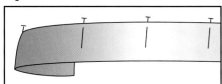

2. Fold one end of ribbon to wrong side at first pin, placing raw end under second pin. Remove second pin; pinch folded ribbon. Wrap gathers tightly with thread. (**Fig. 2**). Continue folding ribbon at pins, pinching ribbon and wrapping with thread to make eight petals (**Fig. 3**). Remove all pins.

Fig. 2

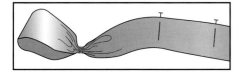

Fig. 3

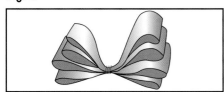

3. Spread petals apart. At folded end of each petal, fold corners to back of petal. Stitch folds together.

4. For center of flower, tie ten to twelve knots in one gold ribbon length. Arrange knots in a spiral with raw ends underneath. Stitch to center of petals.

5. For each leaf, matching ends, fold one green ribbon length in half. Wrap ends with thread. At folded end of leaf, fold corners to back of petal. Stitch folds together.

6. Repeat Steps 1 - 5 to make five flowers and seven leaves. Stitch one or two leaves to back of each flower. Stitch flowers to afghan.

POINSETTIA PILLOW

(Shown on page 109)

You will need 2 1/4"w wired ribbon to wrap around pillow, purchased pillow (we used a 12" x 17" pillow), 44" length of 1 1/2"w red wired ribbon, sewing thread to match ribbons, 18" of 1/2 "w gold ribbon, and a 7" length of green wired ribbon.

1. Crisscrossing center of ribbon at back, wrap 2 1/4"w ribbon around width and length of pillow; tie ends into a bow.

2. Follow Steps 1 - 5 of Poinsettia Afghan and use remaining ribbons to make one poinsettia and one leaf. Stitch leaf to back of poinsettia. Stitch poinsettia to knot of bow.

MEMORY PLATE

(Shown on page 108)

You will need tracing paper; transfer paper; green card stock; light red, red, light green, and green permanent medium-point markers; 1/16" hole punch; decorative-edge craft scissors; color photocopies of photographs; decoupage glue; 10 3/4" dia. clear glass plate; sponge pieces; red acrylic paint; paintbrushes; adhesive size; gold leaf; and clear acrylic spray sealer.

Note: Allow glue, paint, and sealer to dry after each application. Plate is intended for decorative use only.

1. Trace center design and heart D patterns onto tracing paper; cut out. Use transfer paper to transfer design to card stock. Use markers to draw over transferred lines. Punch evenly spaced holes in a circle around design. Cutting 1/4" outside punched holes, use craft scissors to cut out circle. Using heart pattern and craft scissors, cut out photocopies.

2. Use foam brush to apply decoupage glue to right side of center design and photocopies; arrange on back of plate and smooth in place.

3. Use damp sponge to lightly apply red paint over back of plate (do not apply a solid coat of paint). Follow manufacturers' instructions to apply adhesive size and gold leaf over back of plate.

4. Spray back of plate with sealer.

CENTER DESIGN

HEART D

EASY ENTERTAINING

Everyone knows that the best part of Christmas is gathering family and friends to celebrate with love and laughter ... and plenty of good things to eat! Let us help you plan your holiday menus, from elegant hors d'oeuvres to satisfying entrées, savory sides, and sensational sweets. You'll also find ideas for hosting a Yuletide reunion for old friends, complete with decorating tips and party favors!

All Wrapped Up For Christmas

*O*ne of the most enjoyable elements of celebrating Christmas is opening our homes to friends and family. You'll have the menu all wrapped up when you choose from the delicious party recipes in this section — we've even included ways to "package" some of the foods in nifty ways! Guests will love mingling while dazzling their taste buds with scrumptious appetizers and mouth-watering drinks. So whip up a few of your favorite recipes, invite some friendly folks, and let the Yuletide festivities begin!

Spicy Cheddar Cheesecake with Apricot Chutney *(left)* is a savory selection that features a crust of tortilla chips and a hint of cumin for Mexican flair. Dainty finger food, Two-Tone Cucumber Sandwiches *(right)* are layered with cheesy, peppery filling and cool cucumber slices.

SPICY CHEDDAR CHEESECAKE WITH APRICOT CHUTNEY

Both the cheesecake and chutney can be made a day ahead.

CRUST
- 3/4 cup finely crushed tortilla chips
- 1/2 cup finely shredded sharp Cheddar cheese
- 2 tablespoons butter or margarine, melted
- 1/2 teaspoon ground cumin

FILLING
- 2 packages (8 ounces each) cream cheese, softened
- 2 eggs
- 1 cup (4 ounces) finely shredded sharp Cheddar cheese
- 1/3 cup finely chopped green onions
- 1 teaspoon Worcestershire sauce
- 1 teaspoon hot pepper sauce
- 1/2 teaspoon curry powder
- 1/4 teaspoon salt

CHUTNEY
- 1 tablespoon olive oil
- 2 tablespoons minced onion
- 1 clove garlic, minced
- 2 jars (12 ounces each) apricot preserves
- 1/4 cup orange juice
- 2 tablespoons apple cider vinegar

Preheat oven to 325 degrees. For crust, process tortilla chips, cheese, melted butter, and cumin in a food processor until blended. Press mixture into bottom of an ungreased 9-inch springform pan. Bake 15 minutes or until firm.

For filling, beat cream cheese and eggs in a medium bowl until well blended. Stir in Cheddar cheese, green onions, Worcestershire sauce, pepper sauce, curry powder, and salt. Spread mixture over crust. Bake 25 to 30 minutes or until center is set. Cool in pan. Remove sides of pan. Cover and chill at least 2 hours to let flavors blend.

For chutney, combine olive oil, onion, and garlic in a medium saucepan. Sauté over medium heat about 5 minutes or until vegetables are tender. Add preserves, orange juice, and vinegar. Stirring frequently, cook over medium heat until mixture comes to a boil. Reduce heat to medium low and simmer uncovered 17 minutes or until chutney thickens. Remove from heat and cool to room temperature. Store in an airtight container in refrigerator.

Chock-full of chopped tomatillos and avocado, Fresh Salsa Verde is a chunky treat that demands a second dip!

To serve, let chutney come to room temperature. Spoon about 1 cup chutney over chilled cheesecake. Cut into 20 small wedges; serve with remaining chutney.
Yield: 20 servings

TWO-TONE CUCUMBER SANDWICHES

Filling can be made a day ahead.

- 12 ounces cream cheese, softened
- 2 tablespoons finely chopped onion
- 1 teaspoon dried dill weed
- 1 teaspoon dried parsley flakes
- 1 teaspoon prepared horseradish
- 1/2 teaspoon salt
- 1/8 teaspoon hot pepper sauce
- 1 loaf (24 ounces) swirled wheat and white combination bread
- 1 medium cucumber, scored and thinly sliced
- 5 to 7 radishes, thinly sliced

In a medium bowl, beat cream cheese, onion, dill weed, parsley, horseradish, salt, and pepper sauce until well blended. Store in an airtight container in refrigerator until ready to serve.

To serve, let filling come to room temperature. Trim crusts from bread slices. Spread each slice with 1 tablespoon cream cheese mixture; cut each slice into 4 squares. Place a cucumber slice on half of bread squares; top with remaining bread squares, filling side down. Place 1 radish slice on a party pick and insert into each sandwich. Store in an airtight container in refrigerator.
Yield: about 2 1/2 dozen sandwiches

FRESH SALSA VERDE

- 1 pound fresh tomatillos, hulled and finely chopped
- 3/4 cup finely chopped onion
- 1/4 cup water
- 1/2 teaspoon salt
- 1 avocado, seeded, peeled, and chopped
- 1/4 cup chopped fresh cilantro
- 2 tablespoons freshly squeezed lime juice
- 2 to 3 cloves garlic, minced
- 1 small fresh jalapeño pepper, seeded and chopped
- 1/4 teaspoon ground black pepper
  Tortilla chips to serve

In a medium saucepan over medium heat, combine tomatillos, onion, water, and salt. Cover and cook about 15 minutes or until tomatillos are tender; drain. In a medium bowl, combine tomatillo mixture and remaining ingredients. Cover and chill 2 hours to let flavors blend. Serve with tortilla chips.
Yield: about 2 cups salsa

Give ordinary salsa a twist with Cherry Salsa *(left)*, a tart and tangy sensation. Plump with a seasoned mushroom filling, Savory Mushroom Pillows *(right)* are packaged in wonton wrappers and deep fried.

CHERRY SALSA

This salsa would also make a good accompaniment to grilled meat.

- 2 cans (15 ounces each) dark, sweet, pitted cherries in heavy syrup, drained and coarsely chopped
- 3 tablespoons chopped red onion
- 3 tablespoons chopped fresh basil leaves
- 3 tablespoons finely chopped green pepper
- 3 tablespoons honey
- 2 tablespoons finely chopped fresh jalapeño pepper
- 1 tablespoon freshly squeezed lemon juice
- 1 teaspoon grated lemon zest
- 1/2 teaspoon salt
  Tortilla chips to serve

In a medium bowl, combine cherries, onion, basil, green pepper, honey, jalapeño pepper, lemon juice, lemon zest, and salt. Cover and chill 2 hours to let flavors blend. Serve salsa with tortilla chips.

Yield: about 2 cups salsa

SAVORY MUSHROOM PILLOWS

This is another great make-ahead appetizer.

- 1 pound fresh mushrooms
- 3 tablespoons butter
- 1 tablespoon vegetable oil
- 1/4 cup finely chopped green onions
- 2 cloves garlic, minced
- 2 tablespoons dry white wine
- 1 teaspoon chopped fresh thyme leaves
- 1/2 teaspoon salt
- 1/2 teaspoon ground black pepper
- 4 ounces cream cheese, softened
- 1 package (12 ounces) wonton wrappers
  Vegetable oil

Process mushrooms in a food processor until finely chopped. Melt butter with 1 tablespoon oil in a large skillet over medium heat. Add mushrooms, green onions, and garlic; sauté about 20 minutes or until liquid from mushrooms evaporates. Stirring constantly, add wine and cook until liquid evaporates. Stir in thyme, salt, and pepper. Remove from heat and add cream cheese; stir until melted. Place 1 teaspoon mixture on lower half of each wonton wrapper. Brush edges with water; fold sides over filling. Fold lower edge of wrapper over filling and roll. Press edges to seal. Place, seam side down, on baking sheet. Cover and refrigerate until ready to serve.

To serve, deep fry appetizers in hot oil until browned, about 1 to 2 minutes. Drain on paper towels. Serve warm.

Yield: about 4 dozen appetizers

FALAFEL APPETIZERS WITH YOGURT MUSTARD SAUCE

SAUCE
- 2 containers (8 ounces each) plain yogurt
- 3 to 4 tablespoons Dijon-style mustard
- 2 teaspoons balsamic vinegar
- 2 teaspoons honey

APPETIZERS
- 2 cans (19 ounces each) chick peas, drained
- 1 egg, beaten
- 1/4 cup chopped onion
- 3 tablespoons chopped fresh parsley
- 1 1/2 tablespoons freshly squeezed lemon juice
- 4 cloves garlic, minced
- 3/4 teaspoon ground cumin
- 3/4 teaspoon salt
- 1/4 teaspoon ground black pepper
- 1/4 cup finely shredded carrots
- 1/4 cup purchased plain bread crumbs
- 2/3 cup sesame seeds, toasted

For sauce, combine yogurt, mustard, vinegar, and honey in a small bowl. Cover and chill until ready to serve.

For appetizers, process chick peas in a food processor just until puréed. Add egg, onion, parsley, lemon juice, garlic, cumin, salt, and pepper; pulse process until blended. Transfer mixture to a medium bowl. Stir in carrots and bread crumbs. Shape mixture into 1-inch balls. Place on an ungreased baking sheet; cover and chill 2 hours or until ready to serve.

To serve, preheat oven to 375 degrees. Roll falafel balls in toasted sesame seeds and return to baking sheet. Bake 18 to 22 minutes or until heated through. Serve warm with sauce.

Yield: about 6 dozen appetizers and 2 cups sauce

SPARKLING CHAMPAGNE PUNCH

- 2 bottles (750 ml each) champagne, chilled
- 1 bottle (750 ml) white wine, chilled
- 2 cups orange juice, chilled
- 2 cups cranberry juice, chilled
- 1/4 cup freshly squeezed lemon juice

Combine champagne, wine, orange juice, cranberry juice, and lemon juice in a 1-gallon container. Serve immediately.

Yield: about 13 1/2 cups punch

Easy-to-make Sparkling Champagne Punch will signal the beginning of the festivities. Toasted sesame seeds add texture to the delicate taste of Falafel Appetizers with Yogurt Mustard Sauce.

VIETNAMESE SPRING ROLLS WITH GARLIC-GINGER SAUCE

Spring rolls can be made ahead and refrigerated until ready to serve.

SPRING ROLLS
- 14 spring roll wrappers, 8 1/2 inches in diameter (available at Oriental food stores)
- 2 cups coarsely chopped cooked shrimp (about 1 pound)
- 1 cup shredded carrots
- 1 cup shredded romaine lettuce
- 1 cup coarsely chopped fresh cilantro
- 1 tablespoon finely chopped fresh jalapeño pepper
- 1 clove garlic, minced
- 3 tablespoons freshly squeezed lime juice
- 1 tablespoon sesame oil
- 1/2 teaspoon salt

GARLIC-GINGER SAUCE
- 1 tablespoon cornstarch
- 1/2 cup low-sodium beef broth
- 3 cloves garlic, coarsely chopped
- 1 ounce fresh ginger, peeled and cut into small pieces (about 3 tablespoons)
- 1/4 cup freshly squeezed lime juice
- 3 tablespoons fish sauce (available at Oriental food stores)
- 3 tablespoons sugar
- 1 tablespoon soy sauce

For spring rolls, place spring roll wrappers in a shallow dish; cover with cool water. In a medium bowl, combine shrimp, carrots, lettuce, cilantro, jalapeño pepper, and garlic. In a small bowl, combine lime juice, sesame oil, and salt; pour over shrimp mixture. For each spring roll, remove 1 wrapper from water and place on a paper towel. Pat top dry. Place 1/4 cup filling in lower half of wrapper. Fold sides over filling. Fold lower edge of wrapper over filling and roll. Cover and chill until ready to serve.

For garlic-ginger sauce, dissolve cornstarch in beef broth in a small bowl. Process garlic and ginger in a small food processor until minced. In a small saucepan, combine garlic mixture, beef broth mixture, lime juice, fish sauce, sugar, and soy sauce. Stirring constantly, cook over medium heat about 10 minutes or until thickened; cool. Serve sauce at room temperature with spring rolls.

Yield: 14 spring rolls and 1 cup sauce

Seasoned Pita Wedges and zesty Sun-Dried Tomato Dip *(top)* make perfect partners for munching. *(Bottom)* Friends will love nibbling on robust Blue Cheese and Bacon-Stuffed Artichokes along with chilled Vietnamese Spring Rolls dipped in Garlic-Ginger Sauce.

BLUE CHEESE AND BACON-STUFFED ARTICHOKES

- 3 cans (14 ounces each) artichoke bottoms, drained
- 4 ounces cream cheese, softened
- 1/4 cup mayonnaise
- 2 ounces blue cheese, crumbled
- 3 slices bacon, cooked and crumbled
- 1 teaspoon dried chives
- 1 tablespoon purchased plain bread crumbs

Preheat oven to 350 degrees. If necessary, trim bottoms of artichokes so they will sit flat. In a medium bowl, combine cream cheese, mayonnaise, and blue cheese; beat until well blended. Stir in bacon and chives. Spoon about 1/2 tablespoon cheese mixture onto each artichoke. Place on a lightly greased baking sheet. Cover and chill until ready to serve.

To serve, sprinkle stuffed artichokes with bread crumbs. Bake 24 to 28 minutes or until heated through and golden brown. Serve warm or at room temperature.

Yield: about 2 1/2 dozen appetizers

SUN-DRIED TOMATO DIP

1 container (15 ounces) ricotta
    cheese
1 jar (8 ounces) oil-packed
    sun-dried tomatoes, drained and
    chopped
1/2 cup mayonnaise
1/4 cup finely chopped green onions
1 clove garlic, minced
1 tablespoon freshly squeezed lemon
    juice
1/4 teaspoon salt

In a medium bowl, combine ricotta cheese, tomatoes, mayonnaise, green onions, garlic, lemon juice, and salt. Stir until well blended. Serve with Seasoned Pita Wedges.
Yield: about 3 cups dip

SEASONED PITA WEDGES

Thin pita bread makes crisper wedges than thick bread.

5 pita bread rounds
1/2 cup butter or margarine
2 teaspoons dried parsley flakes
1/2 teaspoon garlic salt
1/4 teaspoon ground black pepper

Cut each bread round in half to form 2 pockets. Split each pocket in half. Cut each half into 3 wedges. Preheat broiler. Place bread on an ungreased baking sheet. In a small saucepan, melt butter over medium heat. Stir in parsley, garlic salt, and black pepper. Remove from heat. Brush butter mixture over both sides of bread. Watching closely, broil 4 to 6 minutes or until golden brown, turning once about halfway through broiling time. Serve warm.
Yield: 60 wedges

MAKE-AHEAD SAUCY RIBS

5 pounds pork loin back ribs
    Salt
    Ground black pepper
1 cup finely chopped onion
1 cup finely chopped green pepper
3 tablespoons vegetable oil
1 bottle (28 ounces) ketchup
1 1/2 cups firmly packed brown sugar
3/4 cup orange marmalade
3/4 cup apple cider vinegar
1 tablespoon hot pepper sauce
1 teaspoon salt
3/4 teaspoon ground black pepper

Because most of the preparation can be done the night before, Make-Ahead Saucy Ribs are a great choice for holiday parties.

Preheat oven to 350 degrees. Place rib racks in a single layer in foil-lined baking pans. Sprinkle ribs with salt and pepper. Cover with foil and bake 1 hour or until fully cooked. Let cool.

While ribs are cooking, sauté onion and green pepper in oil in a large saucepan over medium heat until tender. Stir in ketchup, brown sugar, marmalade, vinegar, pepper sauce, 1 teaspoon salt, and 3/4 teaspoon black pepper. Stirring constantly, bring sauce to a simmer. Reduce heat to medium low. Stirring frequently, cook sauce 30 minutes (mixture will be thick). Remove from heat and let cool.

Cut racks into individual ribs. Transfer to a heavy-duty resealable plastic bag. Pour 2 cups sauce over ribs; refrigerate overnight to let ribs marinate. Store remaining sauce in an airtight container in refrigerator.

To serve, preheat oven to 425 degrees. Place ribs in foil-lined baking pans. Spoon sauce from plastic bag over ribs. Bake uncovered 1 hour or until sauce cooks onto ribs, turning every 15 minutes and basting with remaining sauce. Serve warm.
Yield: about 3 dozen ribs

(Clockwise from left) Topped with toasted chopped walnuts, Nutty Blue Cheese Spread turns plain crackers into hearty appetizers. Sips of Hot Spiced Fruit Tea will tickle the taste buds with the inviting flavors of fruit juices and fresh ginger. As pleasing to the eye as they are to the palate, Green Olive and Jalapeño Roll-Ups add zest to the table.

NUTTY BLUE CHEESE SPREAD

- 1 package (8 ounces) cream cheese, softened
- 1 package (4 ounces) blue cheese, crumbled
- 2 tablespoons sour cream
- 1/4 teaspoon ground red pepper
- 1/4 cup finely chopped celery
- 1/4 cup finely chopped green onions
- 1 1/2 cups chopped walnuts, toasted, finely chopped, and divided
  Crackers to serve

Process cream cheese, blue cheese, sour cream, and red pepper in a food processor until smooth. Add celery, green onions, and 1 cup walnuts; process just until blended. Transfer to a 2 1/2-cup serving container. Cover with plastic wrap and chill 2 hours to let flavors blend.

To serve, bring cheese spread to room temperature. Sprinkle with remaining 1/2 cup walnuts. Serve with crackers.
Yield: about 2 1/4 cups cheese spread

GREEN OLIVE AND JALAPEÑO ROLL-UPS

- 1 package (8 ounces) cream cheese, softened
- 1/2 cup mayonnaise
- 1 cup sliced pimiento-stuffed olives, chopped
- 1/2 cup chopped pecans, toasted and finely chopped
- 1 1/2 tablespoons chopped pickled jalapeño pepper
- 4 flavored tortilla wraps, 12 inches in diameter (we used spinach-herb and tomato-basil flavors)

In a medium bowl, combine cream cheese and mayonnaise; beat until smooth. Add olives, pecans, and jalapeño pepper; stir until well blended. Spread about 1/2 cup mixture onto each tortilla. Tightly roll up tortillas and wrap in plastic wrap. Chill 2 hours. Cut into 1/2-inch slices.
Yield: about 7 1/2 dozen slices

HOT SPICED FRUIT TEA

- 1 bottle (64 ounces) apple juice
- 4 cups water
- 1 can (6 ounces) frozen lemonade concentrate, thawed
- 10 orange-spice tea bags
- 1 two-inch-long piece fresh ginger, peeled and thinly sliced
- 1/2 cup firmly packed brown sugar
  Lemon slices to serve

Combine apple juice, water, and lemonade concentrate in a Dutch oven. Add tea bags and ginger slices. Bring to a simmer over medium-high heat. Reduce heat to low; simmer 15 minutes. Remove tea bags and ginger. Stir in brown sugar. Simmer 10 minutes. Serve warm with lemon slices.
Yield: about 12 cups tea

HERBED PIMIENTO DIP

- 1 container (8 ounces) fat-free sour cream
- 4 ounces fat-free cream cheese, softened
- 1/2 cup fat-free mayonnaise
- 1 clove garlic, minced
- 1 jar (7 ounces) sliced pimientos, drained
- 1 tablespoon chopped fresh basil leaves
- 1 tablespoon chopped fresh oregano leaves
- 1 teaspoon lemon pepper
- 1/2 teaspoon salt
  Fresh vegetables to serve

Process sour cream, cream cheese, mayonnaise, and garlic in a food processor until smooth. Add pimientos, basil, oregano, lemon pepper, and salt. Pulse process until blended. Transfer to a serving bowl. Cover and refrigerate 2 hours to let flavors blend. Serve with vegetables.
Yield: about 2 1/2 cups dip

1 serving (1 tablespoon): 14.3 calories, 0.1 gram fat, 1.0 gram protein, 2.2 grams carbohydrate

CHEESY CRAB PUFFS

Puffs can be prepared ahead of time and chilled or frozen until time to bake.

- 1 can (6 ounces) crabmeat, drained
- 4 ounces cream cheese, softened
- 1 cup (4 ounces) shredded Swiss cheese
- 1/4 cup finely chopped red pepper (we used an equal amount of sweet and jalapeño peppers)
- 2 tablespoons finely chopped green onion
- 2 tablespoons purchased plain bread crumbs
- 1 teaspoon freshly squeezed lemon juice
- 1 teaspoon prepared horseradish
- 1 teaspoon Worcestershire sauce
- 1/2 teaspoon garlic salt
- 1/8 teaspoon ground red pepper
- 1 package (17 1/4 ounces) frozen puff pastry, thawed according to package directions

In a medium bowl, combine crabmeat, cream cheese, Swiss cheese, chopped red pepper, green onion, bread crumbs, lemon juice, horseradish, Worcestershire sauce, garlic salt, and ground red pepper; beat until well blended. On a

Cheesy Crab Puffs *(top)* are wrapped in puff pastry and baked for a tummy-warming treat. For a refreshingly lighter snack, try dipping vegetable sticks into Herbed Pimiento Dip *(bottom)* made with fat-free ingredients.

lightly floured surface, use a floured rolling pin to roll each pastry sheet into a 10-inch square. Cut pastry into 2-inch squares. Press a pastry square into each ungreased cup of a non-stick miniature muffin pan. Spoon 1 teaspoon crab mixture into center of each square.

(Pastries may be covered and chilled or frozen at this time.)

Preheat oven to 400 degrees. Bake 19 to 21 minutes or until golden brown. (If puffs were chilled, bake 22 to 24 minutes. If puffs were frozen, bake 25 to 27 minutes.) Serve warm.
Yield: about 4 dozen puffs

NEW ENGLAND HOLIDAY BRUNCH

*Softly swirling snow, newly arrived guests, and heavily laden sideboards paint a
nostalgic picture of a festive New England meal. This bold-spirited region and its rich
culinary heritage set the tone for a grand assortment of succulent foods. Begin the
feast with a beverage flavored with fruit from the area's marshy cranberry bogs and top
it off with a traditional Massachusetts holiday dessert, Marlborough Pie. For a
heartwarming, palate-pleasing Yuletide brunch that promises to be long remembered,
choose from dishes inspired by the land of our Pilgrim forefathers.*

Tinged with saffron and accented with a kaleidoscope of rice and vegetables, Paella is a mouth-watering dish served in the
two-handled pan from which it derives its name. This version of the popular Spanish creation blends sausage, artichoke
hearts, and marinated shrimp and chicken with seasonings.

PAELLA

Marinate chicken and shrimp in advance.

- 1/2 cup plus 2 tablespoons olive oil, divided
- 3 tablespoons freshly squeezed lemon juice
- 4 cloves garlic, divided and minced
- 1 tablespoon chopped fresh thyme leaves
- 1 teaspoon ground black pepper
- 1/4 teaspoon salt
- 2 pounds boneless chicken breasts, cut into large bite-size pieces
- 1/2 pound medium shrimp, peeled and deveined with tails left on
- 1/2 pound chorizo sausage, sliced
- 1 cup chopped onion
- 3 plum tomatoes, peeled and quartered
- 1 jar (4 ounces) whole pimiento, drained and cut into strips
- 2 cups uncooked arborio rice
- 1 can (14 ounces) quartered artichoke hearts, drained
- 1/4 cup chopped fresh parsley
- 1 tablespoon paprika
- 1 tablespoon drained capers
- 1/2 teaspoon saffron
- 1/2 cup white wine
- 3 cups hot chicken broth
- 1 package (10 ounces) frozen small green peas, thawed
- Chopped fresh parsley to garnish

In a large container, combine 1/4 cup plus 2 tablespoons olive oil, lemon juice, 2 cloves minced garlic, thyme, black pepper, and salt. Add chicken and shrimp to marinade; cover and chill 3 to 5 hours, stirring occasionally.

Remove shrimp from marinade; drain. In a 13-inch-diameter paella pan or heavy skillet, heat remaining 1/4 cup olive oil. Stirring constantly, cook shrimp in oil over medium-high heat about 2 minutes or just until shrimp turns pink. Transfer to a bowl. Remove chicken pieces from marinade; drain. Turning frequently, cook in pan about 15 minutes or until browned. Transfer to another bowl. Stirring frequently, cook sausage in pan about 4 minutes or until browned. Transfer sausage to bowl containing shrimp. Reduce heat to medium. Cook onion and remaining 2 cloves minced garlic in pan 4 minutes or until onion is translucent. Add tomatoes and pimiento; continue to cook 5 minutes. Add rice, artichoke hearts, 1/4 cup chopped parsley, paprika, and capers; stir until blended. Add saffron to wine. Stir wine mixture, hot chicken broth, and chicken pieces into rice mixture. Increase heat to

An elegant beverage with a festive twist, Cranberry Champagne Cocktail imparts a golden glow to the holiday table. From flaky crust to creamy topping, Savory Tomato and Olive Pastries are rich, full-bodied delicacies.

medium-high. Bring liquid to a boil. Reduce heat to medium. Cover and simmer about 15 minutes or until liquid is absorbed and rice is tender. Stir in shrimp, sausage, and peas. Remove from heat. Cover pan and let stand 15 minutes before serving. Garnish with parsley.
Yield: 10 to 12 servings

SAVORY TOMATO AND OLIVE PASTRIES

- 6 ounces cream cheese, softened
- 1/3 cup finely chopped green onions
- 1/3 cup finely chopped fresh mushrooms
- 1/2 teaspoon ground black pepper
- 1 sheet frozen puff pastry, thawed
- 6 ounces thinly sliced Provolone cheese
- 3/4 cup dried tomatoes marinated in olive oil, drained and cut into strips
- 1 can (2 1/4 ounces) sliced black olives, drained

Preheat oven to 400 degrees. In a medium bowl, beat cream cheese until fluffy. Stir in green onions, mushrooms, and pepper. On a lightly floured surface,

use a lightly floured rolling pin to roll out pastry into a 10 1/2-inch square. Cut pastry in half. Transfer pastry pieces to an ungreased baking sheet. Dampen edges of pastries with water. Fold edges of pastries 1/2 inch and press to seal. Spread cream cheese mixture over pastries. Place cheese slices over cream cheese mixture. Sprinkle with tomatoes and olives. Bake 15 to 17 minutes or until cheese melts and pastries are golden brown. Let stand 5 minutes. Cut each pastry in half lengthwise, then cut into 1-inch slices. Serve warm.
Yield: about 3 dozen appetizers

CRANBERRY CHAMPAGNE COCKTAIL

- 1/4 cup cranberry-flavored liqueur
- 2 tablespoons Grand Marnier liqueur
- 1 tablespoon sweet vermouth
- 1 bottle (750 ml) champagne, chilled

In a 2-quart container, combine cranberry liqueur, Grand Marnier, and vermouth. Add champagne to mixture. Serve immediately.
Yield: about 3 1/2 cups cocktail

CHEESY TRIANGLE PUFFS

1 container (16 ounces) small-curd
    cottage cheese
2 cups all-purpose flour
$^1/_2$ teaspoon baking powder
$^3/_4$ cup butter or margarine, softened
1 tablespoon lemon pepper

In a large bowl, beat cottage cheese,
flour, baking powder, butter, and lemon
pepper with an electric mixer until well
blended. Divide dough into fourths.
Wrap in plastic wrap and chill 2 hours
or until firm.

Preheat oven to 350 degrees. On a
heavily floured surface, use a floured
rolling pin to roll out one fourth of dough
into a 10-inch square. Cut dough into
2-inch squares. Cut each square in half
diagonally, forming 2 triangles. Transfer
to a lightly greased baking sheet. Bake
12 to 14 minutes or until lightly
browned. Repeat with remaining dough.
Serve warm.
Yield: about 16$^1/_2$ dozen puffs

ROSEMARY-SWEET POTATO SOUP

2 cans (14$^1/_2$ ounces each) chicken
    broth
1 pound fresh sweet potatoes, peeled
    and sliced (about 2 medium
    sweet potatoes)
1$^3/_4$ cups carrots, sliced (about 2 large
    carrots)
2 teaspoons finely chopped fresh
    rosemary leaves
2 tablespoons butter or margarine
1$^1/_4$ cups chopped onion
1 large clove garlic, minced
$^1/_2$ cup orange juice
$^1/_2$ teaspoon salt
$^1/_4$ teaspoon ground white pepper
    Pinch ground red pepper
    Chopped fresh rosemary leaves to
    garnish

In a Dutch oven over medium-high
heat, combine chicken broth, sweet
potatoes, carrots, and 2 teaspoons
rosemary. Bring to a boil. Reduce heat to
low, cover and simmer 20 minutes or
until vegetables are tender.

In a medium skillet, combine butter,
onion, and garlic over medium heat.
Stirring constantly, cook 8 minutes or
until onion is translucent; transfer to a
large food processor. Reserving liquid,
transfer vegetables from sweet potato
mixture to food processor; process until
smooth. Stir puréed mixture back into

Light and delicate Cheesy Triangle Puffs offer a hint of lemon. Rosemary-Sweet
Potato Soup is a flavorful mixture of puréed vegetables.

liquid. Stir in orange juice, salt, and
peppers. Return to low heat; cook
10 minutes or until heated through.
Garnish each serving with rosemary.
Yield: about 6 cups soup

TURKEY QUICHE LORRAINE

1 unbaked 9-inch pie crust
8 slices bacon
$^1/_4$ cup finely chopped onion
1$^1/_2$ cups (about 6 ounces) shredded
    Gruyère cheese
1 cup diced cooked turkey
1$^1/_2$ cups half and half
4 eggs
$^1/_2$ teaspoon dry mustard
$^1/_4$ teaspoon salt

Preheat oven to 350 degrees. Bake
crust 8 minutes or until lightly browned.
Cook bacon in a medium skillet
until crisp; remove bacon, reserving
1 tablespoon drippings in skillet. Drain
and crumble bacon; set aside. Sauté
onion in reserved drippings over
medium-low heat until tender. Sprinkle
cheese, turkey, bacon, and onion into
bottom of pie crust. In a medium bowl,
beat half and half, eggs, dry mustard,
and salt until well blended. Pour egg
mixture into pie crust. Bake 40 to 50
minutes or until a knife inserted in center
of quiche comes out clean. Let stand 5
minutes before serving. Serve warm.
Yield: about 8 servings

(Clockwise from bottom left) Turkey Quiche Lorraine updates a versatile favorite. A faint touch of citrus and flecks of dill add zip to Lemon-Dill Biscuits. Tangy Minted Cranberry-Pear Relish blends sweetened fresh cranberries and pears, lemon juice, and chopped mint.

LEMON-DILL BISCUITS

- 2 cups all-purpose flour
- 1 tablespoon baking powder
- 1/4 teaspoon salt
- 1/4 teaspoon ground black pepper
- 1/3 cup chilled butter or margarine, cut into pieces
- 3/4 cup milk
- 1 tablespoon chopped fresh dill weed
- 1 teaspoon grated lemon zest

Preheat oven to 425 degrees. In a medium bowl, combine flour, baking powder, salt, and pepper. Using a pastry blender or 2 knives, cut butter into dry ingredients until mixture resembles coarse meal. In a small bowl, combine milk, dill weed, and lemon zest. Add to dry ingredients; stir just until moistened. On a lightly floured surface, use a floured rolling pin to roll out dough to 1/2-inch thickness. Use a 2-inch-diameter biscuit cutter to cut out biscuits. Transfer to an ungreased baking sheet. Bake 11 to 13 minutes or until golden brown. Serve warm.

Yield: about 1 1/2 dozen biscuits

MINTED CRANBERRY-PEAR RELISH

- 1 package (12 ounces) fresh cranberries
- 2 fresh unpeeled pears, cored and coarsely chopped
- 2 cups sugar
- 1/4 cup freshly squeezed lemon juice
- 1/4 cup chopped fresh mint leaves
  Whole fresh mint leaves to garnish

Process all ingredients in a food processor until finely chopped. Transfer to an airtight container; cover and chill. To serve, garnish with whole mint leaves.

Yield: about 4 cups relish

With a sprinkling of nuts and dates, Stuffed Baked Apples taste as yummy as they look! Served chilled, festive Zucchini Medley layers sliced fresh mozzarella cheese with vegetables that have been marinated and baked.

STUFFED BAKED APPLES

    5 unpeeled red baking apples
 1/2 cup apple juice
 1/2 cup applejack
    2 tablespoons lemon juice
    1 cup firmly packed brown sugar
 1/4 cup butter or margarine
    1 teaspoon ground cinnamon
 2/3 cup chopped walnuts, toasted
 2/3 cup chopped dates
    1 teaspoon vanilla extract
    1 to 2 tablespoons cornstarch

Preheat oven to 350 degrees. Cut apples in half through stem end. Trim 1/2 inch peel from apples. Core and place in an ungreased 9 x 13-inch baking pan. In a medium saucepan, combine next 6 ingredients. Stirring constantly, cook over medium heat until sugar dissolves. Remove from heat. Stir in walnuts, dates, and vanilla. Spoon mixture over apples. Cover and bake 45 to 50 minutes or until apples are tender, spooning syrup over apples every 10 minutes. Transfer apples to a serving dish. Measure remaining syrup and transfer to a small saucepan. Using 1 tablespoon cornstarch for each cup apple syrup, combine cornstarch with an equal amount of water in a small bowl. Bring syrup to a boil over medium heat. Stir in cornstarch mixture. Stirring constantly, cook until syrup thickens. Spoon over baked apples. Serve warm.
Yield: 10 servings

ZUCCHINI MEDLEY

    1 cup olive oil
    2 tablespoons chopped fresh thyme leaves
    2 tablespoons chopped fresh tarragon leaves
    2 tablespoons chopped fresh basil leaves
    2 cloves garlic, minced
    1 teaspoon salt
 1/2 teaspoon crushed red pepper flakes
 1/8 teaspoon ground black pepper
    4 unpeeled zucchini, sliced lengthwise
    2 sweet red peppers, cut into rings
    5 plum tomatoes, peeled and sliced
    4 ounces fresh mozzarella cheese (packed in water), sliced

In a medium bowl, combine first 8 ingredients. Place zucchini, pepper rings, and marinade in a large resealable plastic bag. Let stand at room temperature 2 hours, turning frequently to coat vegetables.

Preheat oven to 350 degrees. Reserving marinade, place zucchini and peppers on an ungreased broiler pan. Chill marinade. Bake vegetables 30 minutes, turning after 15 minutes. Cool on pan 10 minutes. Store in an airtight container in refrigerator until ready to serve.

To serve, alternate zucchini, tomatoes, cheese, and peppers on serving platter. Brush vegetables with reserved marinade.
Yield: 6 to 8 servings

HAZELNUT COFFEE CAKE

CAKE

    1 cup butter or margarine, softened
 1 1/3 cups granulated sugar
    3 eggs
 1 1/2 teaspoons vanilla extract
 2 1/2 cups sifted cake flour
    1 teaspoon baking powder
    1 teaspoon baking soda
 1/8 teaspoon salt
 1 1/3 cups sour cream
 1 1/4 cups chopped hazelnuts, toasted
 1/2 cup firmly packed brown sugar
    1 teaspoon ground cinnamon

ICING

    2 ounces bittersweet baking chocolate
    4 teaspoons hazelnut-flavored liqueur
    1 tablespoon light corn syrup

Preheat oven to 325 degrees. For cake, cream butter and granulated sugar in a large bowl until fluffy. Add eggs and vanilla; beat until smooth. In a medium bowl, combine cake flour, baking powder, baking soda, and salt. Alternately beat dry ingredients and sour cream into creamed mixture, beating just until blended. Spoon one-third of batter into bottom of a greased and floured 9-inch springform pan with a tube insert. In a small bowl, combine hazelnuts, brown sugar, and cinnamon. Sprinkle one-third of hazelnut mixture over batter. Continue layering batter and hazelnut mixture, ending with hazelnut mixture. Bake 55 to 65 minutes or until a toothpick inserted in center of cake comes out clean. Cool cake in pan on a wire rack 10 minutes. Run a knife around edge of pan; remove sides of pan. Cool completely. Carefully remove bottom of pan; transfer cake to a serving plate.

For icing, place chocolate, liqueur, and corn syrup in top of a double boiler over hot water. Stirring frequently, cook until chocolate melts and mixture is smooth. Drizzle chocolate mixture over cake. Store in an airtight container.
Yield: about 16 servings

(From left) Sliced almonds embedded in white icing give lemony Pinecone Cookies their prickly appearance. Drizzled with a stunning chocolate glaze, light-textured Hazelnut Coffee Cake has a crunchy topping that's echoed in the tasty filling. Delicious either warm or cold, handsome Marlborough Pie adds tasty apples, whipping cream, sherry, and cinnamon to a rich custard.

PINECONE COOKIES

COOKIES
- ³/₄ cup butter or margarine, softened
- ¹/₂ cup sugar
- 1 egg
- 1 tablespoon freshly squeezed lemon juice
- ¹/₂ teaspoon grated lemon zest
- ¹/₂ teaspoon vanilla extract
- 1 ³/₄ cups all-purpose flour
- ¹/₄ teaspoon salt

ICING
- 4 cups sifted confectioners sugar
- 2 tablespoons plus 2 teaspoons water
- 2 tablespoons freshly squeezed lemon juice
- ¹/₂ teaspoon grated lemon zest
- ¹/₂ teaspoon vanilla extract
- 1 ¹/₂ cups sliced almonds, toasted

For cookies, cream butter and sugar in a large bowl until fluffy. Add egg, lemon juice, lemon zest, and vanilla; beat until smooth. In a small bowl, combine flour and salt. Add dry ingredients to creamed mixture; stir until a soft dough forms. Divide dough in half. Wrap in plastic wrap and chill 2 hours or until dough is firm enough to handle.

Preheat oven to 375 degrees. On a lightly floured surface, use a floured rolling pin to roll out dough to ¹/₄-inch thickness. Use a 2 ¹/₂-inch-wide by 3 ¹/₂-inch-long oval crinkled-edge cookie cutter to cut out cookies. Transfer to a greased baking sheet. Bake 8 to 10 minutes or until bottoms are lightly browned. Transfer cookies to a wire rack to cool.

For icing, combine confectioners sugar, water, lemon juice, lemon zest, and vanilla in a medium bowl; beat until smooth. Working with 3 cookies at a time, spread icing on cookies. Before icing hardens, place almonds on cookies to resemble pinecones. Let icing harden. Store in a single layer in an airtight container.

Yield: about 2 dozen cookies

MARLBOROUGH PIE

- 4 eggs
- 1 cup sugar
- 1 cup whipping cream
- ¹/₄ cup cream sherry
- 1 tablespoon butter, melted
- ¹/₂ teaspoon ground cinnamon
- ¹/₈ teaspoon salt
- 2 cups unpeeled, cored, and finely chopped Granny Smith apples
- 1 unbaked 9-inch pie crust

Preheat oven to 400 degrees. In a medium bowl, beat eggs and sugar until smooth. Add whipping cream, sherry, melted butter, cinnamon, and salt; beat until well blended. Stir in apples. Pour into crust. Bake 10 minutes. Reduce temperature to 350 degrees. Bake 40 to 50 minutes or until center is firm. Let stand 1 ¹/₂ hours before serving. Store in an airtight container in refrigerator.

Yield: about 8 servings

CANDLELIGHT CREOLE DINNER

*D*eep in the heart of the Delta lies a tradition of cooking passed down through generations of French Creole families. Seafood, vegetables, and robust sauces highlight the recipes that have made the Louisiana bayou famous. You can share this zesty style when you create a Yuletide feast using foods from this mouth-watering menu. Begin with spicy fried oysters or shrimp salad followed by a dish of grillades and grits to satisfy hearty appetites. From creamy soup to praline-covered cake, entice your guests with scrumptious foods from this feisty region of the South. Laissez le bon temps rouler *(Let the good times roll)!*

(From left) A rich concoction for quenching the thirst, Milk Punch with Bourbon *(in glass)* is a perky party potable. Toast wedges topped with tart and spicy Tapenade make scrumptious holiday appetizers. Fried Oysters with Spicy Tartar Sauce bring New Orleans flair to the table, and hearty stuffed Sausage-Cheese Bread is almost a meal in itself.

MILK PUNCH WITH BOURBON

6 cups milk
3 cups whipping cream
1 cup superfine sugar
3 tablespoons vanilla extract
3/4 cup bourbon
Freshly grated nutmeg to serve

In a 4-quart container, combine milk, whipping cream, superfine sugar, and vanilla; stir until sugar dissolves. Stir in bourbon. Cover and store in refrigerator about 2 hours or until chilled.

To serve, garnish individual servings with nutmeg.

Yield: about 11 cups punch

FRIED OYSTERS WITH SPICY TARTAR SAUCE

SPICY TARTAR SAUCE
3/4 cup mayonnaise
3 tablespoons Dijon-style mustard
1 tablespoon finely chopped onion
1 tablespoon finely chopped fresh parsley
1 tablespoon drained capers
1 teaspoon freshly squeezed lemon juice
1/2 teaspoon hot pepper sauce

OYSTERS
1 egg
3 tablespoons milk
3/4 cup yellow cornmeal
1/4 cup all-purpose flour
1/2 teaspoon salt
1/4 teaspoon ground black pepper
1/8 teaspoon ground red pepper
3 dozen shucked oysters **or** 2 containers (10 ounces each) fresh oysters, drained
Vegetable oil

For spicy tartar sauce, combine mayonnaise, Dijon mustard, onion, parsley, capers, lemon juice, and pepper sauce in a small bowl. Cover and chill 2 hours to let flavors blend.

For oysters, beat egg and milk in a small bowl. In another small bowl, combine cornmeal, flour, salt, and peppers. Dip each oyster into milk mixture, then into cornmeal mixture. Deep fry in hot oil until golden brown. Transfer to paper towels to drain. Serve warm with sauce.

Yield: about 3 dozen oysters and 1 cup sauce

Perfect for the salad course, Shrimp Rémoulade (*recipe on page 150*) is a light delicacy featuring chilled shrimp and thin vegetable strips topped with a deliciously tangy sauce.

TAPENADE

2 jars (10 ounces each) Kalamata olives, pitted
1 jar (3 1/4 ounces) capers, drained
1 can (6 ounces) oil-packed tuna
3 tablespoons olive oil
1 teaspoon freshly squeezed lemon juice
1 clove garlic, chopped
1/4 teaspoon red pepper flakes
Toasted white cocktail bread

Pulse process olives, capers, undrained tuna, olive oil, lemon juice, garlic, and red pepper flakes in a food processor just until mixture forms a coarse paste. Serve with toast.

Yield: about 3 cups spread

SAUSAGE-CHEESE BREAD

3 to 3 1/2 cups all-purpose flour, divided
2 packages dry yeast
1 tablespoon sugar
1 teaspoon salt
1/2 teaspoon dry mustard
1/4 teaspoon garlic powder
1/4 teaspoon onion powder
1/8 teaspoon ground red pepper
1/2 cup butter or margarine
1 cup milk
2 cups (8 ounces) shredded sharp Cheddar cheese
Vegetable cooking spray
8 ounces andouille sausage (or other spicy sausage), browned, drained, and crumbled
1 egg white, beaten

In a large bowl, combine 2 cups flour, yeast, sugar, salt, dry mustard, garlic powder, onion powder, and red pepper. In a small saucepan, combine butter and milk over medium-low heat; stir until butter melts. Pour milk mixture into flour mixture; stir until well blended. Gradually stir in 1 cup flour and cheese. Turn onto a lightly floured surface. Knead about 5 minutes or until dough becomes smooth and elastic, using additional flour as necessary. Place in a large bowl sprayed with cooking spray, turning once to coat top of dough. Cover and let rise in a warm place (80 to 85 degrees) 1 1/2 hours or until doubled in size.

(Continued on page 150)

Turn dough onto a lightly floured surface and punch down. Divide dough into thirds. With a lightly floured rolling pin, roll one third of dough into a 6 x 15-inch rectangle. Sprinkle one third of sausage lengthwise down center of dough. Beginning at 1 long edge, roll up dough jellyroll style. Pinch seam to seal. Repeat with remaining dough and sausage. On a lightly greased baking sheet, braid ropes with seam sides down. Pinch ends of ropes together to seal; turn ends under. Spray top of dough with cooking spray, cover, and let rise in a warm place 45 minutes or until doubled in size.

Preheat oven to 350 degrees. Brush egg white over dough. Bake 30 to 35 minutes or until bread is golden brown and sounds hollow when tapped. Cover with aluminum foil if top browns too quickly. Serve warm or transfer to a wire rack to cool completely. Cut into 1/2-inch slices, then cut each slice in half.
Yield: about 2 dozen servings

SHRIMP RÉMOULADE
(Shown on page 149)

    2   cups mayonnaise
    1   cup finely chopped green onions
  1/2   cup finely chopped celery
  1/4   cup chopped fresh parsley
    2   tablespoons Creole mustard
    1   tablespoon freshly squeezed lemon juice
    1   tablespoon finely chopped sour pickles
    1   tablespoon drained capers
    2   cloves garlic, minced
    1   teaspoon paprika
    1   teaspoon prepared horseradish
    1   teaspoon anchovy paste
  1/2   teaspoon finely chopped fresh tarragon leaves
        Romaine lettuce, shredded
 1 1/4 pounds medium shrimp, cooked, shelled (leaving tails on), deveined, and chilled
    1   sweet red pepper, sliced
    1   green pepper, sliced

In a medium bowl, combine mayonnaise, green onions, celery, parsley, Creole mustard, lemon juice, pickles, capers, garlic, paprika, horseradish, anchovy paste, and tarragon; stir until well blended. Cover and chill overnight.

To serve, place lettuce on 8 serving plates. Top with shrimp and pepper slices. Spoon rémoulade sauce onto each salad.
Yield: 8 servings

Creamy Corn Muffins baked in mini muffin pans are bite-size munchies for accompanying steaming bowls of thick Cream of Artichoke Soup. Both recipes require little preparation, so you can take time to enjoy them with your guests.

CREAM OF ARTICHOKE SOUP

    2   tablespoons olive oil
    2   tablespoons butter
    1   cup chopped onion
  1/2   cup chopped celery
    2   cans (14 1/2 ounces each) chicken broth
    2   cans (14 ounces each) artichoke hearts, drained and chopped
    1   large carrot, sliced
    2   tablespoons freshly squeezed lemon juice
  1/2   teaspoon salt
  1/2   teaspoon ground white pepper
    1   cup half and half
  1/4   cup freshly grated Parmesan cheese
        Celery leaves to garnish

In a Dutch oven, combine olive oil and butter over medium heat; stir until butter melts. Sauté onion and celery in oil mixture until onion is translucent. Stir in chicken broth, artichokes, carrot, lemon juice, salt, and white pepper. Cover and cook about 30 minutes or until vegetables are tender. Remove from heat. Purée vegetables in batches in a food processor. Return to Dutch oven. Stir in half and half and cheese. Serve warm or store in an airtight container in refrigerator.

To reheat, cook over medium-low heat uncovered about 20 minutes or until heated through, stirring frequently. Garnish individual servings with celery leaves.
Yield: about 8 cups soup

CREAMY CORN MUFFINS

    1   cup yellow cornmeal
    1   cup all-purpose flour
    2   tablespoons sugar
    1   tablespoon baking powder
  3/4   teaspoon salt
  1/2   teaspoon baking soda
    1   can (8 1/2 ounces) cream-style corn
    1   cup sour cream
  1/4   cup butter or margarine, melted
    1   egg

Preheat oven to 375 degrees. In a medium bowl, combine cornmeal, flour, sugar, baking powder, salt, and baking soda. In a small bowl, beat corn, sour cream, melted butter, and egg until well blended. Add to dry ingredients; stir just until blended. Spoon batter into lightly greased miniature muffin pans. Bake 16 to 18 minutes or until tops are lightly browned. Serve warm.
Yield: about 4 dozen muffins

GRILLADES AND GRITS

- 2 pounds beef or veal round roast (we used eye of round)
- 1/2 cup all-purpose flour
- 2 tablespoons salt
- 1 tablespoon ground black pepper
- 1/2 teaspoon ground red pepper
  Vegetable oil
- 1 cup finely chopped white onion
- 1/2 cup finely chopped green onions
- 1 cup finely chopped green pepper
- 1 cup finely chopped celery
- 2 cloves garlic, minced
- 1 can (14 1/2 ounces) diced tomatoes
- 1 can (8 ounces) tomato sauce
- 1 tablespoon Worcestershire sauce
- 1 bay leaf
- 4 cups cooked grits

Cut meat into 8 slices. Pound each piece to about 1/2-inch thickness. In a medium bowl, combine flour, salt, black pepper, and red pepper. Dredge pieces of meat in flour mixture. In a large skillet over medium-high heat, brown both sides of meat in oil. Transfer meat to a warm plate. Reserving about 3 tablespoons oil in skillet, sauté onions, green pepper, celery, and garlic until vegetables are tender. Add undrained tomatoes, tomato sauce, Worcestershire sauce, and bay leaf; bring to a simmer. Return meat to skillet. Reduce heat to low. Cover and simmer about 1 hour or until meat is tender, turning meat occasionally. Serve with hot grits.
Yield: 8 servings

RATATOUILLE

This dish can be made ahead and reheated.

- 10 slices bacon
- 1 medium eggplant, peeled and cubed
- 2 unpeeled zucchini, cubed
- 2 green peppers, chopped
- 1 cup finely chopped onion
- 2 cloves garlic, minced
- 2 cans (14 1/2 ounces each) diced tomatoes
- 1 package (10 ounces) frozen sliced okra, thawed
- 3 tablespoons balsamic vinegar
- 2 tablespoons finely chopped fresh parsley
- 1 teaspoon salt
- 1/2 teaspoon dried marjoram leaves
- 1/2 teaspoon dried thyme leaves
- 1/4 teaspoon ground black pepper

Cook bacon in a Dutch oven until crisp. Drain and crumble bacon;

Packed with flavor, Ratatouille (*top*) combines vegetables and herbs for a tasty make-ahead side dish. Smothered in a robust red gravy, meaty Grillades and Grits (*bottom*) are mouth-watering Creole fare.

set aside. Reserving 2 tablespoons drippings in pan, sauté eggplant, zucchini, green peppers, onion, and garlic over medium heat until vegetables are tender. Add undrained tomatoes, okra, vinegar, parsley, salt, marjoram, thyme, and black pepper. Cover and cook 20 minutes or until vegetables are tender, stirring frequently. Transfer to a serving dish. Sprinkle bacon over vegetables. Serve warm.
Yield: about 18 servings

CHEESE-STUFFED MIRLITONS

Mirlitons, also known as chayotes, are members of the squash family.

4 mirlitons (about 2 1/2 pounds)
2 teaspoons plus 1/2 teaspoon salt, divided
2 1/4 cups fresh bread crumbs, divided
1/2 cup freshly grated Parmesan cheese, divided
1/4 cup finely chopped green onions
1 egg
2 tablespoons chopped fresh parsley, divided
1 to 2 cloves garlic, minced
1/8 teaspoon ground black pepper
1/8 teaspoon ground red pepper
3 tablespoons butter or margarine, melted

Cut mirlitons in half lengthwise. Place in a large Dutch oven; cover with water and add 2 teaspoons salt. Bring to a boil over medium-high heat. Cover and reduce heat to medium low. Simmer until vegetables are barely tender (about 20 minutes). Drain mirlitons and cool.

Preheat oven to 350 degrees. Scoop seeds from mirlitons and discard. Scoop pulp into a medium bowl, leaving about a 1/8-inch-thick shell. Stir 2 cups bread crumbs, 1/4 cup cheese, green onions, egg, 1 tablespoon parsley, garlic, peppers, and remaining 1/2 teaspoon salt into pulp. Spoon mixture into each shell. Place in a greased 9 x 13-inch baking dish. In a small bowl, combine remaining 1/4 cup bread crumbs, 1/4 cup cheese, and remaining 1 tablespoon parsley; sprinkle over squash. Drizzle with melted butter. Bake 45 minutes or until tops are golden brown. Serve warm.
Yield: 8 servings

CREAMED SPINACH

1/4 cup butter or margarine
1 clove garlic, cut in half
6 tablespoons all-purpose flour
2 1/4 cups hot whipping cream
3/4 teaspoon salt
1/4 teaspoon ground white pepper
2 bags (10 ounces each) fresh spinach, stemmed and coarsely chopped
1/2 cup freshly grated Parmesan cheese

In a large skillet, melt butter over medium heat. Add garlic and sauté until garlic starts to brown; remove garlic.

With a scrumptious topping of bread crumbs and Parmesan cheese baked to a golden brown, Cheese-Stuffed Mirlitons (*bottom*) are a warm addition to the holiday table. Folks will want second helpings of quick-to-fix Creamed Spinach (*top*) seasoned with fresh garlic and Parmesan cheese.

Stirring constantly, add flour; stir until mixture is smooth. Cook 2 minutes. Stir in hot whipping cream, salt, and white pepper. Stirring constantly, bring to a boil and cook 2 minutes. Gradually stir in spinach. Reduce heat to medium low. Stirring frequently, cover and cook about 10 minutes or until spinach is tender. Stir in cheese. Serve warm.
Yield: about 9 servings

What would the holidays be without dessert! Our Sweet Potato Pie with Marshmallow Meringue puts a new twist on an old favorite. Top off a delicious meal with cups of spicy Café Brûlot, which is prepared by pouring strong coffee into a flaming mixture of spices and brandy.

SWEET POTATO PIE WITH MARSHMALLOW MERINGUE

Spoon meringue onto hot pie for best results.

PIE
- 1 can (29 ounces) sweet potatoes in syrup, drained and mashed
- 1 cup firmly packed brown sugar
- 2 tablespoons butter or margarine, softened
- 3 egg yolks
- 1 teaspoon pumpkin pie spice
- 1 teaspoon vanilla extract
- 1/4 teaspoon salt
- 1 can (5 ounces) evaporated milk
- 1 unbaked 9-inch deep-dish pie crust

MERINGUE
- 1/2 cup water
- 2 tablespoons sugar
- 1 tablespoon cornstarch
- 1/8 teaspoon salt
- 3 egg whites
- 1/4 teaspoon cream of tartar
- 1 jar (7 ounces) marshmallow creme
- 1/2 teaspoon vanilla extract

Preheat oven to 400 degrees. For pie, combine sweet potatoes, brown sugar, butter, egg yolks, pumpkin pie spice, vanilla, and salt in a medium bowl; beat until well blended. Stir in evaporated milk. Pour mixture into crust. Bake 10 minutes. Reduce heat to 350 degrees. Bake 40 minutes or until center is almost set and edges are cracked and lightly browned.

About 25 minutes after placing pie in oven, combine water, sugar, cornstarch, and salt in a small saucepan for meringue. Stirring constantly, cook over medium heat about 5 minutes or until mixture is clear. Transfer to a heatproof bowl. Cool about 15 minutes.

In a medium bowl, beat egg whites and cream of tartar until foamy. Add cornstarch mixture; beat until well blended. Gradually add marshmallow creme and vanilla; beat until soft peaks form. Top hot pie with meringue, sealing edges to crust; return pie to oven. Bake 12 to 15 minutes or until meringue is lightly browned. Let stand 30 minutes; serve warm.

Yield: about 8 servings

CAFÉ BRÛLOT

Use caution when igniting mixture.

- Shaved zest from half of an orange
- Shaved zest from half of a lemon
- 6 whole cloves
- 6 whole allspice
- 2 teaspoons superfine sugar
- 1/2 cup brandy
- 1 tablespoon Curaçao liqueur
- 4 cups hot strongly brewed coffee

Combine orange zest, lemon zest, cloves, allspice, and superfine sugar in a chafing dish over a heat source. Add brandy and liqueur; stir until sugar dissolves. As mixture begins to simmer, use a ladle to remove a small amount of brandy mixture. Ignite mixture in ladle and return to remaining mixture (flame will spread over surface). Slowly pour in coffee, stirring until flame goes out. Serve immediately.

Yield: about 4 cups coffee

Decorated with icing curlicues and an elegant monogram, French Quarter Cake is a dark, sweet ending to your holiday meal. Three layers of decadent cake are separated by an espresso-flavored chocolate filling, capturing the unique flavor of Bourbon Street.

FRENCH QUARTER CAKE

CAKE
1 ¹/₂ cups all-purpose flour
1 ¹/₄ cups sugar
3 tablespoons cocoa
2 teaspoons baking soda
¹/₂ teaspoon salt
4 eggs
¹/₂ cup buttermilk
¹/₂ cup coffee-flavored liqueur
¹/₃ cup vegetable oil
1 teaspoon vanilla extract
2 packages (3 ounces each) cream cheese, softened
6 ounces semisweet baking chocolate, melted

FILLING
¹/₂ cup whipping cream
2 teaspoons instant espresso powder
2 ounces semisweet baking chocolate, finely chopped

ICING
3 cups confectioners sugar
²/₃ cup butter or margarine, softened
3 tablespoons cocoa
2 to 3 tablespoons milk
1 teaspoon vanilla extract

DECORATING ICING
2 cups confectioners sugar
2 tablespoons plus 1 teaspoon cocoa, divided
3 to 4 tablespoons coffee-flavored liqueur
1 teaspoon vanilla extract

Preheat oven to 350 degrees. For cake, grease three 8-inch round cake pans. Line bottoms with waxed paper; grease waxed paper. In a large bowl, combine flour, sugar, cocoa, baking soda, and salt. In a medium bowl, whisk eggs, buttermilk, liqueur, oil, and vanilla.

Add egg mixture to dry ingredients; stir until well blended. In a medium bowl, beat cream cheese and chocolate until well blended. Beat cream cheese mixture into batter. Pour batter into prepared pans. Bake 18 to 23 minutes or until a toothpick inserted in center of cake comes out clean. Cool in pans 10 minutes; remove from pans and cool completely on a wire rack.

For filling, combine whipping cream and espresso powder in a small saucepan. Bring to a boil over medium-high heat; pour mixture into a small bowl. Add chocolate; stir until smooth. Chill 10 minutes or until chocolate is cool but not set. Beat chocolate mixture until thickened (about 5 minutes). Spread filling between cake layers. Cover cake and chill 15 minutes or until filling is set.

For icing, combine confectioners sugar, butter, cocoa, milk, and vanilla in a large bowl; beat until smooth. Spread icing on top and sides of cake.

For decorating icing, combine confectioners sugar, 2 tablespoons cocoa, liqueur, and vanilla in a medium bowl; stir until smooth. Spoon icing into a pastry bag fitted with a small round tip. Using a toothpick, mark a 4-inch-diameter circle at center top of cake. Beginning at edge of circle, pipe connecting swirls onto top and sides of cake. Fill in circle with decorating icing. Pipe a small bead border around circle and top edge of cake. Allow icing to harden.

Transfer remaining decorating icing to a small bowl. Add remaining 1 teaspoon cocoa to icing to darken; stir until smooth. Return icing to pastry bag. Pipe desired initial in center of cake. Store in an airtight container in refrigerator. Serve at room temperature.

Yield: about 16 servings

Finish the feast with slices of Praline Angel Food Cake, a heavenly combination of airy cake covered with a crunchy praline topping.

PRALINE ANGEL FOOD CAKE

CAKE
- 10 egg whites
- 1 1/2 teaspoons cream of tartar
- 1 teaspoon salt
- 1 teaspoon vanilla extract
- 1 teaspoon almond extract
- 2 cups firmly packed brown sugar, sifted and divided
- 1 1/4 cups sifted cake flour
- 1 cup almond brickle chips

PRALINE TOPPING
- 1 cup firmly packed brown sugar
- 1 1/2 tablespoons dark corn syrup
- 1 tablespoon water
- 1 tablespoon butter or margarine
- 1/2 teaspoon vanilla extract
- 1/2 teaspoon almond extract
- 1/2 cup almond brickle chips

Preheat oven to 350 degrees. For cake, beat egg whites in a large bowl until foamy. Add cream of tartar and salt; beat until soft peaks form. Add extracts. Gradually adding 1 cup brown sugar, beat until stiff peaks form. Sift remaining 1 cup brown sugar and cake flour over egg whites; fold into mixture. Fold in brickle chips. Pour into an ungreased 10-inch tube pan with a removable bottom. Bake 44 to 48 minutes or until top is golden brown. Invert pan; cool completely. Transfer cake to a serving plate.

For praline topping, butter sides of a heavy small saucepan. Combine brown sugar, corn syrup, water, and butter in saucepan. Stirring constantly, cook over medium-low heat until sugar dissolves. Using a pastry brush dipped in hot water, wash down any sugar crystals on sides of pan. Bring topping to a boil over medium heat; boil, without stirring, 3 minutes. Remove from heat; cool 5 minutes. Stir in extracts and brickle chips. Quickly pour glaze over cake. Let glaze harden.

Yield: about 16 servings

Ski Lodge Supper

Whether you live in Maine or Miami, you can create a setting with the cozy atmosphere of a ski lodge for your holiday meal. Our collection of hearty and flavorful dishes is rich in well-seasoned items influenced by foods from south of the border and fresh from the country's heartland. To satisfy appetites stimulated by an exhilarating day on the slopes or a cliff-hanger football game, our mountain-high menu is a surefire crowd pleaser!

Turkey Enchiladas with Sweet Red Pepper Sauce add a festive touch to a Mexican standard. A good use for leftover turkey, the cilantro-garnished dish is flavored with Monterey Jack and Cheddar cheeses as well as sour cream. Golden Citrus Cider Punch is a sweet, slightly tangy blend of lemon-lime and apple. For a stronger beverage, serve bottled draft cider.

TURKEY ENCHILADAS WITH SWEET RED PEPPER SAUCE

- 3 sweet red peppers
- 1/2 cup plus 3 tablespoons finely chopped onion, divided
- 2 cloves garlic, minced
- 2 tablespoons vegetable oil
- 1 can (28 ounces) crushed tomatoes
- 1 can (14 1/2 ounces) chicken broth
- 1/2 teaspoon salt
- 1/2 teaspoon ground cumin
- 1/4 teaspoon dried oregano leaves, crushed
- 4 cups finely chopped cooked turkey
- 1 container (8 ounces) sour cream
- 20 corn tortillas (6 inches in diameter)
- 4 cups combined shredded Monterey Jack and Cheddar cheeses, divided
  Chopped fresh cilantro to garnish

To roast red peppers, cut in half lengthwise; remove seeds and membranes. Place, skin side up, on an ungreased baking sheet; flatten with hand. Broil about 3 inches from heat 12 to 15 minutes or until skin is evenly blackened. Immediately seal peppers in a plastic bag and allow to steam 10 to 15 minutes. Remove charred skin. Cut peppers into 1/2-inch x 1-inch strips.

In a heavy large saucepan, sauté 1/2 cup onion and garlic in oil over medium-high heat until vegetables are tender. Stir in pepper strips, tomatoes, chicken broth, salt, cumin, and oregano. Bring mixture to a boil. Stirring frequently, reduce heat to medium-low and simmer about 20 minutes or until sauce thickens.

Preheat oven to 375 degrees. Spread 2/3 cup sauce in each of 2 greased 7 x 11-inch baking dishes. In a medium bowl, combine turkey, remaining 3 tablespoons chopped onion, and sour cream. Soften tortillas in a microwave according to package directions. Place 2 rounded tablespoons turkey mixture and 2 tablespoons cheese on each tortilla. Tightly roll up tortillas and place, seam side down, in baking dishes. Spoon remaining sauce down each side of baking dishes, covering ends of tortillas. Sprinkle remaining cheese over middle of enchiladas. Bake 12 to 15 minutes or until heated through and cheese melts. Garnish with cilantro. Serve warm.

Yield: 20 enchiladas

What a culinary surprise — Christmas Pasta Snacks are crisp and crunchy instead of al dente! To make this tasty treat, lightly sauté colorful tree-shaped pasta, then sprinkle with spiced-up Parmesan cheese. Terrific as an appetizer, Seafood-Stuffed Jalapeños *(recipe on page 158)* have a not-too-spicy shrimp and crab filling. The crunchy buttermilk coating goes well with our zesty horseradish sauce.

CITRUS CIDER PUNCH

We made apple cider ice cubes to serve in our punch.

- 1 gallon apple cider, chilled
- 1 can (12 ounces) frozen limeade concentrate
- 1 can (12 ounces) frozen lemonade concentrate
- 1 bottle (2 liters) lemon-lime soft drink, chilled
  Lemon and lime slices and maraschino cherries with stems to garnish

In a 2-gallon container, combine cider and concentrates. Stir until concentrates thaw. Stir in soft drink. Garnish servings with lemon and lime slices and maraschino cherries. Serve immediately.

Yield: about 27 cups punch

CHRISTMAS PASTA SNACKS

- 2 tablespoons grated Parmesan cheese
- 1 teaspoon ground cumin
- 3/4 teaspoon ground oregano
- 3/4 teaspoon salt
- 1/2 teaspoon garlic powder
  Vegetable oil
- 8 ounces tree-shaped pasta, cooked, drained, and patted dry

In a small bowl, combine cheese, cumin, oregano, salt, and garlic powder. In a heavy medium saucepan, heat oil to 375 degrees. Stirring occasionally, deep fry 1 cup pasta 4 to 5 minutes or until pasta is golden brown and oil stops bubbling. Drain on paper towels. Transfer warm pasta to lightly greased aluminum foil. Sprinkle about 2 teaspoons cheese mixture over warm pasta. Repeat with remaining pasta and cheese mixture. Cool completely and store in an airtight container.

Yield: about 4 1/2 cups snack mix

SEAFOOD-STUFFED JALAPEÑOS (Shown on page 157)

HORSERADISH SAUCE

1 ½ cups sour cream
¾ cup mayonnaise
4 to 5 tablespoons prepared horseradish

PEPPERS

30 medium jalapeño peppers
1 package (8 ounces) cream cheese, softened
1 can (6 ounces) small shrimp, drained
1 can (6 ounces) crabmeat, drained
2 tablespoons finely chopped onion
1 tablespoon Worcestershire sauce
1 tablespoon freshly squeezed lemon juice
¼ teaspoon garlic powder
1 cup buttermilk
1 egg, beaten
1 ½ cups corn flake crumbs
¾ cup self-rising cornmeal mix
Vegetable oil

For horseradish sauce, combine sour cream, mayonnaise, and horseradish in a small bowl. Cover and chill 4 hours to let flavors blend.

For peppers, cut peppers in half lengthwise and seed (protect hands with gloves). To blanch peppers, cover with water in a large saucepan. Cover and bring to a boil over medium-high heat; boil 5 minutes. Being careful to avoid steam, drain peppers and rinse with cold water. Drain on paper towels.

In a medium bowl, combine cream cheese, shrimp, crabmeat, onion, Worcestershire sauce, lemon juice, and garlic powder; beat until well blended. Transfer cream cheese mixture to a quart-size resealable plastic bag. Cut off 1 corner of bag and pipe mixture into each pepper half. Place on a baking sheet lined with waxed paper; freeze about 1 hour or until filling is frozen.

Combine buttermilk and egg in a small bowl. In a medium bowl, combine corn flake crumbs and cornmeal mix. Dip each pepper into buttermilk mixture and roll in crumb mixture. Return to baking sheet. Cover and freeze 1 hour.

To serve, heat oil to 350 degrees in a heavy medium saucepan. Removing about 6 peppers at a time from freezer, deep fry peppers about 2 minutes or until golden brown. Drain on paper towels. Serve warm with sauce.
Yield: about 2 ½ cups sauce and 5 dozen appetizers

Elegant Pear and Spinach Salad is a choice blend of textures and flavors. For an unforgettable start to your meal, top this unique salad with Mango Buttermilk Dressing, a creamy accent with a hint of curry.

PEAR AND SPINACH SALAD

12 cups washed and torn fresh spinach
3 avocados
3 cans (15¼ ounces each) pear slices in heavy syrup, drained
2 cups fresh grapefruit segments (about 3 grapefruit)
1 cup (4 ounces) shredded Cheddar cheese
⅓ cup sliced almonds, toasted and coarsely chopped

Place 1 cup spinach on each serving plate. Peel each avocado and cut into 12 slices. Arrange about 3 slices each of pear, grapefruit, and avocado on each plate. Garnish each serving with about 1 tablespoon cheese and 1 teaspoon almonds. Serve with Mango Buttermilk Dressing.
Yield: 12 servings

MANGO BUTTERMILK DRESSING

Chilled jars of mango slices can be found in the produce department.

1 cup mayonnaise
¼ cup buttermilk
½ teaspoon curry powder
1 cup finely chopped mango
1 tablespoon chopped fresh parsley
2 teaspoons finely chopped onion

In a small bowl, combine mayonnaise, buttermilk, and curry powder; whisk until well blended. Stir in mango, parsley, and onion. Serve with Pear and Spinach Salad.
Yield: about 2 cups dressing

HEARTY CORN CHOWDER

1/4 cup butter or margarine
1 1/4 cups chopped sweet red pepper
1/2 cup finely chopped celery
1/2 cup chopped onion
3 cups peeled and diced potatoes
1 can (14 1/2 ounces) chicken broth
2 1/4 cups half and half, divided
3 tablespoons all-purpose flour
2 packages (10 ounces each) frozen
   whole kernel corn, thawed
1 teaspoon salt
1/2 teaspoon ground white pepper

In a large Dutch oven, melt butter over medium-high heat. Add red pepper, celery, and onion; sauté until tender. Add potatoes and chicken broth; bring to a boil. Reduce heat to medium-low. Cover and cook 15 minutes or until potatoes are tender.

In a medium bowl, combine 1/4 cup half and half and flour; whisk until smooth. Whisk in remaining 2 cups half and half. Stir corn, half and half mixture, salt, and white pepper into soup. Increase heat to medium. Stirring frequently, cook 15 minutes longer or until heated through and thickened. Serve warm.

Yield: about 8 1/2 cups soup

BLACK BEAN SALSA

1 can (15 ounces) black beans,
   rinsed and drained
1 cup seeded and chopped fresh
   plum tomatoes
1 cup chopped sweet yellow pepper
1/2 cup chopped fresh cilantro
1/2 cup sliced green onions
1 jalapeño pepper, seeded and
   chopped
3 tablespoons freshly squeezed lime
   juice
1 tablespoon olive oil
1 tablespoon red wine vinegar
1 clove garlic, minced
1 teaspoon salt
1/2 teaspoon ground cumin
   Tortilla chips to serve

In a medium bowl, combine beans, tomatoes, yellow pepper, cilantro, green onions, and jalapeño pepper. In a small bowl, combine lime juice, olive oil, vinegar, garlic, salt, and cumin; stir until blended. Pour lime juice mixture over bean mixture and gently toss. Cover and chill 2 hours to let flavors blend. Serve with tortilla chips.

Yield: about 3 1/2 cups salsa

Hearty Corn Chowder is a rich, filling dish that's good to the last yummy drop. Chilled to combine its distinct tastes, colorful Black Bean Salsa is a sauce with "wow!" An excellent make-ahead dish, cheesy Green Chili Rice Timbales have just the right amount of zip to complement our enchiladas.

GREEN CHILI RICE TIMBALES

Timbales may be made ahead and chilled.

1 can (4 ounces) whole green
   chiles, drained
2 cans (4 1/2 ounces each) chopped
   green chiles, drained
1/2 cup salsa
1/2 teaspoon salt
1/2 teaspoon ground cumin
6 cups hot cooked rice
1 cup (4 ounces) shredded Monterey
   Jack cheese
1 cup (4 ounces) shredded mild
   Cheddar cheese

Preheat oven to 325 degrees. Slice whole green chiles into twenty-two 1/2-inch-wide strips. Cross 2 strips in bottom of each of 11 greased 6-ounce baking cups. In a large bowl, combine chopped green chiles, salsa, salt, and cumin; stir until blended. Stir in rice and cheeses. Spoon rice mixture into prepared baking cups. Cover and chill until ready to serve.

To serve, bake covered 25 to 30 minutes or until heated through. Let stand 5 minutes. Invert onto serving plates; serve warm.

Yield: 11 servings

159

A sumptuous butter and honey mixture is brushed between three layers of sour cream-moistened Honey Spice Cake. Toasted pecan pieces are pressed into the sides for a rustic finish.

HONEY SPICE CAKE

CAKE
- 1/2 cup butter or margarine, softened
- 1/2 cup granulated sugar
- 1/2 cup firmly packed brown sugar
- 1 container (8 ounces) sour cream
- 3 eggs
- 1/4 cup honey
- 1 3/4 cups plus 2 tablespoons all-purpose flour
- 2 teaspoons ground cinnamon
- 1 teaspoon baking soda
- 1/2 teaspoon ground allspice
- 1/2 teaspoon salt
- 3/4 cup chopped pecans, toasted

SYRUP
- 1/4 cup honey
- 2 tablespoons butter or margarine

ICING
- 1 cup firmly packed brown sugar
- 3/4 cup butter or margarine
- 1 tablespoon light corn syrup
- 1/3 cup milk
- 1 teaspoon vanilla extract
- 2 1/4 cups sifted confectioners sugar
- 1 cup finely chopped pecans, toasted

Preheat oven to 325 degrees. For cake, grease three 8-inch round cake pans and line bottoms with waxed paper; set aside. In a large bowl, cream butter and sugars until well blended. Add sour cream, eggs, and honey; beat until smooth. In a medium bowl, combine flour, cinnamon, baking soda, allspice, and salt. Add dry ingredients to creamed mixture; beat until well blended. Stir in pecans. Pour batter into prepared pans. Bake 20 to 25 minutes or until a toothpick inserted in center of cake comes out clean. Cool in pans 10 minutes. Remove from pans and cool completely on a wire rack.

For syrup, combine honey and butter in a small saucepan over medium heat. Stir constantly until butter melts. Brush syrup between cake layers.

For icing, combine brown sugar, butter, and corn syrup in a heavy medium saucepan. Whisking constantly, cook over medium heat until mixture comes to a full boil (about 8 minutes); boil 5 minutes. Turn off heat, leaving pan on burner. Slowly whisk in milk and vanilla until smooth. Transfer to a heatproof bowl and let cool 20 minutes. Place bowl of icing in a larger bowl filled with ice. Beat in confectioners sugar, beating until mixture is smooth and begins to hold its shape (about 3 minutes). Spread icing on top and sides of cake. Press pecans into sides of cake. Let icing harden. Store in an airtight container.
Yield: 12 to 14 servings

ORANGE-WALNUT PIE

CRUST
1 1/4 cups all-purpose flour
1/2 teaspoon salt
1/2 teaspoon grated orange zest
1/3 cup vegetable shortening
3 to 4 tablespoons cold orange juice

FILLING
3 eggs
1 cup light corn syrup
1/2 cup sugar
1/4 teaspoon salt
1/4 cup butter or margarine, melted
1/2 teaspoon orange extract
1 cup chopped walnuts

For crust, combine flour, salt, and orange zest in a medium bowl. Using a pastry blender or 2 knives, cut in shortening until mixture resembles coarse meal. Sprinkle with orange juice; mix until a soft dough forms. On a lightly floured surface, use a floured rolling pin to roll out dough. Transfer to a 9-inch pie plate and use a sharp knife to trim edge of dough. Flute edge of dough.

Preheat oven to 400 degrees. For filling, beat eggs, corn syrup, sugar, and salt in a medium bowl until blended. Add melted butter and orange extract; beat until well blended. Stir in walnuts. Pour mixture into prepared crust. Bake 10 minutes. Reduce temperature to 350 degrees. Bake 35 to 40 minutes longer or until center is almost set. Cool completely. Store in an airtight container in refrigerator.

Yield: about 8 servings

FROSTED CINNAMON BARS

1/2 cup butter or margarine, softened
3 cups sugar, divided
1 egg
1 egg yolk
1 teaspoon vanilla extract
1 1/2 cups all-purpose flour
1 tablespoon ground cinnamon
1/2 teaspoon baking powder
1/4 teaspoon salt
2 egg whites
2 cups finely chopped pecans

Preheat oven to 325 degrees. Line a 10 1/2 x 15 1/2-inch jellyroll pan with aluminum foil, extending foil over ends of pan. In a large bowl, cream butter and 1 cup sugar until fluffy. Add egg, egg yolk, and vanilla; beat until well blended. In a small bowl, combine flour, cinnamon, baking powder, and salt. Stir dry ingredients into creamed mixture.

A walnut version of the ever-popular pecan pie, Orange-Walnut Pie has a delightful citrus taste from flaky crust to exquisite filling. Frosted Cinnamon Bars have a meringue-like covering with a pecan-flavored crunch.

Use lightly greased hands to press mixture into bottom of prepared pan. In a medium bowl, beat egg whites until foamy. Gradually add remaining 2 cups sugar; beat about 3 minutes or until well blended (sugar will not dissolve). Fold in pecans. Spread topping evenly over crust. Bake 26 to 30 minutes or until top is lightly browned and firm to touch. Cool in pan on a wire rack. Lift from pan using ends of foil. Use a serrated knife and a sawing motion to cut into 2-inch squares. Store in an airtight container.

Yield: about 3 dozen bars

YULETIDE REUNION

Reuniting faraway friends around the dinner table for food and fellowship makes for a truly memorable Yuletide event. Even before the first course is served, the house is filled with conversation and laughter as guests renew memories of years past and share the latest news. Photographs are passed around the table along with the bread and wine, and cameras flash as each moment is captured on film. Whether your friends have come from across the country or across the street, their hearts will be warmed by the festive mood and our collection of savory dishes and mouth-watering sweets.

ROASTED RED PEPPER SOUP

- 4 sweet red peppers
- 3 tablespoons butter or margarine
- 1 3/4 cups chopped onions
- 1/2 cup sliced carrot
- 3 cloves garlic, minced
- 2 tablespoons all-purpose flour
- 2 cans (14 1/2 ounces each) chicken broth
- 1 can (14 1/2 ounces) whole tomatoes
- 1 cup whipping cream
- 1/4 cup white wine
- 2 tablespoons freshly squeezed lemon juice
- 1 teaspoon honey
- 1 teaspoon salt
- 1/4 teaspoon ground white pepper
  Parsley to garnish

To roast peppers, cut in half lengthwise and remove seeds and membranes. Place, skin side up, on a greased baking sheet; flatten with hand. Broil about 3 inches from heat about 15 to 20 minutes or until skin of peppers blackens. Immediately seal peppers in a plastic bag and allow to steam 10 to 15 minutes. Remove and discard charred skin.

In a large Dutch oven, melt butter over medium heat. Sauté onions, carrot, and garlic about 5 minutes or until onion is tender. Stirring constantly, add flour and cook about 2 minutes. Stir in chicken broth, tomatoes, and peppers; bring to a simmer. Reduce heat to medium low. Stirring occasionally, cover and simmer about 25 minutes or until vegetables are tender. Process mixture in batches in a food processor until vegetables are puréed. Return mixture to Dutch oven. Stir in whipping cream, wine, lemon juice, honey, salt, and white pepper. Cook until heated through (do not boil). Garnish individual servings with parsley, if desired.

Yield: about 7 cups soup

Guests can warm up to a bowl of creamy Roasted Red Pepper Soup. Complete the course with homemade Parmesan Cheese Crisps and finish with a glass of spirited Christmas Sangria.

Set the scene for good food and good cheer with your best holiday china and table linens; tie shining ribbon around napkins and goblet stems. Instead of place cards, hang a handmade stocking for each guest and trim it with a colorful glass ornament painted with his or her name; invite everyone to bring little gifts to tuck in the stockings! To complete the setting, fill the table with brilliant poinsettias and add photographs of past gatherings to the arrangement.

PARMESAN CHEESE CRISPS

These crackers freeze well.

- 1 cup butter, softened
- 1 clove garlic, minced
- 2 cups all-purpose flour
- 1 cup freshly grated Parmesan cheese
- 2 tablespoons dried parsley flakes

Process butter and garlic in a large food processor until smooth. Add flour, Parmesan cheese, and parsley flakes; process until well blended. Shape cheese mixture into two 10-inch-long rolls. Wrap in plastic wrap and chill 2 hours or until firm enough to slice.

Preheat oven to 350 degrees. Cut rolls into 1/4-inch slices. Place slices on an ungreased baking sheet. Bake 13 to 15 minutes or until crackers are golden brown. Transfer to a wire rack to cool. Store in an airtight container.

Yield: about 6 1/2 dozen crackers

CHRISTMAS SANGRIA

- 4 navel oranges, sliced
- 2 lemons, sliced
- 1 1/2 cups sugar
- 2 bottles (750 ml each) dry white wine, chilled
- 1 can (12 ounces) frozen cranberry juice cocktail concentrate, thawed
- 2 tablespoons orange-flavored liqueur
- 2 tablespoons brandy
- 1 bottle (1 liter) club soda, chilled

Place fruit slices in a large bowl. Pour sugar over fruit; stir with a wooden spoon until fruit is coated with sugar. Cover and let stand at room temperature 1 hour.

In a large container combine fruit mixture, wine, cranberry juice concentrate, liqueur, and brandy. Cover and chill 2 hours.

To serve, transfer wine mixture to a 5-quart serving container; stir in club soda. Serve immediately.

Yield: about 14 cups wine

ELEGANT CRANBERRY SALAD

- 1 can (8 ounces) crushed pineapple in juice
- 1 cup boiling water
- 2 packages (3 ounces each) cranberry gelatin
- 1 cup cold water
- 1 can (16 ounces) whole berry cranberry sauce
- 1 cup chopped walnuts
- 1 cup chopped unpeeled red apple (we used Red Delicious)
- 1/2 cup finely chopped celery
  Lettuce leaves to serve

Drain pineapple, reserving juice in a measuring cup. Add enough water to juice to make 1 cup. In a medium bowl, stir boiling water into gelatin; stir until gelatin dissolves. Add pineapple juice mixture, cold water, and cranberry sauce; stir until well blended. Chill gelatin mixture about 45 minutes or until partially set, stirring occasionally.

Fold pineapple, walnuts, apple, and celery into gelatin mixture. Pour into a lightly oiled 9 x 13-inch baking dish. Cover and chill about 2 hours or until firm.

Cut gelatin into 3-inch squares. Serve on lettuce leaves.
Yield: about 12 servings

CORN SOUFFLÉS

Soufflés can be made ahead and chilled until ready to bake.

- 1 1/2 cups water
- 3/4 cup yellow cornmeal
- 2 cups (8 ounces) shredded sharp Cheddar cheese
- 1 can (11 ounces) whole kernel corn, drained
- 1 small clove garlic, minced
- 1/2 teaspoon salt
- 1/8 teaspoon ground white pepper
- 3/4 cup milk
- 4 eggs, separated

Preheat oven to 325 degrees. In a large saucepan, combine water and cornmeal. Stirring constantly, cook over medium heat 3 to 4 minutes or until mixture thickens. Reduce heat to low. Add cheese, corn, garlic, salt, and white pepper; stir until cheese melts. Remove from heat. In a small bowl, combine milk and egg yolks; beat until blended. Stir into cornmeal mixture. In a medium bowl, beat egg whites until stiff.

Delight friends with a scrumptious spread of holiday fare. Begin with Elegant Cranberry Salad featuring crunchy celery, walnuts, and chopped apples. A light side dish, time-saving Corn Soufflés can be made ahead and baked just before serving. Our Brie-Stuffed Chicken Breasts with Green Peppercorn Sauce are bursting with the robust flavor of Dijon mustard.

Fold egg whites into cornmeal mixture. Spoon into 7 greased 1-cup ramekins. (Mixture may be covered and chilled until ready to bake.) Bake 30 to 35 minutes (40 to 45 minutes if chilled) or until puffed and lightly browned. Serve immediately.
Yield: 7 servings

BRIE-STUFFED CHICKEN BREASTS WITH GREEN PEPPERCORN SAUCE

CHICKEN BREASTS
- 6 boneless, skinless chicken breasts
- 1/4 cup mayonnaise
- 2 tablespoons Dijon-style mustard
- 1/2 teaspoon ground white pepper
- 8 ounces Brie cheese, rind removed and shredded
- 1/2 cup purchased plain bread crumbs
- 1/2 cup chopped pecans, toasted and ground
- 1 tablespoon finely chopped fresh parsley

GREEN PEPPERCORN SAUCE
- 1/4 cup butter or margarine
- 1/4 cup minced onion
- 2 tablespoons green peppercorns, crushed
- 1 can (14 1/2 ounces) chicken broth
- 1/4 cup finely chopped fresh parsley

The zesty flavor of Golden Lemon Biscuits (*left*) is enhanced with dollops of Lemon Butter (*recipes on page 166*). A cool and tangy recipe made with red wine vinegar, Marinated Mushrooms (*recipe on page 166*) add vibrant color to the table. Tasty Oven-Roasted Vegetables are delicately seasoned with fresh ginger and thyme for a delicious complement to any meal.

2   tablespoons Dijon-style mustard
³/₄ teaspoon salt
2   cups half and half
2   tablespoons cornstarch
¹/₄ cup water

Preheat oven to 350 degrees. Place chicken between sheets of waxed paper. Using a mallet, gently pound chicken pieces until ¹/₄-inch thick. In a small bowl, combine mayonnaise and mustard. Spread 1 tablespoon mixture over each chicken breast. Sprinkle chicken breasts with white pepper. Place ¹/₄ cup cheese in center of each chicken piece. Beginning at 1 short edge, roll up chicken jellyroll style; secure with a toothpick. (Chicken may be covered and chilled until ready to bake.) In a shallow bowl, combine bread crumbs, pecans, and parsley. Coat chicken with crumb mixture. Place chicken in a lightly greased jellyroll pan. Bake 35 minutes (40 minutes if chilled) or until juices run clear when pierced with a fork.

For green peppercorn sauce, melt butter in a medium saucepan over medium heat. Sauté onion and peppercorns in butter about 5 minutes or until onion is tender; stir in chicken broth. Stirring occasionally, cook mixture 25 minutes or until volume is reduced by half. Add parsley, mustard, and salt; stir until well blended. Stirring frequently, add half and half and bring mixture to a simmer over medium-high heat. In a small bowl, combine cornstarch and water. Stirring constantly, add cornstarch mixture and cook about 1 minute or until sauce is bubbly and thickened. Serve warm or store in an airtight container in refrigerator until ready to serve.

To reheat sauce, place in a medium microwave-safe bowl. Microwave on medium-high power (80%) about 6 minutes or until heated through, stirring every 2 minutes. Remove toothpicks from chicken. Serve ¹/₂ cup sauce with each chicken piece.
Yield: 6 servings

OVEN-ROASTED VEGETABLES

1   package (16 ounces) frozen bean and carrot blend, thawed
1   package (16 ounces) frozen peas with baby corn and snow peas, thawed
³/₄ cup butter or margarine
2   tablespoons freshly grated ginger
1¹/₂ tablespoons finely chopped fresh thyme leaves
1   teaspoon salt
¹/₂ teaspoon ground black pepper
1   jar (15 ounces) whole small onions, drained

Preheat oven to 400 degrees. In a large roasting pan, combine first 2 ingredients. In a small saucepan, combine butter, ginger, thyme, salt, and pepper. Stirring constantly, cook over medium-low heat until butter melts. Pour over vegetables. Bake 30 minutes, stirring after 15 minutes. Stir in onions and bake 15 minutes or until vegetables are tender and lightly browned.
Yield: about 6 cups vegetables

LEMON BUTTER
(Shown on page 165)

- 1/2 cup butter or margarine, softened
- 2 teaspoons freshly squeezed lemon juice
- 1 teaspoon grated lemon zest

In a small bowl, combine butter, lemon juice, and lemon zest; beat until well blended. Cover and store in refrigerator.
Yield: about 1/2 cup butter

GOLDEN LEMON BISCUITS
(Shown on page 165)

- 2 cups all-purpose flour
- 2 tablespoons sugar
- 2 teaspoons baking powder
- 1/2 teaspoon salt
- 1/2 cup chilled butter or margarine
- 2 eggs, beaten
- 3 tablespoons milk
- 2 tablespoons freshly squeezed lemon juice
- 2 teaspoons grated lemon zest

Preheat oven to 400 degrees. In a medium bowl, combine flour, sugar, baking powder, and salt. Using a pastry blender or 2 knives, cut in butter until mixture resembles coarse meal. Stir in eggs, milk, lemon juice, and lemon zest just until blended. On a lightly floured surface, knead dough about 1 minute or until smooth. Roll out dough to 1/2-inch thickness; use a 2-inch biscuit cutter to cut out biscuits. Place biscuits 2 inches apart on an ungreased baking sheet. Bake 12 to 15 minutes or until tops are golden brown. Serve warm with Lemon Butter.
Yield: about 1 1/2 dozen biscuits

MARINATED MUSHROOMS
(Shown on page 165)

- 1 pound fresh mushrooms (we used white, shiitake, and golden Italian)
- 1 bottle (16 ounces) red wine vinegar and oil salad dressing
- 1/4 cup chopped fresh parsley
- 2 tablespoons drained capers

Clean, trim, and slice mushrooms. Place in a medium container. Stir in salad dressing, parsley, and capers. Cover and chill overnight, stirring mushrooms several times. Serve chilled.
Yield: about 4 3/4 cups mushrooms

An eye-catching Yuletide display, our Eggnog Trifle contrasts rich pudding with colorful oranges and cherries, all layered with slices of moist pound cake.

EGGNOG TRIFLE

- 2 packages (3 ounces each) vanilla pudding mix
- 1 carton (1 quart) eggnog
- 1/4 teaspoon freshly grated nutmeg (optional)
- 2 loaves (10 3/4 ounces each) pound cake
- 1/3 cup cream sherry
- 2 1/4 cups whipping cream, divided
- 3 cans (11 ounces each) mandarin oranges, drained
- 1 jar (10 ounces) maraschino cherry halves, drained
- 2 tablespoons confectioners sugar
- 1 teaspoon vanilla extract

Combine pudding mix and eggnog in a medium saucepan. Stirring constantly, cook over medium heat until mixture comes to a full boil. Pour mixture into a large heatproof bowl. Stir in nutmeg, if desired. Place plastic wrap directly on surface of pudding; chill 1 hour.

Cut top of pound cake flat and trim edges from cake. Cut cake into 1/2-inch slices. Place slices on waxed paper. Brush slices with sherry. Beat 1 1/4 cups whipping cream in a medium bowl until stiff peaks form. Fold whipped cream into pudding. Place one-third of cake slices in bottom of a 16-cup trifle bowl. Spoon 2 cups pudding over cake. Using 1 1/2 cups oranges, line outside edge of bowl and place remaining oranges over pudding. Using 1/2 cup cherries, line outside edge of bowl and place remaining cherries over oranges. Continue layering using half of remaining cake, 2 cups pudding, 1 1/2 cups oranges, 1/2 cup cherries, remaining cake, and remaining pudding. Cover and chill until ready to serve.

To serve, beat remaining 1 cup whipping cream, confectioners sugar, and vanilla in a small bowl until stiff peaks form. Spoon whipped cream into a pastry bag fitted with a large star tip. Pipe dollops of whipped cream onto top of trifle.
Yield: about 24 servings

CHOCOLATE PEPPERMINT PATTIES

  7 cups confectioners sugar
  7 tablespoons cocoa
  1 can (14 ounces) sweetened
        condensed milk
 $1/2$ cup butter, softened
  1 teaspoon peppermint extract
 24 ounces chocolate candy coating,
        chopped
  1 package (12 ounces) semisweet
        chocolate chips

In a large bowl, combine confectioners sugar and cocoa. Add sweetened condensed milk, butter, and peppermint extract; beat until well blended. Shape mixture into 1-inch balls and flatten each ball to make a 1 $1/2$-inch-diameter patty. Place patties on baking sheets lined with waxed paper. Freeze patties 30 minutes or until thoroughly chilled.

In top of a double boiler, melt candy coating and chocolate chips over hot, not simmering, water. Remove double boiler from heat. Remove 1 dozen patties at a time from freezer. Placing each patty on a fork and holding over saucepan, spoon chocolate mixture over patties. Return to baking sheets lined with waxed paper. Let chocolate harden. Store in an airtight container in refrigerator.
Yield: about 7 $1/2$ dozen patties

FAVOR STOCKINGS
(Shown on page 162)

For each stocking, you will need tracing paper, $1/3$ yd. of plaid taffeta for stocking, 1 $1/4$ yds. of $1/8$ "w gold cord with lip, $1/4$ yd. of red velvet for hanger and cuff, pressing cloth, straight pins, gold fine-tip paint pen, red satin glass ornament, and 18" of $1/16$ "w gold cord.

Note: Match right sides and raw edges and use a $1/2$" seam allowance for all sewing unless otherwise indicated. Use pressing cloth for all pressing.

1. Aligning arrows and dotted lines, trace stocking top B and stocking bottom patterns, page 95, onto tracing paper. For seam allowance, draw a second line $1/2$" outside the first. Cut out pattern along outer line.
2. Matching short edges, fold taffeta in half. Using pattern, cut out stocking pieces.
3. Matching raw edges on right side of taffeta, baste lip of cord along side and bottom edges of front of stocking.

Refreshing Chocolate Peppermint Patties *(left, on plate)* are a great way to end a satisfying meal. Give each guest a decorated photo album to hold snapshots of the festivities. The memories will last a lifetime!

4. Using a zipper foot and stitching as close to cord as possible, sew stocking pieces together. Clip curves and turn right side out.
5. For hanger, cut a 2 $1/4$" x 14" strip from velvet. Press long edges $1/2$" to wrong side. Matching wrong sides and long edges, press in half; stitch close to pressed edges. Matching short ends, fold hanger in half to form a loop. Matching raw edges, pin loop inside stocking at heel seam.
6. For cuff, cut a 7" x 16" piece from velvet. Sew short edges together; press seam open.
7. Matching wrong sides and raw edges, fold cuff in half. Matching raw edges, place cuff inside top of stocking. Sew cuff to stocking. Turn cuff to outside of stocking.
8. Use gold pen to write name and draw holly leaves and berries on ornament. Use $1/16$"w cord to tie ornament to stocking.

FRIENDSHIP PHOTO ALBUM

You will need a 2 $1/2$" dia. gold frame, 3" square of ecru card stock, black permanent fine-point marker, 18" of $7/8$ "w red wired ribbon with gold edges, hot glue gun, and a 5" x 6 $1/2$" photo album.

1. Trace around frame on card stock. Cut out circle just inside drawn line. Use marker to write "Friendship grows from pleasures shared" on circle. Mount circle in frame.
2. Tie ribbon into a bow with 5" streamers. Glue bow and frame to album.

Angel Food

Create your own seventh heaven when you treat a gathering of friends and family to the most celestial desserts ever! Our fabulous collection of goodies will satisfy anyone's sweet tooth — and we've even included a few low-fat items. With so many extravagant delicacies, it's not easy to choose a favorite. You'll want to share each and every one of them with the "angels" who grace your holiday table.

Billowy swirls of white icing finish this decadent Lady Baltimore Cake, which features a fruity filling. Light in texture and rich in flavor, the traditional cake is just right for entertaining family and special friends.

LADY BALTIMORE CAKE

FRUIT FILLING
- 1 cup chopped dried figs
- 1/2 cup chopped golden raisins
- 1/2 cup orange juice

CAKE
- 1 cup butter or margarine, softened
- 2 cups sugar
- 1 teaspoon grated orange zest
- 3 cups sifted cake flour
- 1 tablespoon baking powder
- 1/4 teaspoon salt
- 1/2 cup orange juice
- 1/2 cup water
- 2 teaspoons vanilla extract
- 8 egg whites

ICING
- 1 1/2 cups sugar
- 5 tablespoons water
- 2 egg whites
- 2 tablespoons light corn syrup
- 1/4 teaspoon cream of tartar
- 1 teaspoon vanilla extract
- 1 cup chopped pecans

For fruit filling, combine figs, raisins, and orange juice in a small bowl; set aside.

Preheat oven to 350 degrees. For cake, grease three 9-inch round cake pans. Line bottom of pans with waxed paper; grease waxed paper. In a large bowl, cream butter, sugar, and orange zest. In a medium bowl, combine cake flour, baking powder, and salt. In a small bowl, combine orange juice, water, and vanilla. Alternately add dry ingredients and orange juice mixture to creamed mixture, beating until well blended. In a medium bowl, beat egg whites until stiff peaks form. Fold egg whites into batter; pour into prepared pans. Bake 20 to 25 minutes or until a toothpick inserted in center of cake comes out clean. Cool in pans 10 minutes. Remove from pans and cool completely on a wire rack.

For icing, drain fruit mixture; set aside. In top of a double boiler, combine sugar, water, egg whites, corn syrup, and cream of tartar. Beat with an electric mixer until sugar is well blended. Place over simmering water; beat about 7 minutes or until soft peaks form. Remove from heat and add vanilla. Continue beating 2 minutes longer or until icing is desired consistency. In a medium bowl, fold fruit mixture and pecans into 1 cup icing. Spread filling between layers. Ice top and sides of cake with remaining icing. Store in an airtight container in refrigerator.

Yield: about 12 servings

Delicate and unmistakably sweet, Heavenly Angel Cookies live up to their name. These buttery, melt-in-your-mouth cookies are embellished with ethereal icing so they look as good as they taste.

HEAVENLY ANGEL COOKIES

COOKIES
- 3/4 cup butter or margarine, softened
- 1 package (3 ounces) cream cheese, softened
- 1 3/4 cups sifted confectioners sugar
- 1 egg
- 1/2 teaspoon vanilla extract
- 1/2 teaspoon almond extract
- 2 cups all-purpose flour
- 3/4 teaspoon baking powder

ICING
- 3 cups sifted confectioners sugar
- 2 1/2 to 3 tablespoons water
- 2 teaspoons light corn syrup
- 1/2 teaspoon vanilla extract
  Pink paste food coloring

For cookies, cream butter, cream cheese, and confectioners sugar in a large bowl. Beat in egg and extracts. In a small bowl, combine flour and baking powder. Add dry ingredients to creamed mixture; stir until a soft dough forms.

Divide dough into fourths. Wrap in plastic wrap and chill 2 hours or until firm enough to handle.

Preheat oven to 350 degrees. On a lightly floured surface, use a floured rolling pin to roll out one fourth of dough to 1/8-inch thickness. Use a 4-inch-wide by 4 1/4-inch-high angel-shaped cookie cutter to cut out cookies. Transfer to an ungreased baking sheet. Bake 7 to 9 minutes or until bottoms are lightly browned. Transfer cookies to a wire rack to cool.

For icing, combine confectioners sugar, water, corn syrup, and vanilla in a medium bowl; tint pink. Spoon icing into a pastry bag fitted with a small round tip. Pipe hair, face, and wing design onto each cookie. Use a medium tip to outline and fill in dresses with icing. Allow icing to harden. Store in a single layer in an airtight container.

Yield: about 1 1/2 dozen cookies

CRANBERRY ANGEL DESSERT

- 1 cup fresh cranberries
- 1/2 unpeeled orange, seeded
- 1 package (3 ounces) cranberry gelatin
- 1/3 cup boiling water
- 1/3 cup cold water
- 1 package (16 ounces) angel food cake mix
- 2 containers (8 ounces each) fat-free frozen whipped topping, thawed
- 1/2 teaspoon orange extract
  Fresh cranberries and orange zest to garnish

Process 1 cup cranberries and orange half in a food processor until coarsely ground. Transfer to a small bowl; cover and chill.

In a medium bowl, combine gelatin and boiling water; stir until gelatin dissolves. Stir in cold water; cover and chill 30 minutes, stirring after 15 minutes. Stir in chilled cranberry mixture. Cover and chill up to 2 hours.

Preheat oven to 350 degrees. Line bottom of a 9 x 13-inch baking pan with waxed paper. Prepare cake mix according to package directions. Pour batter into prepared pan. Bake 30 to 35 minutes or until top is golden brown and cake pulls away from sides of pan. Cool cake in pan.

Remove cake from pan and cut in half horizontally. Place bottom layer on a serving plate. Spread gelatin mixture over bottom layer. Replace top layer. Place whipped topping in a medium bowl. Sprinkle orange extract over topping; fold into topping. Ice cake with whipped topping. Garnish cake with cranberries and orange zest.
Yield: about 20 servings

1 serving (1 slice): 143 calories, 0.1 gram fat, 2.4 grams protein, 31.7 grams carbohydrate

COCONUT CREAMS WITH PINEAPPLE RUM SAUCE

COCONUT CREAMS
- 1 envelope unflavored gelatin
- 1/4 cup cold water
- 1/2 cup shredded unsweetened frozen coconut
- 3 eggs
- 1/2 cup sugar
- 1/8 teaspoon salt
- 1 1/4 cups milk
- 1 1/2 teaspoons vanilla extract
- 1 cup whipping cream

Light, fluffy cake is layered with fruity gelatin to make flavorful low-fat Cranberry Angel Dessert *(top)*. Pineapple Rum Sauce bathes our luscious Coconut Creams with sweetness.

SAUCE
- 1 can (15 1/4 ounces) pineapple tidbits in juice
- 1 1/2 tablespoons cornstarch
- 1/2 cup sugar
- 1/4 cup coconut-flavored rum

For coconut creams, sprinkle gelatin over water in a small bowl; let stand. Process coconut in a food processor until finely chopped. In a small bowl, beat eggs, sugar, and salt until well blended. Combine egg mixture, coconut, and milk in top of a double boiler over simmering water. Stirring constantly, cook about 15 minutes or until mixture coats the back of a spoon. Stir in gelatin mixture and vanilla; continue stirring 1 minute or until gelatin dissolves. Remove from heat. Transfer custard to a medium heatproof bowl; chill 35 minutes or until thickened, stirring every 5 minutes.

In a medium bowl, beat whipping cream until stiff peaks form. Fold whipped cream into chilled custard mixture. Spoon into lightly oiled 1/2-cup shortcake molds. Cover and chill 1 hour.

For sauce, combine 2 tablespoons pineapple juice and cornstarch in a small bowl. In a heavy small saucepan, combine pineapple, remaining juice, and sugar. Stirring constantly, bring to a boil over medium-high heat. Add cornstarch mixture; cook 3 minutes or until sauce thickens. Remove from heat. Stir in rum; cool. Unmold custards onto serving plates; top with sauce.
Yield: about 9 servings

FRUIT CUPS WITH LEMON YOGURT SAUCE

- 1 can (15 1/4 ounces) pineapple tidbits in juice, drained
- 1 can (15 ounces) mandarin oranges in light syrup, drained
- 1 jar (10 ounces) maraschino cherries, drained and chopped
- 1 package (8 ounces) Neufchâtel cheese, softened
- 1 container (8 ounces) nonfat lemon yogurt
- 3/4 cup plus 1 1/2 teaspoons sifted confectioners sugar, divided
- 12 sheets frozen phyllo pastry, thawed and divided
  Butter-flavored vegetable cooking spray

In a medium bowl, combine pineapple, oranges, and cherries. Cover and chill.

In a medium bowl, beat cheese until fluffy. Add yogurt and 3/4 cup confectioners sugar; beat until smooth. Cover and chill.

Preheat oven to 350 degrees. Stack 6 pastry sheets. Cover remaining pastry with a damp cloth. Spray top layer with cooking spray. Cut pastry into 5-inch squares. Working with 1 stack of pastry squares at a time, arrange layers with corners staggered. Place in every other cup of a greased 12-cup muffin pan. Bake 5 to 7 minutes or until lightly browned. Transfer pastries to a wire rack to cool. Repeat with remaining 6 pastry sheets.

To serve, sift remaining 1 1/2 teaspoons confectioners sugar over pastries. Spoon 1 rounded tablespoon yogurt sauce into each pastry. Spoon 1/4 cup fruit into each pastry cup. Top fruit with 1 rounded tablespoon yogurt sauce. Serve immediately.

Yield: about 12 servings

1 serving (1 pastry): 172 calories, 3.8 grams fat, 4.3 grams protein, 31.1 grams carbohydrate

LEMON-RASPBERRY POUND CAKE

SAUCE

- 1 1/4 cups seedless raspberry jam
- 1 1/2 cups whipping cream
- 3 tablespoons raspberry liqueur

CAKE

- 1/2 cup seedless raspberry jam
- 2 cups butter or margarine, softened
- 2 1/2 cups sugar
- 8 eggs

Fruit Cups with Lemon Yogurt Sauce *(left)* offer a less sinful way to enjoy holiday pastries! Lemon-Raspberry Pound Cake is served atop a tantalizing raspberry sauce made with jam and liqueur.

- 3 1/4 cups all-purpose flour
- 1/2 teaspoon baking powder
- 1/4 teaspoon salt
- 1 tablespoon freshly squeezed lemon juice
- 1 1/2 teaspoons lemon extract

For sauce, melt jam in a small saucepan over medium-low heat. Remove from heat and slowly whisk in whipping cream. Whisk in liqueur. Transfer to an airtight container and chill.

Preheat oven to 325 degrees. For cake, beat jam in a small bowl with an electric mixer just until smooth; set aside. In a large bowl, cream butter and sugar. Add eggs, 1 at a time, beating well after each addition. Sift flour, baking powder, and salt into a medium bowl. Add dry ingredients to creamed mixture; beat until

well blended. Beat in lemon juice and lemon extract. Pour half of batter into a greased and floured 10-inch tube pan with a removable bottom. Spoon half of jam over batter. Repeat with remaining batter and jam. Gently swirl batter with a knife, pulling up from bottom through batter and folding over. Bake 1 hour 25 minutes to 1 hour 40 minutes or until a toothpick inserted in center of cake comes out clean. Cool cake in pan 15 minutes. Run a knife around edge of pan; remove sides of pan. Allow cake to cool completely. Run knife around bottom of cake; transfer to a cake plate.

To serve, spoon about 2 tablespoons sauce onto each serving plate. Place a slice of cake on sauce.

Yield: about 16 servings cake and 2 1/2 cups sauce

BANANA-ORANGE SPONGE CAKE

CAKE
1 1/4 cups sugar, divided
2 egg yolks
1 tablespoon orange juice
1 teaspoon grated orange zest
1 teaspoon vanilla extract
3/4 cup mashed bananas
1 3/4 cups sifted cake flour
1/2 teaspoon salt
7 egg whites
1/2 teaspoon cream of tartar

GLAZE
1 1/2 cups sifted confectioners sugar
2 tablespoons light corn syrup
2 tablespoons orange juice
1/2 teaspoon grated orange zest

Preheat oven to 325 degrees. For cake, beat 1 cup sugar, egg yolks, orange juice, orange zest, and vanilla in a large bowl until mixture is fluffy and lightens in color. Add bananas; beat until well blended. In a small bowl, combine flour and salt. Gradually fold dry ingredients into banana mixture. In a medium bowl, beat egg whites until soft peaks form. Gradually add remaining 1/4 cup sugar and cream of tartar; beat until stiff peaks form. Stir 1 cup egg white mixture into banana mixture to lighten batter. Fold remaining egg white mixture into batter. Spoon batter into an ungreased 10-inch tube pan with a removable bottom. Bake 50 to 60 minutes or until the top of cake springs back when lightly touched. Invert pan onto a bottle to cool. Remove cake from pan and place on a serving plate.

For glaze, combine confectioners sugar, corn syrup, orange juice, and orange zest in a small bowl; stir until smooth. Drizzle glaze over cake.
Yield: 16 servings

1 serving (1 slice): 170 calories, 0.8 gram fat, 2.9 grams protein, 38.9 grams carbohydrate

PEANUT BUTTER CREAM PIE

FILLING
2/3 cup firmly packed brown sugar
2 tablespoons all-purpose flour
4 eggs
1/2 cup smooth peanut butter
2 cups half and half
1 1/2 teaspoons vanilla extract

COCOA CRUST
1 cup all-purpose flour
3 tablespoons cocoa

Drizzled with orange glaze, this Banana-Orange Sponge Cake *(top)* makes a delightfully light finale to a holiday feast. Peanut Butter Cream Pie is a rich dessert bursting with creamy chocolate and nutty flavors.

2 tablespoons firmly packed brown sugar
2 tablespoons granulated sugar
1/4 teaspoon salt
1/3 cup chilled butter or margarine
1 egg

TOPPING
1 cup whipping cream
1/4 cup sugar
2 tablespoons shaved semisweet baking chocolate
Shaved chocolate to garnish

For filling, combine brown sugar and flour in top of a double boiler. Add eggs and peanut butter; beat until well blended. Add half and half; beat until smooth. Stirring constantly, cook over simmering water about 30 minutes or until mixture thickens and has the consistency of pudding. Stir in vanilla. Transfer filling to a bowl. Place plastic wrap directly on surface of filling. Chill 2 hours. Chill a medium bowl and beaters from an electric mixer in freezer.

Preheat oven to 400 degrees. For cocoa crust, combine flour, cocoa, sugars, and salt in a medium bowl. Using a pastry blender or 2 knives, cut in butter until mixture resembles coarse meal. Add egg; stir until well blended. Between sheets of plastic wrap, roll out dough to 1/8-inch thickness. Transfer to a 9-inch pie plate and use a sharp knife to trim edge of dough. Flute edge of dough. Chill crust 15 minutes.

Prick bottom of pie crust with a fork. Bake 12 to 15 minutes or until firm. Cool completely on a wire rack.

To serve, spoon filling into crust. For topping, beat whipping cream in chilled bowl until soft peaks form. Gradually add sugar and beat until stiff peaks form. Fold in 2 tablespoons shaved chocolate. Spread topping onto pie. Garnish with chocolate.
Yield: about 8 servings

CARAMEL BROWNIE SUNDAES

Caramel sauce is best if made early in the day and chilled.

CARAMEL SAUCE
- 2 cups sugar
- 1/2 cup water
- 1 1/2 cups whipping cream
- 1 quart vanilla ice cream, softened

BROWNIES
- 1/3 cup butter or margarine, softened
- 1 1/2 cups firmly packed brown sugar
- 2 eggs
- 1 1/4 teaspoons vanilla extract
- 1 1/3 cups all-purpose flour
- 1 teaspoon baking powder
- 1/8 teaspoon salt
- 1 cup chopped pecans, toasted
  Toasted pecan halves to garnish

For caramel sauce, combine sugar and water in a heavy large saucepan over medium heat. Stir constantly until sugar dissolves. Using a pastry brush dipped in hot water, wash down any sugar crystals on sides of pan. Increase heat to medium-high. Swirling pan occasionally, cook without stirring until syrup is dark golden brown (about 10 minutes). Remove from heat. Using a long-handle whisk, slowly whisk in whipping cream. Return to medium heat. Whisking constantly, cook about 3 minutes or until color darkens. (Sauce will thicken as it cools.) Pour sauce into a heatproof container. Cool to room temperature. Cover and store in refrigerator. Spread ice cream into a 9-inch square baking pan. Cover and freeze 4 hours or until firm.

Preheat oven to 350 degrees. For brownies, cream butter and brown sugar in a large bowl until fluffy. Add eggs and vanilla; beat until smooth. In a small bowl, combine flour, baking powder, and salt. Add dry ingredients to creamed mixture; stir until well blended. Stir in chopped pecans. Spread batter into a greased 9-inch square baking pan. Bake 33 to 38 minutes or until crust starts to pull away from sides of pan. Cool in pan. Cut into 2-inch squares.

For each sundae, place 1 brownie on a serving plate. Cut ice cream into 2-inch squares. Place 1 ice cream square on brownie. Spoon 2 tablespoons caramel sauce over sundae. Garnish with a pecan half.

Yield: about 16 servings

For an elegant presentation, serve divine Caramel Brownie Sundaes topped with a rich homemade sauce and pecan halves. Refreshingly robust cups of Cappuccino Mousse will please coffee lovers.

CAPPUCCINO MOUSSE

- 1 teaspoon unflavored gelatin
- 1/4 cup cold water
- 1 tablespoon instant espresso powder
- 1 can (14 ounces) sweetened condensed milk
- 1 teaspoon vanilla extract
- 1 cup whipping cream
  Whipped cream and ground cinnamon to garnish

Chill a medium bowl and beaters from an electric mixer in freezer. Sprinkle gelatin over water in a small saucepan; let stand 1 minute. Stirring constantly, cook over low heat until gelatin dissolves. Add espresso powder, stirring constantly until powder dissolves. Remove from heat. In a large bowl, combine sweetened condensed milk, vanilla, and espresso mixture; stir until well blended. In chilled bowl, beat whipping cream until stiff peaks form. Fold into espresso mixture. Spoon into cups; cover and chill.

To serve, garnish with whipped cream and sprinkle with cinnamon.

Yield: about 6 servings

SWEET NIGHT BEFORE CHRISTMAS

*For generations, children have eagerly awaited the most magical night of the year —
Christmas Eve. Cater to their imaginations with heavenly delicacies that seem to be taken
straight from the lines of Clement Moore's famous poem. Character cookies iced to
perfection and candies that melt in your mouth create a storybook display to behold. With
goodies that look as delightful as they taste, this scrumptious section will have folks
young and old dreaming of a visit from old Saint Nick!*

Amish Sugar Cookies are easy-to-make treats! Using one basic recipe, you can vary the ingredients to create an
assortment of delicious cookies.

AMISH SUGAR COOKIES

Variations on basic cookie are listed below.

- 1/2 cup butter or margarine, softened
- 1 1/2 cups sugar
- 1/2 cup sour cream
- 2 eggs
- 1 1/2 teaspoons vanilla extract
- 2 cups all-purpose flour
- 1 teaspoon baking powder
- 1/4 teaspoon salt

Preheat oven to 375 degrees. In a large bowl, cream butter and sugar until fluffy. Add sour cream, eggs, and vanilla; beat until smooth. In a small bowl, combine flour, baking powder, and salt. Add dry ingredients to creamed mixture; stir until a soft dough forms. Drop teaspoonfuls of dough 2 inches apart onto a lightly greased baking sheet. Bake 8 to 10 minutes or until bottoms are lightly browned. Transfer cookies to a wire rack to cool. Store in an airtight container.
Yield: about 6 1/2 dozen cookies

Chocolate-Chocolate Chip Cookies: Make Amish Sugar Cookies, adding 2 ounces melted semisweet baking chocolate to butter and sour cream mixture. Add 1 cup semisweet chocolate mini chips to dough.

Cherry-Almond Cookies: Make Amish Sugar Cookies, using 1 teaspoon almond extract instead of vanilla extract. Add 3/4 cup finely chopped red candied cherries and 3/4 cup finely chopped, toasted slivered almonds to dough.

Lemon-Pecan Cookies: Make Amish Sugar Cookies, using 1 teaspoon lemon flavoring instead of vanilla extract. Add 1 cup finely chopped, toasted pecans to dough.

Spice-Walnut Cookies: Make Amish Sugar Cookies, adding 3/4 teaspoon ground cinnamon and 1/8 teaspoon ground cloves to dry ingredients. Add 1 cup chopped walnuts to dough.

FROSTED CANDY CANES

- 5 ounces vanilla candy coating, chopped
- 12 6-inch-long candy canes
  Coarse red decorating sugar
  White non-pareils

In a small saucepan, melt candy coating. Spoon coating over curved ends of candy canes. Sprinkle decorating sugar and non-pareils on coating before

These snacks look almost too good to eat! Easy Microwave Fudge whips up in a snap, and Frosted Candy Canes are made in two simple steps. Children and adults alike will have fun decorating Mice Cookies using peanut halves, shoestring licorice, and decorating sugar.

coating hardens. Place candy canes on waxed paper to let coating harden. Store in an airtight container.
Yield: 12 candy canes

EASY MICROWAVE FUDGE

- 1/2 cup butter or margarine
- 1 1/2 cups sugar
- 1 can (5 ounces) evaporated milk
- 2 cups miniature marshmallows
- 1 package (6 ounces) semisweet chocolate chips
- 1 teaspoon vanilla extract

(**Note:** This recipe was tested in a 700-watt microwave.) Line an 8-inch square baking pan with aluminum foil, extending foil over 2 sides of pan; grease foil. In a large microwave-safe bowl, microwave butter until melted. Stir in sugar and milk. Microwave on high power (100%) 8 minutes, stirring every 2 minutes. Add marshmallows, chocolate chips, and vanilla; stir until smooth. Pour mixture into prepared pan; chill 2 hours or until firm.

Use ends of foil to lift fudge from pan. Cut into 1-inch squares. Store in an airtight container in refrigerator.
Yield: about 4 dozen pieces fudge

MICE COOKIES

- 3/4 cup butter or margarine, softened
- 1/2 cup smooth peanut butter
- 1 cup firmly packed brown sugar
- 1 egg
- 1 teaspoon vanilla extract
- 2 1/2 cups all-purpose flour
- 1/3 cup peanuts
  Red shoestring licorice
  Black coarse decorating sugar

Preheat oven to 325 degrees. In a large bowl, cream butter, peanut butter, and brown sugar until fluffy. Add egg and vanilla; beat until smooth. Add flour to creamed mixture; stir until a soft dough forms. Shape dough into 1-inch balls. Pinch each ball to form a nose. Decorate each cookie using peanut halves for ears, small pieces of licorice for eyes, and a sugar crystal for nose. Use a toothpick to poke a hole in back of each cookie for tail. Transfer to an ungreased baking sheet. Bake 10 to 12 minutes or until bottoms are lightly browned. Transfer cookies to a wire rack. While cookies are warm, insert 2-inch-long pieces of licorice into holes for tails. Cool completely. Store in an airtight container.
Yield: about 4 1/2 dozen cookies

You won't find these stockings hanging by the chimney! Bright icings give Almond Stocking Cookies a glossy painted look. Apricot-Nut Balls are covered in tasty coatings of coconut, toasted almonds, and confectioners sugar.

ALMOND STOCKING COOKIES

COOKIES
- 1 can (8 ounces) almond paste, coarsely crumbled
- ³/₄ cup butter or margarine, softened
- ¹/₂ cup granulated sugar
- ¹/₂ cup confectioners sugar
- 1 egg
- 1 teaspoon almond extract
- 2¹/₄ cups all-purpose flour
- ¹/₄ teaspoon salt

ICING
- 5 cups confectioners sugar
- 5¹/₂ to 6¹/₂ tablespoons water
- 1¹/₂ teaspoons almond extract
  Red and green paste food coloring

Preheat oven to 350 degrees. For cookies, place almond paste in a large microwave-safe bowl. Microwave on high power (100%) 25 seconds or until paste softens. Add butter and sugars; cream until fluffy. Add egg and almond extract; beat until smooth. In a medium bowl, combine flour and salt. Add dry ingredients to creamed mixture; stir until a soft dough forms. On a lightly floured surface, use a floured rolling pin to roll out half of dough to ¹/₄-inch thickness. Use a 2 x 3¹/₄-inch stocking-shaped cookie cutter to cut out cookies. Transfer cookies to a lightly greased baking sheet. Bake 10 to 12 minutes or until bottoms are lightly browned. Transfer cookies to a wire rack to cool. Repeat with remaining dough.

For icing, combine confectioners sugar, water, and almond extract in a medium bowl; beat until smooth. Transfer icing into 3 small bowls; tint red and green, leaving remaining bowl white. Spoon icing into pastry bags fitted with small round tips. Outline "cuff" and fill in with white icing; let icing harden. Pipe "toe" and "heel" shapes on each cookie using red or green icing; let icing harden. Outline remainder of cookie and fill in with red or green icing; let icing harden. Using red or green icing and a very small round tip, pipe words on cuffs of stockings; let icing harden. Store in an airtight container.
Yield: about 2 dozen cookies

APRICOT-NUT BALLS

- 1 package (6 ounces) chopped dried apricots
- ¹/₂ cup apricot brandy
- 1¹/₃ cups slivered almonds, toasted, coarsely ground, and divided
- ¹/₂ cup light corn syrup
- ¹/₂ cup confectioners sugar, divided
- 1 package (11 ounces) vanilla wafers, finely crushed
- ¹/₂ cup flaked coconut

In a small bowl, combine apricot pieces and brandy. Cover and let stand 1 hour.

In a medium bowl, combine apricot mixture, 1 cup almonds, corn syrup, ¹/₄ cup confectioners sugar, and cookie crumbs. With greased hands, shape mixture into 1-inch balls. Roll one-third of balls in remaining ¹/₃ cup almonds, one-third in coconut, and one-third in remaining ¹/₄ cup confectioners sugar; transfer to waxed paper. Let stand 15 minutes; roll sugar-coated balls in confectioners sugar again. Store in an airtight container in refrigerator.
Yield: about 5 dozen candies

BEDTIME COOKIES

COOKIES

- ¹/₂ cup butter or margarine, softened
- ¹/₃ cup vegetable shortening
- 1 cup sugar
- ¹/₄ cup molasses
- 1 egg
- 1 teaspoon vanilla extract
- 3 cups all-purpose flour
- 1 teaspoon ground cinnamon
- ¹/₄ teaspoon salt

DECORATING ICING

- 2¹/₂ cups confectioners sugar
- 3 to 4 tablespoons water
- ¹/₂ teaspoon vanilla extract
  Green, red, and yellow paste food coloring

GLAZE

- 3¹/₃ cups confectioners sugar
- 4 to 5 tablespoons water
- 1 teaspoon vanilla extract
  Yellow paste food coloring

Preheat oven to 350 degrees. For cookies, cream butter, shortening, and sugar in a medium bowl until fluffy. Add molasses, egg, and vanilla; beat until smooth. In a another medium bowl, combine flour, cinnamon, and salt. Add dry ingredients to creamed mixture; stir until a soft dough forms. Divide dough in half. On a lightly floured surface, use a floured rolling pin to roll out half of dough to ¹/₈-inch thickness. Use a 2¹/₄ x 3¹/₂-inch boy-shaped cookie cutter to cut out cookies. Transfer to a greased baking sheet. Bake 5 to 7 minutes or until bottoms are lightly browned. Transfer cookies to a wire rack to cool. Repeat with remaining dough and use a 2¹/₄ x 3¹/₂-inch girl-shaped cookie cutter to cut out cookies.

For decorating icing, combine confectioners sugar, water, and vanilla in a medium bowl; stir until smooth. Transfer icing into 3 small bowls; tint green, red, and yellow. Spoon icing into pastry bags fitted with small round tips. Pipe green icing onto each boy cookie to outline pajamas. Pipe red icing onto each girl cookie to outline nightgown. Pipe yellow icing onto each cookie to outline hair. Cover pastry bag tips with plastic wrap. Let icing on cookies harden.

For glaze, combine confectioners sugar, water, and vanilla in a small bowl; stir until smooth (icing should be thin enough to flow easily). Transfer ¹/₂ cup glaze into a small bowl; tint yellow. Spoon white and yellow glazes into

Dressed in icing pajamas, Bedtime Cookies make a great offering for old Saint Nick. For truly munchable morsels, try serving Fruity Brittle that features gumdrops surrounded by crunchy candy.

2 pastry bags fitted with medium round tips. Pipe yellow glaze onto cookies, filling in hair outlines. Pipe white glaze onto cookies, filling in pajama and nightgown outlines. Let glaze harden.

Using decorating icing, pipe green eyes and red mouths onto cookies. Pipe green stripes onto pajamas of boy cookies and red dots onto nightgowns of girl cookies. Let icing harden. Store in an airtight container.

Yield: about 3¹/₂ dozen cookies

FRUITY BRITTLE

- 1 cup chopped soft green and red fruit-flavored candy slices **or** small gumdrops
- 1¹/₂ cups sugar
- ¹/₂ cup light corn syrup
- ¹/₄ cup water
- 2 tablespoons butter or margarine
- ¹/₂ teaspoon salt
- 1 teaspoon baking soda

Line a baking sheet with aluminum foil; grease foil. Sprinkle candy in a

10 x 12-inch area on prepared baking sheet. Butter sides of a heavy medium saucepan. Combine sugar, corn syrup, and water in saucepan. Stirring constantly, cook over medium-low heat until sugar dissolves. Using a pastry brush dipped in hot water, wash down any sugar crystals on sides of pan. Attach a candy thermometer to pan, making sure thermometer does not touch bottom of pan. Increase heat to medium and bring to a boil. Cook, without stirring, until mixture reaches hard-crack stage (approximately 300 to 310 degrees) and turns light golden brown in color. Test about ¹/₂ teaspoon mixture in ice water. Mixture will form brittle threads in ice water and will remain brittle when removed from water. Remove from heat and add butter and salt; stir until butter melts. Add baking soda (mixture will foam); stir until soda dissolves. Pour mixture over candy. Cool completely. Break into pieces. Store in an airtight container.

Yield: about 1 pound, 5 ounces brittle

CHOCOLATE-DIPPED CHERRIES

    1 jar (10 ounces) maraschino
         cherries with stems
    2 ounces semisweet baking
         chocolate
    2 ounces chocolate candy coating

Drain cherries and pat dry with paper towels. Melt chocolate and candy coating in a small saucepan over low heat. Dip three-fourths of each cherry into melted chocolate. Place dipped cherries on a baking sheet lined with waxed paper. Chill until chocolate hardens. Place in candy cups and store in an airtight container in refrigerator.
Yield: about 2 1/2 dozen cherries

SURPRISE OATMEAL MUFFINS

MUFFINS

    1 cup all-purpose flour
 1/2 cup firmly packed brown sugar
    2 teaspoons baking powder
 1/2 teaspoon salt
 1/4 teaspoon ground cinnamon
    1 cup quick-cooking oats
    1 cup milk
 1/4 cup vegetable oil
    1 egg, beaten
 1/3 cup plus 1 tablespoon seedless
         raspberry jam

ICING

    1 package (3 ounces) cream
         cheese, softened
    3 tablespoons butter or margarine,
         softened
1 1/2 cups confectioners sugar
 1/2 teaspoon vanilla extract

Preheat oven to 375 degrees. For muffins, combine first 5 ingredients in a medium bowl. Stir in oats. In a small bowl, combine milk, oil, and egg. Add milk mixture to dry ingredients; stir just until blended. Spoon 1 tablespoon batter into each greased cup of a miniature muffin pan. Drop 1/2 teaspoonful jam into center of batter in each cup. Bake 14 to 16 minutes or until lightly browned on top. Cool in pan 5 minutes. Transfer muffins to a wire rack to cool completely.

For icing, beat cream cheese and butter in a small bowl until fluffy. Add confectioners sugar and vanilla; beat until smooth. Spoon icing into a pastry bag fitted with a large round tip. Pipe icing onto center of each muffin. Store in an airtight container in refrigerator.
Yield: about 2 1/2 dozen muffins

(Clockwise from top) Perfect morning snacks, Surprise Oatmeal Muffins have secret fruity middles and rich cream cheese icing. Our Chocolate-Dipped Cherries are a cinch to make by dipping maraschino cherries into melted chocolate coating. No one will be able to eat just one of these chunky Fruitcake Bars, which boast lots of candied fruit and nuts.

FRUITCAKE BARS

1/4 cup frozen orange juice
   concentrate, thawed
1/3 cup honey
2 cups raisins
2/3 cup butter or margarine, softened
1/3 cup granulated sugar
1/3 cup firmly packed brown sugar
3 eggs
1 teaspoon vanilla extract
1 1/4 cups all-purpose flour
1 teaspoon ground cinnamon
1/2 teaspoon baking powder
1/4 teaspoon ground allspice
1/4 teaspoon salt
1 cup graham cracker crumbs
1 cup finely chopped pecans
1/2 cup flaked coconut
1 package (4 ounces) red candied
   cherries, chopped
1 package (4 ounces) green candied
   cherries, chopped
1 package (4 ounces) candied
   pineapple, chopped

Line a 10 1/2 x 15 1/2-inch jellyroll pan with aluminum foil, extending foil over ends of pan; grease foil. In a medium microwave-safe bowl, combine juice concentrate and honey. Cover and microwave on high power (100%) about 4 minutes or until liquid boils. Stir in raisins; cover and let stand 30 minutes.

Preheat oven to 350 degrees. In a medium bowl, cream butter and sugars until fluffy. Add eggs and vanilla; beat until smooth. In a small bowl, combine flour, cinnamon, baking powder, allspice, and salt. Add dry ingredients to creamed mixture; stir until well blended. Stir in raisin mixture, cracker crumbs, pecans, coconut, and candied fruit. Spread mixture into prepared pan. Bake 19 to 21 minutes or until a toothpick inserted in center of fruitcake comes out clean. Cool in pan.

Use ends of foil to lift fruitcake from pan. Use a serrated knife to cut fruitcake into 1 1/2 x 2-inch bars. Store in an airtight container.
Yield: about 4 dozen bars

PEANUT BUTTER CANDY BARS

CRUST
1 1/2 cups quick-cooking oats
1/2 cup firmly packed brown sugar
1/2 cup salted peanuts
1/4 cup butter or margarine, softened
3 tablespoons light corn syrup
2 tablespoons smooth peanut butter
1/2 teaspoon vanilla extract

Layered with a crunchy crust, a super rich filling, and a chewy, gooey topping, Peanut Butter Candy Bars are a triple treat!

FILLING
1 jar (7 ounces) marshmallow
   creme
2 cups sugar
1/2 cup water
1/2 cup light corn syrup
1/8 teaspoon salt
1/2 cup smooth peanut butter
1/2 teaspoon vanilla extract

TOPPING
1 package (14 ounces) caramels
2 tablespoons water
1/2 cup salted peanuts, coarsely
   ground
1/2 cup milk chocolate chips
4 ounces chocolate candy coating,
   chopped

Line a 10 1/2 x 15 1/2-inch jellyroll pan with aluminum foil, extending foil over ends of pan; grease foil. For crust, process oats, brown sugar, peanuts, butter, corn syrup, peanut butter, and vanilla in a large food processor. Press mixture into bottom of prepared pan.

For filling, spoon marshmallow creme into a large bowl; set aside. Butter sides of a heavy medium saucepan. Combine sugar, water, corn syrup, and salt in saucepan. Stirring constantly, cook over medium-low heat until sugar dissolves. Using a pastry brush dipped in hot water, wash down any sugar crystals on sides of pan. Attach a candy thermometer to pan, making sure thermometer does not touch bottom of pan. Increase heat to medium and bring to a boil. While mixture is cooking, microwave peanut butter in a small microwave-safe bowl until hot. Cook candy mixture, without stirring, until mixture reaches hard-ball stage (approximately 250 to 268 degrees). Test about 1/2 teaspoon mixture in ice water. Mixture will roll into a hard ball in ice water and will remain hard when removed from water; remove from heat. While beating with an electric mixer at medium speed, slowly pour candy mixture over marshmallow creme. Add peanut butter and vanilla; beat at high speed just until mixture holds its shape (about 3 minutes). Spread filling over crust.

For topping, combine caramels and water in a small microwave-safe bowl. Microwave on high power (100%) 3 minutes or until caramels melt, stirring after each minute. Stir in peanuts; spread caramel mixture over filling. In a small microwave-safe bowl, combine chocolate chips and candy coating. Microwave on medium-high power (80%) 2 minutes or until chocolate softens; stir until smooth. Spread chocolate over caramel mixture. Chill uncovered until firm enough to cut.

Use ends of foil to lift candy from pan. Cut into 1-inch squares. Store in an airtight container in refrigerator.
Yield: about 12 1/2 dozen candies

Treats in Toyland

Visions of sugarplums and a wonderland of playthings create a magical formula for Christmas excitement. For sweets to please kids of all ages, start with childhood favorites, from crispy rice cereal and peanut butter to chocolate and cherries. The result is a delightful collection of melt-in-your-mouth treats. Shaped into prancing reindeer, cuddly teddy bears, and clever cowboy gear, these goodies are guaranteed to make dreams come true.

For a sure holiday hit, serve crunchy Maple Clusters *(left)* enriched with walnuts, whipping cream, and maple syrup. Decorated with candied cherries and crushed peppermints, Christmas Fudge makes a pretty package.

CHRISTMAS FUDGE

    2 cups sugar
 $^3/_4$ cup evaporated milk
    3 tablespoons butter or margarine
 $^1/_2$ teaspoon salt
    3 cups miniature marshmallows
    1 package (11 $^1/_2$ ounces) milk
        chocolate chips
 1 $^1/_2$ teaspoons vanilla extract
        Candied cherry halves and
          peppermint pieces to decorate

Line a 9 x 13-inch baking pan with aluminum foil, extending foil over sides of pan; grease foil. Butter sides of a heavy large saucepan. Combine sugar, evaporated milk, butter, and salt in pan. Stirring constantly, cook over medium-low heat until sugar dissolves. Using a pastry brush dipped in hot water, wash down any sugar crystals on sides of pan. Attach a candy thermometer to pan, making sure thermometer does not touch bottom of pan. Increase heat to medium and bring to a boil. Cook, without stirring, until mixture reaches soft-ball stage (approximately 234 to 240 degrees). Test about $^1/_2$ teaspoon mixture in ice water. Mixture will easily form a ball in ice water but will flatten when held in your hand. Remove from heat. Add marshmallows, chocolate chips, and vanilla; stir until smooth. Pour into prepared pan. Chill 2 hours.

Use ends of foil to lift fudge from pan. Cut into 1-inch squares. Decorate fudge with cherries and peppermint. Store in an airtight container in refrigerator.
Yield: about 7 $^1/_2$ dozen pieces fudge

MAPLE CLUSTERS

    1 cup firmly packed brown sugar
    1 cup granulated sugar
 $^1/_2$ cup maple syrup
 $^1/_2$ cup whipping cream
    1 tablespoon light corn syrup
 $^1/_8$ teaspoon salt
    1 tablespoon butter or margarine
    1 teaspoon vanilla extract
    2 cups chopped walnuts

Butter sides of a heavy large saucepan. Combine sugars, maple syrup, whipping cream, corn syrup, and salt in pan. Stirring constantly, cook over medium-low heat until sugars dissolve. Using a pastry brush dipped in hot water, wash down any sugar crystals on sides of pan. Attach a candy thermometer to pan, making sure thermometer does not touch bottom of pan. Increase heat to medium and bring to a boil. Cook,

Dancer and Prancer will never be as handsome as our Fun Reindeer Cookies! Prepared with almond and vanilla, these buttery cookies are festively iced and embellished.

without stirring, until mixture reaches 234 degrees. Test about $^1/_2$ teaspoon mixture in ice water. Mixture will easily form a ball in ice water but will flatten when held in your hand. Remove from heat and stir in butter, vanilla, and walnuts. Using medium speed of an electric mixer, beat until candy thickens and begins to lose it gloss (about 3 minutes). Drop by teaspoonfuls onto waxed paper; cool completely. Store in an airtight container.
Yeild: about 5 dozen candies

FUN REINDEER COOKIES

COOKIES
 $^3/_4$ cup butter or margarine, softened
 $^1/_2$ cup sugar
    1 egg
    1 teaspoon almond extract
 $^1/_2$ teaspoon vanilla extract
 1 $^3/_4$ cups all-purpose flour
    3 tablespoons cornstarch
 $^1/_2$ teaspoon baking powder
 $^1/_8$ teaspoon salt

ICING
 2 $^3/_4$ cups sifted confectioners sugar
 $^1/_4$ cup warm water
    2 tablespoons meringue powder
    1 teaspoon almond extract
        Red, green, brown, and copper
          paste food coloring

Preheat oven to 350 degrees. For cookies, cream butter and sugar in a large bowl until fluffy. Add egg and extracts; beat until smooth. In a small bowl, combine remaining ingredients. Add dry ingredients to creamed mixture; stir until a soft dough forms. On a lightly floured surface, use a floured rolling pin to roll out dough to $^1/_4$-inch thickness. Use a 4 $^1/_2$ x 2 $^3/_4$-inch reindeer-shaped cookie cutter to cut out cookies. Transfer to a greased baking sheet. Bake 10 to 12 minutes or until bottoms are lightly browned. Transfer cookies to a wire rack to cool.

For icing, beat all ingredients at high speed of an electric mixer in a medium bowl 10 to 12 minutes or until stiff. Place $^1/_4$ cup icing in each of 2 small bowls; tint red and green. Tint remaining icing using brown and a small amount of copper food coloring. Adding $^1/_4$ teaspoon water at a time, add enough water to each icing until icing begins to flow from a spoon (about $^3/_4$ teaspoon water in red and green and about 3 $^3/_4$ teaspoons water in brown). Spoon each icing into a pastry bag fitted with a small round tip. Outline and fill in each reindeer with brown icing. Let icing set up 30 minutes. Pipe green icing onto each reindeer for spots and eye. Pipe red icing for collar and nose. Let icing harden. Store in an airtight container.
Yield: about 1 $^1/_2$ dozen cookies

For a cowboy-style Christmas, fill up the chuck wagon with spicy Western Cookies! These boots, stars, and hats are edged in red icing and flavored with molasses. A kid-pleasing, pop-in-your-mouth treat, Porcupine Candies are a jumble of cocoa-flavored rice cereal, chocolate-covered raisins, and slivered almonds.

WESTERN COOKIES

    1   cup butter or margarine, softened
  ³/₄   cup plus 2 tablespoons sugar
    1   egg
    3   tablespoons molasses
    1   teaspoon vanilla extract
 2 ½   cups all-purpose flour
    1   tablespoon ground cinnamon
 1 ½   teaspoons baking powder
  ½   teaspoon salt
  ½   teaspoon ground cloves
    2   tubes (4 ¼ ounces each) red
        decorating icing

For cookies, cream butter and sugar in a large bowl until fluffy. Add egg, molasses, and vanilla; beat until smooth. In a medium bowl, combine flour, cinnamon, baking powder, salt, and cloves. Add dry ingredients to creamed mixture; stir until a soft dough forms.

Divide dough into thirds and wrap in plastic wrap; chill 1 hour.

Preheat oven to 375 degrees. On a lightly floured surface, use a floured rolling pin to roll out dough to slightly thicker than ¹/₈ inch. Use about 1 ³/₄-inch-wide Western-shaped cookie cutters to cut out cookies (we used a hat, boot, and star). Place 1 inch apart on an ungreased baking sheet. Bake 4 to 6 minutes or until bottoms are lightly browned. Transfer cookies to a wire rack to cool.

Transfer icing into a pastry bag fitted with a small round tip. Pipe icing onto cookies. Let icing harden. Store in an airtight container.
Yield: about 13 dozen cookies

PORCUPINE CANDIES

    5   cups cocoa-flavored crispy rice
        cereal
    1   cup chocolate-covered raisins
  ½   cup slivered almonds
    3   cups miniature marshmallows
  ¼   cup butter or margarine
  ½   teaspoon vanilla extract

In a large bowl, combine cereal, raisins, and almonds. Combine marshmallows and butter in a large saucepan. Stirring constantly, cook over low heat until smooth. Remove from heat. Stir in vanilla. Pour marshmallow mixture over cereal mixture; stir until well coated. Use greased hands to shape cereal mixture into 1 ½-inch balls. Place on greased waxed paper; cool completely. Store in an airtight container in a cool place.
Yield: about 3 dozen candies

CREAMY CHERRY BROWNIES

- 1 jar (16 ounces) maraschino cherries, divided
- 1 package (22 1/2 ounces) fudge brownie mix and ingredients to prepare brownies
- 1 package (3 ounces) cream cheese, softened
- 6 tablespoons butter or margarine, softened
- 2 1/4 cups sifted confectioners sugar

Preheat oven to 350 degrees. Drain cherries, reserving syrup. Line a 9 x 13-inch baking pan with aluminum foil, extending foil over ends of pan; grease foil. To prepare brownie mix, use reserved syrup plus enough water to equal water measurement in recipe. In a large bowl, combine brownie mix and required ingredients; stir until blended. Stir in 1 cup cherries. Spread mixture into prepared pan. Bake 27 to 30 minutes or until brownies begin to pull away from sides of pan and are firm. Cool in pan.

Finely chop remaining cherries; drain on paper towels and pat dry. In a medium bowl, beat cream cheese and butter until fluffy. Stir in confectioners sugar and chopped cherries. Spread icing over brownies. Cover and chill 2 hours or until icing is firm.

Lift brownies from pan using ends of foil. Cut into 2-inch squares. Store in an airtight container in refrigerator.
Yield: about 2 dozen brownies

PEANUT BUTTER BALLS

- 1 1/4 cups smooth peanut butter
- 2/3 cup butter or margarine, softened
- 1 teaspoon vanilla extract
- 1 package (16 ounces) confectioners sugar
- 8 ounces chocolate candy coating
- 1 package (6 ounces) semisweet chocolate chips
  Chocolate sprinkles

In a large bowl, beat peanut butter, butter, and vanilla until well blended. Gradually beat in confectioners sugar. Shape mixture into 1-inch balls and place on a baking sheet lined with waxed paper. Chill 45 minutes or until firm.

In top of a double boiler, melt candy coating and chocolate chips over hot water. Dip peanut butter balls into melted chocolate. Return to baking sheet; sprinkle with chocolate sprinkles. Chill until chocolate hardens. Store in an airtight container in refrigerator.
Yield: about 6 1/2 dozen candies

Ideal for a tea party, our Creamy Cherry Brownies feature fluffy cream cheese icing atop fudgy morsels. Picture-perfect Peanut Butter Balls, with yummy peanutty centers, are first dipped in chocolate, then topped with chocolate sprinkles.

BROWN SUGAR COOKIES

COOKIES
- 1/2 cup butter or margarine, softened
- 1 cup firmly packed brown sugar
- 1 egg
- 1 teaspoon vanilla extract
- 1 1/2 cups all-purpose flour
- 1/2 teaspoon baking powder
- 1/2 teaspoon ground cinnamon
- 1/4 teaspoon salt

ICING
- 1 1/2 cups sifted confectioners sugar
- 1 1/2 tablespoons cocoa
- 2 tablespoons milk
- 1/2 teaspoon vanilla extract

In a large bowl, cream butter and brown sugar until fluffy. Add egg and vanilla; beat until smooth. In a small bowl, combine flour, baking powder, cinnamon, and salt. Add dry ingredients to creamed mixture; stir until a soft dough forms. Divide dough in half. Wrap in plastic wrap and chill 2 hours.

Preheat oven to 375 degrees. On a lightly floured surface, use a floured rolling pin to roll out dough to 1/8-inch thickness. Use a 3 1/4 x 4-inch bear-shaped cookie cutter to cut out cookies. Transfer to an ungreased baking sheet. Bake 4 to 6 minutes or until edges are lightly browned. Transfer cookies to a wire rack to cool.

For icing, combine confectioners sugar, cocoa, milk, and vanilla in a small bowl; stir until smooth. Spoon icing into a pastry bag fitted with a medium petal tip. Pipe icing onto neck of each bear for scarf. Use a small round tip to pipe icing onto bear for eyes, nose, ear, and scarf fringe. Let icing harden. Store in an airtight container.

Yield: about 1 1/2 dozen cookies

BAKED BOSTON PEANUTS

- 2 cups raw Spanish peanuts
- 1 cup sugar
- 1/2 cup water
- 1 teaspoon salt

Preheat oven to 350 degrees. In a heavy medium skillet, cook peanuts, sugar, and water over medium heat until all liquid is absorbed and peanuts are coated with sugar (about 20 minutes). Sprinkle with salt. Transfer to a greased 10 1/2 x 15 1/2-inch jellyroll pan. Bake 10 minutes, stirring after 5 minutes. Spread on aluminum foil to cool. Store in an airtight container.

Yield: about 4 cups peanuts

As cute as their furry, full-sized friends, these "beary" sweet Brown Sugar Cookies have cocoa-flavored scarves. Irresistibly crunchy, Baked Boston Peanuts are made by baking sugar-coated peanuts.

CRISPY CHRISTMAS TREES

Let the kids press mixture into cookie cutters and decorate trees.

4 1/2 cups miniature marshmallows
  3 tablespoons butter or margarine
 1/8 teaspoon green liquid food coloring
  6 cups crispy rice cereal
     Small red cinnamon candies

Lightly grease twenty-two 3 1/2 by 3 1/4-inch tree-shaped cookie cutters and place on a greased baking sheet. Combine marshmallows and butter in a heavy Dutch oven over medium heat; stir until smooth. Tint mixture green. Stir in cereal. When cool enough to handle, use lightly greased hands to press about 1/4 cup of mixture into each cookie cutter. Press candies onto trees. Store in an airtight container in a cool place.
Yield: 22 trees

PEANUT PLANK CANDY

3 1/2 cups sugar
  1 cup dark corn syrup
 3/4 cup whipping cream
  5 cups chopped salted peanuts
  1 tablespoon vanilla extract
 1/2 teaspoon baking soda

Line a 10 1/2 x 15 1/2-inch jellyroll pan with aluminum foil, extending foil over ends of pan; grease foil. Butter sides of a heavy Dutch oven. Combine sugar, corn syrup, and whipping cream in pan. Stirring constantly, cook over medium-low heat until sugar dissolves. Using a pastry brush dipped in hot water, wash down any sugar crystals on sides of pan. Attach a candy thermometer to pan, making sure thermometer does not touch bottom of pan. Continuing to stir constantly, increase heat to medium and bring to a boil. Stir in peanuts. Cook, without stirring, until mixture reaches soft-ball stage (approximately 234 to 240 degrees). Test about 1/2 teaspoon mixture in ice water. Mixture will easily form a ball in ice water but will flatten when held in your hand. Remove from heat and stir in vanilla and baking soda (mixture will foam). Beat about 3 minutes or until candy begins to thicken. Pour into prepared pan; cool. Use foil to lift candy from pan. Cut into 1 x 2-inch pieces. Store in an airtight container.
Yield: about 6 dozen pieces candy

Packed into tree-shaped cookie cutters and trimmed with red cinnamon candies, Crispy Christmas Trees *(top)* make great party favors. Peanut Plank Candy, made with whipping cream and corn syrup, features crunchy chunks of peanut. Rolled in sugar and cinnamon before baking, Chocodoodles add a chocolate twist to the traditional snickerdoodle cookie recipe.

CHOCODOODLES

  1 cup butter or margarine, softened
1 1/2 cups plus 3 tablespoons sugar, divided
  2 eggs
  1 teaspoon vanilla extract
2 1/4 cups all-purpose flour
 1/2 cup cocoa
2 3/4 teaspoons ground cinnamon, divided
  1 teaspoon cream of tartar
  1 teaspoon baking soda
 1/4 teaspoon salt

Preheat oven to 375 degrees. In a large bowl, cream butter and 1 1/2 cups sugar until fluffy. Add eggs and vanilla; beat until smooth. In a medium bowl, combine flour, cocoa, 1 teaspoon cinnamon, cream of tartar, baking soda, and salt. Add dry ingredients to creamed mixture; stir until a soft dough forms. In a small bowl, combine remaining 3 tablespoons sugar and 1 3/4 teaspoons cinnamon. Shape dough into 1-inch balls and roll in sugar mixture. Place balls 2 inches apart on a lightly greased baking sheet. Bake 6 to 8 minutes or until bottoms are lightly browned. Transfer cookies to a wire rack to cool. Store in an airtight container.
Yield: about 7 dozen cookies

MAKING PATTERNS

When entire pattern is shown, place tracing paper over pattern and trace pattern. For a more durable pattern, use a permanent marker to trace pattern onto stencil plastic.

When pattern pieces are stacked or overlapped, place tracing paper over pattern and follow a single color to trace pattern. Repeat to trace each pattern separately onto tracing paper.

When only half of pattern is shown (indicated by blue line on pattern), fold tracing paper in half and match fold of paper to blue line of pattern. Trace pattern half; turn folded paper over and draw over traced lines on remaining side of paper.

SEWING SHAPES

1. Center pattern on wrong side of one fabric piece and use fabric marking pen to draw around pattern. Do not cut out shape.
2. Place fabric pieces right sides together. Leaving an opening for turning, carefully sew pieces together directly on drawn line.
3. Leaving a $1/4$" seam allowance, cut out shape. Clip seam allowance at curves and corners. Turn right side out.

CUTTING A FABRIC CIRCLE

1. Cut a square of fabric the size indicated in project instructions.
2. Matching right sides, fold fabric square in half from top to bottom and again from left to right.
3. Tie one end of string to a pencil or fabric marking pen. Measuring from pencil, insert a thumbtack through string at length indicated in project instructions. Insert thumbtack through folded corner of fabric. Holding tack in place and keeping string taut, mark cutting line (**Fig. 1**).

Fig. 1

4. Cut along drawn line through all fabric layers.

MAKING APPLIQUÉS

To prevent darker fabrics from showing through, white or light-colored fabrics may need to be lined with fusible interfacing before applying paper-backed fusible web.

To make reverse appliqué pieces, trace pattern onto tracing paper; turn traced paper over and continue to follow all steps using reversed pattern.

1. Use a pencil to trace pattern or draw around reversed pattern onto paper side of web as many times as indicated for a single fabric. Repeat for additional patterns and fabrics.
2. Follow manufacturer's instructions to fuse traced patterns to wrong side of fabrics. Do not remove paper backing.
3. Cut out appliqué pieces along traced lines. Remove paper backing.
4. Arrange appliqués, web side down, on project, overlapping as necessary. Appliqués can be temporarily held in place by touching appliqués with tip of iron. If appliqués are not in desired position, lift and reposition.
5. Fuse appliqués in place.

MACHINE APPLIQUÉ

1. Pin or baste a piece of stabilizer slightly larger than design to wrong side of background fabric under design.
2. Set sewing machine for a medium width zigzag stitch. Beginning on a straight edge of appliqué if possible, position project under presser foot so that most of stitching will be on appliqué. Take a stitch in fabric and bring bobbin thread to top. Holding both threads toward you, sew over threads for two or three stitches to secure. Stitch over all exposed raw edges of appliqué(s) and along detail lines as indicated in instructions.
3. When stitching is complete, remove stabilizer. Pull loose threads to wrong side of fabric; knot and trim ends.

BINDING

MAKING BINDING

1. To determine length of binding strip needed, measure edges of item to be bound (**Fig. 1**). Add 12" to measurement.

Fig. 1

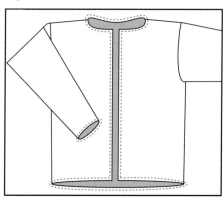

2. To give binding flexibility to fit around corners and curved edges, cut fabric strips on the bias. Cut bias strips the width indicated in project instructions and piece as necessary for determined length.

ADDING SEWN BINDING

1. Matching wrong sides and raw edges, press binding strip in half lengthwise.
2. Press one end of binding strip diagonally (**Fig. 2**).

Fig. 2

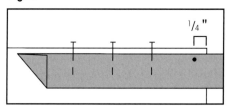

3. Beginning with pressed end several inches from a corner, pin binding to right side of item along one edge.
4. When first corner is reached, mark $1/4$" from corner of item (**Fig. 3**).

Fig. 3

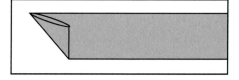

5. Using a $1/4$" seam allowance, sew binding to item, backstitching at beginning and when mark is reached (**Fig. 4**).

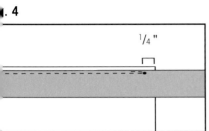

. 4

1/4"

Fold binding up as shown in **Fig. 5**.
ld down and pin binding to adjacent
le (**Fig. 6**). Mark 1/4" from edge of item
next corner.

. 5

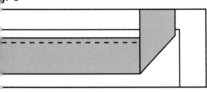

. 6

Backstitching at edge of binding, sew
nned binding to item (**Fig. 7**);
ckstitch when next mark is reached.
t needle and clip thread.

. 7

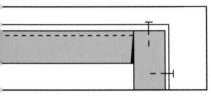

Repeat Steps 6 and 7 to continue
wing binding to item until binding
erlaps beginning end by 2". Trim
cess binding.
If binding a quilt, trim backing and
tting even with edges of quilt top.
). For a mitered corner, fold binding
er to backing of item and pin pressed
ge in place, covering stitching line
ig. 8). Fold adjacent edge over to
cking of item, forming a mitered
rner (**Fig. 9**); pin in place. Repeat for
ch corner.

Fig. 8

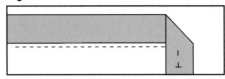

Fig. 9

11. Hand sew binding to backing, taking
care not to stitch through front of item.

MAKING A BOW

Note: Loop sizes given in project
instructions refer to the length of ribbon
used to make one loop of bow.

1. For first streamer, measure desired
length of streamer from one end of
ribbon; twist ribbon between fingers
(**Fig. 1**).

Fig. 1

2. Keeping right side of ribbon facing out,
fold ribbon to front to form desired-size
loop; gather ribbon between fingers
(**Fig. 2**). Fold ribbon to back to form
another loop; gather ribbon between
fingers (**Fig. 3**).

Fig. 2

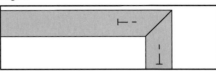

Fig. 3

3. (**Note:** If a center loop is desired,
form half the desired number of loops,
then loosely wrap ribbon around thumb
and gather ribbon between fingers
as shown in **Fig. 4**; form remaining
loops.) Continue to form loops, varying
size of loops as desired, until bow is
desired size.

Fig. 4

4. For remaining streamer, trim ribbon to
desired length.

5. To secure bow, hold gathered loops
tightly. Fold a length of floral wire around
gathers of loops. Hold wire ends behind
bow, gathering all loops forward; twist
bow to tighten wire. Arrange loops and
trim ribbon ends as desired.

PAPER TWIST ROSES

You will need desired color of paper twist,
tracing paper, pencil, and a hot glue gun.

1. For rose center, cut a 13" length of
paper twist; untwist. Cut a 3" x 13" strip
from untwisted paper. Fold one short
edge of strip 1/4" to wrong side. Matching
wrong sides, fold strip in half lengthwise.

2. Beginning with unfolded end and with
long folded edge at top, roll about one
quarter of strip tightly; glue to secure.
Roll remainder of strip loosely, making
small pleats in bottom edge and gluing
to secure. *Rose Petal*

3. Trace rose petal pattern onto tracing
paper. Use pattern to cut four to six petals
from untwisted paper. Wrap side edges of
each petal around a pencil to curl (**Fig. 1**).

Fig. 1

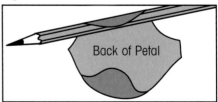

Back of Petal

4. Slightly overlapping petals, glue
desired number of petals around base of
rose center; allow to dry.

CROCHET

Abbreviations:

ch(s)	chain
dc	double crochet(s)
hdc	half double crochet(s)
mm	millimeters
Rnd(s)	Round(s)
sl st	slip stitch
sc	single crochet(s)
sp(s)	space(s)
st(s)	stitch(es)
tr	treble crochet(s)
YO	yarn over

★ - work instructions following ★ as many **more** times as indicated in addition to the first time.

† **to** † - work all instructions from first † to second † **as many** times as specified.

() or [] - work enclosed instructions **as many** times as specified by the number immediately following **or** work all enclosed instructions in the stitch or space indicated **or** contains explanatory remarks.

Colon (:) - the number(s) given after a colon at the end of a row or round denote(s) the number of stitches you should have on that row or round.

SINGLE CROCHET (sc): To work a single crochet, insert hook in stitch or space indicated, YO and pull up a loop, YO and draw yarn through both loops on hook (**Fig. 1**).

Fig. 1

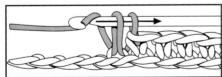

DOUBLE CROCHET (dc): To work a double crochet, YO, insert hook in stitch or space indicated, YO and pull up a loop (3 loops on hook), YO and draw yarn through 2 loops on hook (**Fig. 2**) (2 loops remain on hook), YO and draw yarn through remaining 2 loops on hook (**Fig. 3**).

Fig. 2   **Fig. 3**

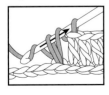   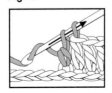

HALF DOUBLE CROCHET (hdc): YO, insert hook in stitch or space indicated, YO and pull up a loop (3 loops on hook), YO and draw yarn through all 3 loops on hook (**Fig. 4**).

Fig. 4

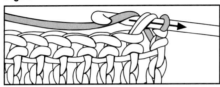

SLIP STITCH (sl st): This stitch is used to attach new yarn, to join work, or to move yarn across a group of stitches without adding height. Insert hook in stitch or space indicated, YO and draw yarn through stitch **and** loop on hook (**Fig. 5**).

Fig. 5

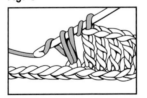

TREBLE CROCHET (tr): YO twice, insert hook in stitch or space indicated, YO and pull up a loop (4 loops on hook) (**Fig. 6**), (YO and draw yarn through 2 loops on hook) 3 times (**Fig. 7**).

Fig. 6

Fig. 7

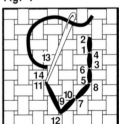

CROSS STITCH

COUNTED CROSS STITCH (X): Work one Cross Stitch for each colored square on chart. For horizontal rows, work stitches in two journeys (**Fig. 1**). For vertical rows, complete each stitch as shown in **Fig. 2**. When the chart shows a Backstitch crossing a colored square (**Fig. 3**), work the Cross Stitch first, then work the Backstitch over the Cross Stitch.

Fig. 1

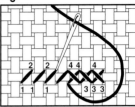

Fig. 2

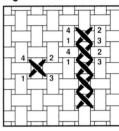

Fig. 3

BACKSTITCH (B'ST): For outline or details, Backstitch (shown in chart and color key by colored straight lines) should be worked after the design has been completed (**Fig. 4**).

Fig. 4

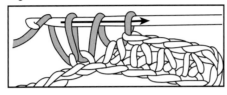

EMBROIDERY STITCHES

BACKSTITCH

Bring needle up at 1; go down at 2. Bring needle up at 3 and back down at 1 (**Fig. 1**). Continue working to make a continuous line of stitches.

Fig. 1

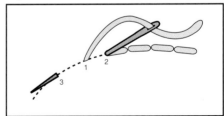

[BL]ANKET STITCH

[Br]ing needle up at 1; keeping thread [be]low point of needle, go down at 2 and [up] at 3 (**Fig. 2**). Continue working as [sh]own in **Fig. 3**.

[Fig]. 2   **Fig. 3**

[C]ROSS STITCH

[Br]ing needle up at 1 and go down at 2. [Co]me up at 3 and go down at 4 [(**F**ig. 4**).

Fig. 4

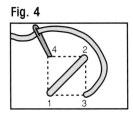

[F]RENCH KNOT

[Br]ing needle up at 1. Wrap thread once [ar]ound needle and insert needle at 2, [ho]lding thread with non-stitching fingers [(**F**ig. 5**). Tighten knot as close to fabric [as] possible while pulling needle back [th]rough fabric.

Fig. 5

[L]AZY DAISY

[Br]ing needle up at 1 and go down at [2] to form a loop; bring needle up at 3, [ke]eping thread below point of needle [(**F**ig. 6**). Go down at 4 to anchor loop [(**F**ig. 7**).

[Fig]. 6   **Fig. 7**

[O]VERCAST STITCH

[Br]ing needle up at 1; take thread over [ed]ge of fabric and bring needle up at 2. [Co]ntinue stitching along edge of fabric [(**F**ig. 8**).

Fig. 8

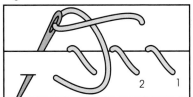

RUNNING STITCH

Make a series of straight stitches with stitch length equal to the space between stitches (**Fig. 9**).

Fig. 9

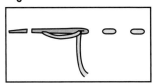

STEM STITCH

Bring needle up at 1. Keeping thread below stitching line, go down at 2 and up at 3. Go down at 4 and up at 5 (**Fig. 10**).

Fig. 10

STRAIGHT STITCH

Bring needle up at 1 and take needle down at 2 (**Fig. 11**). Length of stitches may be varied as desired.

Fig. 11

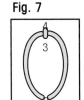

PAINTING TECHNIQUES

PREPARING PROJECT

If painting on a garment, wash, dry, and press garment according to paint manufacturer's recommendations. Insert T-shirt form or iron shiny side of freezer paper to wrong side of garment under area to be painted.

TRANSFERRING PATTERNS

Trace pattern onto tracing paper. Using removable tape, tape pattern to project. Place transfer paper coated side down between project and tracing paper (using old transfer paper will help prevent smudges). If transferring pattern onto a dark surface, use light-colored transfer paper to transfer pattern. Use a pencil to transfer outlines of base coat areas of design to project (press lightly to avoid smudges and heavy lines that are difficult to cover). If necessary, use a soft eraser to remove any smudges.

PAINTING BASE COATS

(**Note:** A disposable plate makes a good palette.) Use medium round brush for large areas and a small round brush for small areas. Do not overload brush. Let paint dry between coats.

TRANSFERRING DETAILS

To transfer detail lines to design, replace pattern and transfer paper over painted base coats and use stylus to lightly transfer detail lines onto project.

PAINTING DETAILS

Side loading (shading and highlighting): Dip one corner of a flat brush in water; blot on a paper towel. Dip dry corner of brush into paint. Stroke brush back and forth on palette until there is a gradual change from paint to water in each brush stroke. Stroke loaded side of brush along detail line on project, pulling brush toward you and turning project if necessary.
For shading, side load brush with a darker color of paint. For highlighting, side load brush with lighter color of paint.
Line work: Let paint dry before beginning line work to prevent smudging lines or ruining pen. Draw over detail lines with permanent pen.
Dots: Dip the tip of a round paintbrush, the handle end of a paintbrush, or one end of a toothpick in paint and touch to project. Dip in paint each time for uniform dots.
Sponge painting: Lightly dampen sponge piece. Dip sponge piece into paint and blot on paper towel to remove excess paint. Use a stamping motion to apply paint. Reapply paint to sponge as necessary.

RECIPE INDEX

PROJECT INDEX

Continued on page 192

CREDITS

We want to extend a warm thank you to the generous people who allowed us to photograph our projects at their homes.

- *Make an Entrance:* John and Anne Childs, David and Christine Jernigan, Casey and Wendy Jones
- *Nature's Glory:* Tom and Barbara Denniston
- *Crimson and Ice:* Mr. and Mrs. Phillip Duncan
- *Radiant White Christmas:* Dr. Jerry and Gwen Holton
- *Redwork Revival:* Duncan and Nancy Porter
- *Keep Christmas in Your Heart:* Rusty and Rhonda Compton
- *A Festival of Wreaths:* William and Nancy Appleton, Charles and Peg Mills, Duncan and Nancy Porter
- *Yuletide Memories:* Charles and Peg Mills

- *Snowman Frolic:* Tom and Robin Steves
- *Snowman Dress* (shown on page 102): Paul and Ann Weaver
- *New England Holiday Brunch:* Duncan and Nancy Porter
- *Candlelight Creole Dinner:* Dr. Dan and Sandra Cook
- *Ski Lodge Supper:* Pinnacle Vista Lodge, Little Rock, Arkansas
- *Yuletide Reunion:* Shirley Held

A special thanks is also extended to Monroe Salt Works of Monroe, Maine, for the use of dishes in Ski Lodge Supper.

We would like to recognize Husqvarna Viking Sewing Machine Company of Cleveland, Ohio, for providing the sewing machines used to make many of our projects.

Our sincere appreciation goes to photographers Ken West, Larry Pennington, Mark Mathews, Karen Shirey, and David Hale, Jr., of Peerless Photography, Little Rock, Arkansas; and Jerry R. Davis of Jerry Davis Photography, Little Rock, Arkansas, for their time, patience, and excellent work.

To the talented people who helped in the creation of the following projects and recipes in this book, we extend a special word of thanks.

- *Santa Patches* cross stitch designs, page 127: Kooler Design Studio
- *Crocheted Vest*, page 130: Margie Wicker
- *Poinsettia Afghan and Poinsettia Pillow* page 131: Nancy Overton
- *Winter Warmer* cross stitch design, page 123: Deborah Lambein
- *Porcupine Candies*, page 182: Susan Warren Reeves